Edward Thomas and World Literary Studies

CREW

CREW series of Critical and Scholarly Studies
General Editor: Professor M. Wynn Thomas (CREW, Swansea University)

This CREW series is dedicated to Emyr Humphreys, a major figure in the literary culture of modern Wales, a founding patron of the *Centre for Research into the English Literature and Language of Wales* and, along with Gillian Clarke and Seamus Heaney, one of CREW's Honorary Associates. Grateful thanks are due to the late Richard Dynevor for making this series possible.

Other titles in the series

Stephen Knight, *A Hundred Years of Fiction* (978-0-7083-1846-1)
Barbara Prys-Williams, *Twentieth-Century Autobiography* (978-0-7083-1891-1)
Kirsti Bohata, *Postcolonialism Revisited* (978-0-7083-1892-8)
Chris Wigginton, *Modernism from the Margins* (978-0-7083-1927-7)
Linden Peach, *Contemporary Irish and Welsh Women's Fiction* (978-0-7083-1998-7)
Sarah Prescott, *Eighteenth-Century Writing from Wales: Bards and Britons* (978-0-7083-2053-2)
Hywel Dix, *After Raymond Williams: Cultural Materialism and the Break-Up of Britain* (978-0-7083-2153-9)
Matthew Jarvis, *Welsh Environments in Contemporary Welsh Poetry* (978-0-7083-2152-2)
Harri Garrod Roberts, *Embodying Identity: Representations of the Body in Welsh Literature* (978-0-7083-2169-0)
M. Wynn Thomas, *In the Shadow of the Pulpit: Literature and Nonconformist Wales* (978-0-7083-2225-3)
Linden Peach, *The Fiction of Emyr Humphreys: Contemporary Critical Perspectives* (978-0-7083-2216-1)
Daniel Westover, *R. S. Thomas: A Stylistic Biography* (978-0-7083-2413-4)
Jasmine Donahaye, *Whose People? Wales, Israel, Palestine* (978-0-7083-2483-7)
Judy Kendall, *Edward Thomas: The Origins of His Poetry* (978-0-7083-2403-5)
Damian Walford Davies, *Cartographies of Culture: New Geographies of Welsh Writing in English* (978-0-7083-2476-9)
Daniel G. Williams, *Black Skin, Blue Books: African Americans and Wales 1845–1945* (978-0-7083-1987-1)

Edward Thomas and World Literary Studies:

Wales, Anglocentrism and English Literature

Writing Wales in English

ANDREW WEBB

UNIVERSITY OF WALES PRESS
CARDIFF
2013

www.uwp.co.uk

British Library Cataloguing-in-Publication Data
A catalogue record for this book is available from the British Library.

ISBN   978-0-7083-2622-0
e-ISBN 978-0-7083-2623-7

THE *ASSOCIATION FOR*
WELSH WRITING IN ENGLISH
CYMDEITHAS LLÊN SAESNEG CYMRU

Typeset in Wales by Eira Fenn Gaunt, Cardiff
Printed by CPI Antony Rowe, Chippenham, Wiltshire

For Kathryn and Thomas

Contents

General Editor's Preface

The aim of this series is to produce a body of scholarly and critical work that reflects the richness and variety of the English-language literature of modern Wales. Drawing upon the expertise both of established specialists and of younger scholars, it will seek to take advantage of the concepts, models and discourses current in the best contemporary studies to promote a better understanding of the literature's significance, viewed not only as an expression of Welsh culture but also as an instance of modern literatures in English worldwide. In addition, it will seek to make available the scholarly materials (such as bibliographies) necessary for this kind of advanced, informed study.

M. Wynn Thomas
*CREW (Centre for Research into the English
Literature and Language of Wales)*
Swansea University

Acknowledgements

I am grateful to trustees of the Edward Thomas Estate for permission to quote from Thomas's letters and diaries. Thank you to colleagues at Bangor University for providing me with the research environment in which to finish this project. Sarah Lewis at the University of Wales Press has been unstinting in her support. The study has benefited enormously from M. Wynn Thomas's generosity, wealth of knowledge and professionalism. I would also like to thank the anonymous reader whose suggestions have been very helpful.

This book would not have been written without the support of all those who contributed to the PhD thesis from which it emerges: Jeremy Treglown and David Morley supervised it, but key suggestions and advice along the way also came from Thomas Docherty, Graeme Macdonald, Nick Lawrence and Michael Bell, all based at Warwick University, and from Tom Paulin, at Oxford, who was the dissertation's external examiner. Thanks to Katie Gramich at Cardiff who, back in 2006, first drew my attention to the Welsh context of Thomas's work. Librarians at Swansea, Oxford, Warwick, Durham, the British Library, the British Newspaper Library and the National Library of Wales have helped to make the research an enjoyable and rewarding activity. Special thanks to Alison Harvey at Cardiff University Library whose knowledge of the Thomas archive there is second to none. Above all, thank you to Kathryn and Thomas for all the patience, understanding and love, and for putting up with all my time away from home. We could not have done any of it without Jill, Hugh, Thelma and Charles.

Abbreviations

References are given in endnotes and subsequently abbreviated in accord-
ance with series practice. Abbreviations for the most commonly cited
sources appear in the text as follows:

ACP   *Edward Thomas: the Annotated Collected Poems*, ed. Edna
        Longley (Newcastle: Bloodaxe, 2008).

BW   Edward Thomas, *Beautiful Wales* (London: A. & C. Black,
        1905).

CET   Edward Thomas, *The Childhood of Edward Thomas: a
        Fragment of Autobiography* (London: Faber and Faber,
        1938).

CS   Edward Thomas, *Celtic Stories* (Oxford: Clarendon Press,
        1911).

EF   *Elected Friends: Robert Frost and Edward Thomas to One
        Another*, ed. Matthew Spencer (New York: Handsel Books,
        2003).

ETAP R. George Thomas, *Edward Thomas: a Portrait* (Oxford:
        Clarendon Press, 1995).

F   Tony Conran, *Frontiers in Anglo-Welsh Poetry* (Cardiff:
        University of Wales Press, 1997).

HGLM Edward Thomas, *The Happy-Go-Lucky Morgans* (London:
        Duckworth & Co., 1913).

HW   John Davies, *A History of Wales* (rev. edn; London: Penguin,
        2007).

I   M. Wynn Thomas, 'Introduction', in Tony Brown and
        Russell Stephens (eds), *Nations and Relations: Writing*

across the British Isles (Cardiff: New Welsh Review, 2000), pp. i–iv.

IW   Edward Thomas, *Icknield Way* (London: Constable and Co., 1916).

LGB   *Letters from Edward Thomas to Gordon Bottomley*, ed. R. George Thomas (London: Oxford University Press, 1968).

NCLW   Meic Stephens (ed.), *The New Companion to the Literature of Wales* (Cardiff: University of Wales Press, 1998).

OOP   Ian Baucom, *Out of Place: Englishness, Empire and the Locations of Identity* (Princeton, N. J.: Princeton University Press, 1999).

P   Edward Thomas, 'The Patriot', *Nationalist* 3/29 (1909), 38–43.

PET   Andrew Motion, *The Poetry of Edward Thomas* (London: Routledge and Kegan Paul, 1980).

PR   Kirsti Bohata, *Postcolonialism Revisited* (Cardiff: University of Wales Press, 2004).

PW   Edna Longley, *Poetry in the Wars* (Newcastle: Bloodaxe, 1986).

R   Edward Thomas, 'Reviews', scrapbooks 1901–17, 6 vols, Edward Thomas Collection, Cardiff University Library, Cardiff.

TUL   Hazel Davies, 'Edward Thomas: twelve unpublished letters to O. M. Edwards', *National Library of Wales Journal*, 28/3 (1994), 335–45.

WRL   Pascale Casanova, *The World Republic of Letters*, trans. M. B. DeBevoise (Cambridge, Mass.: Harvard University Press, 2004).

WWWH   Gwyn A. Williams, *When Was Wales?: a History of the Welsh* (London: Black Raven Press, 1985).

Note:

Edward Thomas's idiosyncrasies of place names and personal names in titles and text (for example 'Llandebie' for Llandybie, or 'Kilhwch' for Culhwch) are retained without comment throughout the text

Introduction

The three million inhabitants of Wales are the inheritors of two principal literary traditions. One is the expression of a modern culture in a Celtic language, a literature central to Welsh national identity, whose writers have, since the sixth century, repeatedly reinvented their tradition to meet changing historical conditions. The other, Anglophone, tradition has emerged more recently, and has already produced a body of literature distinctive from, indeed foreign to, its English counterpart. Its writers include Dylan Thomas, one of the most translated English-language poets of the twentieth century, as well as Raymond Williams, the most influential British critic and theorist since the Second World War. This is not to mention many other writers from both traditions who are deserving of wide critical attention. The reasons for the present relative international obscurity of the two Welsh literatures (in comparison to their Irish, English and even their Scottish equivalents) are complex, but one factor stands out: an historical and continuing Anglocentrism within British literary studies. This has many manifestations, including widespread ignorance within Britain of the Welsh-language literary tradition, and the historical appropriation of many Anglophone Welsh writers and texts by the institutions of an expansive English Literature. The present study critiques such Anglocentrism through its analysis of the work of Edward Thomas, often seen as 'quintessentially English', in the hope of contributing to a discipline of British literary studies that is more sensitive to the full range of national literary traditions within it.

In 'The Patriot', a short story placed in the October 1909 issue of the Cardiff-based journal, *Nationalist*, Edward Thomas describes the last moments of an anonymous soldier, fighting in the British Army in an unnamed war in a distant 'foreign land'.[1] The final minutes of this soldier's life are juxtaposed against his memories of a childhood journey with his father from their home in London back to Wales. When they reach their destination, father and son discover the 'country of their souls', while the 'strange tongue' spoken by the inhabitants is miraculously identified as 'the boy's own' (*P*, p. 40). As the narrative shifts back to the soldier's deathbed, readers are told that 'the country he had been fighting for' – the Britain whose uniform he wore – was not the nation with which he identified (*P*, p. 41). Instead, the soldier realises, in his last moment of consciousness, that 'his country [is] not the country he had fought for' (*P*, p. 43). The narrative is then brought to an abrupt end.

'The Patriot' raises issues that will be explored in this book. It forcefully suggests its author's allegiance to a Welsh nation whose interests, it implies, are not served by fighting imperialist battles for the British. Thomas's story draws on its author's own experience as a London-born Welshman, someone who could, at times, declare his own national identity in unambiguous terms – 'I am Welsh'[2] – in spite of what he described as his 'accidentally cockney nativity' (*TUL*, p. 341). Nor is this an isolated incident. A diary entry for 29 September 1901 records that Thomas talked with a friend 'of patriotism of which I never felt a spark unless it be perhaps to love a few acres of Wales. A Frenchman is to me the same as an Eng[lishman].'[3] Thomas's distance from British imperialism is further suggested by lines from *The South Country* (1909) in which he writes that 'what with Great Britain, the British Empire, Britons, Britishers, and the English-speaking world, the choice offered to whomsoever would be patriotic is embarrassing'.[4] Above all, 'The Patriot' raises the question of whether his literary work can be read in the light of his intention, set out in a letter written at the beginning of his career to his tutor, O. M. Edwards, a key figure in the Welsh literary renaissance, 'to help you and the Welsh cause' (*TUL*, p. 343).

In anticipating Thomas's own death, eight years later, in a British army uniform at the Battle of Arras, the story offers a counter to the majority critical view, which has prevailed since Walter de la Mare's foreword to the first edition of Thomas's *Collected Poems* in 1920, that Thomas's poetry is a 'mirror of England'.[5] The most influential critical intervention in this vein has been that of Edna Longley who, in the 1970s, developing a critical line first articulated by Philip Larkin, identified Thomas as the

'missing link' in a native, English poetic line that stretched between the
Romantics and modern writers.[6] This study challenges Longley's interpretation, and those of the many subsequent critics of Thomas who mention
his self-description as 'mainly Welsh' or '5/8 Welsh' (never simply 'I am
Welsh') but then pass over his Welshness in a paragraph or two. However,
'The Patriot' also challenges Welsh critics of Thomas, one of whom bitterly
comments that 'if Anglo-Welsh writing represents a pilgrim's progress
towards the New Jerusalem of the blue-blooded English, then Edward
Thomas is the success story'.[7]

    Another significant aspect of 'The Patriot' is the fact that Thomas pub-
lished it in Thomas Marchant Williams's Cardiff-based journal, *Nationalist*,
something that critics on both sides of the Welsh-English border have
missed. This raises another key question considered in this book: the
relation between Thomas's national allegiance, and the literary institutions
in England and Wales through which he was able to publish his work.
Put simply, when the British nation's literary infrastructure – its publishing
houses, journalistic outlets, readership, concentration of writers and critics
– is centred on London, what is the impact on the writer with an allegiance
to Wales, the literary infrastructure of which is undeveloped in comparison
to that of London? This is an issue that has been faced by successive
generations of Welsh writers, as well as those from other parts of Britain,
and indeed the wider Anglophone world.

    This book aims to present its subject as a Welsh writer, but to do so
not only as a contribution to the growing field of publications on Edward
Thomas, but as a simultaneous intervention into two other areas: first,
that of the ongoing reconfiguration of the relations between the nations
of these islands – the debate around cultural nationalism, devolution and
independence – and, second, that of recent attempts to theorise the structure
of international literary space – the new field of world literary studies.
My project investigates whether this emerging field of study enables us
to shed new light on British literary space, and in particular, whether it
offers a set of critical tools adequate to the task of unpacking the complex
relations between the national literary traditions within Britain.

The most ambitious recent work on literary devolution within the UK
has taken place in Scotland. In *Devolving English Literature*, first published in 1992, seven years before some measure of political devolution
was achieved in Scotland and Wales, Robert Crawford draws attention
to the Anglocentrism historically inherent in the discipline of English

Literature. He argues that readers should 'remain alert to nuances of cultural politics embedded in [a given text], nuances which set them apart from Anglocentric assumptions but which are ignored when these texts are read in an unexamined context of "English Literature"'.[8] Providing numerous examples of the subject's 'homage to centralism', he contends that English Literature 'is a force which must be countered continually by a devolutionary momentum' (*DEL*, p. 7).

Crawford's project identifies non-English writers who, as a result of the discipline's inherent Anglocentrism, are 'too smoothly assimilated into English Literature', as well as some anti-English writers who are 'awkwardly marginalised' from the canon (*DEL*, p. 7). To exemplify his point, Crawford points to Larkin's 1973 *Oxford Book of Twentieth-Century Verse*, the preface to which focuses on English writers and states that the anthology does not include 'poems by Commonwealth or American writers' (*DEL*, p. 274). The anthology itself, Crawford reveals, gives most of its space to the American expatriate T. S. Eliot and the Irish writer W. B. Yeats, and contains work by the Australian author Peter Porter and the Caribbean poet Derek Walcott. In this manner, the English tradition, argues Crawford, 'is appropriating and incorporating extra-English elements at exactly the same time as it asserts its English purity' (*DEL*, p. 274). The exclusion of Hugh MacDiarmid from the canon of English Literature is an example of how writers who have, at best, an ambivalent attitude towards England, are 'awkwardly marginalised' from the main tradition (*DEL*, p. 7). Crawford's study focuses on Scottish literature as 'a, if not *the*, test case' for deciding 'whether or not we have devolved our view of "English Literature" in order to take full account of the various different cultural traditions which are so easily lumped together under that label' (*DEL*, p. 8). Scottish literature is chosen on the grounds that 'it offers the longest continuing example of a substantial body of literature produced by a culture pressurized by the threat of English cultural domin-ation', and because 'Scottish writing has often formed a model for writers in other countries concerned to escape from being England's cultural provinces' (*DEL*, p. 8). Due to its geography and lack of political independ-ence, it is also 'particularly vulnerable to being subsumed within the English literary tradition' (*DEL*, p. 8).

For the purposes of this book, I want to suggest that, while *Devolving English Literature* opens the door to future development in this area, there are three problems with Crawford's work. Firstly, a significant omission – perhaps the source of his doubts over the status of Scottish literature as 'a, if not *the*, test case' – is serious discussion of literature from Wales.

He mentions in parentheses that his argument about devolution also applies to Welsh writing in English, but does not consider the matter further (*DEL*, p. 8). A second area of concern is the limitation in Crawford's ambition: his aim is to make the discipline's practitioners 'take account of the other cultures which are in part responsible for the initial construction of "English Literature" as a subject' (*DEL*, p. 11). A significant part of his book, as well as his more recent work, is therefore devoted to revealing the eighteenth-century Scottish origins of English Literature as a university discipline. He demands that readers and critics give Scotland due credit for its part in building a newly devolved, yet still structurally coherent, discipline of 'Eng. Lit.'. To this end, *Devolving English Literature* is concerned with *de*-centring – taking canonical writers and suggesting that more attention should be paid to their peripheral origins – rather than attempting the more radical task of trying to *re*-centre a literary tradition in a formerly peripheral space. Thirdly, as one of his critics suggests, he avoids 'the English question': by exploring the regional identity of non-Oxbridge or non-London-based English writers in the same breath as he restores the national identity of Scottish writers, Crawford appears to equate the English provinces with the Scottish nation.[9] In this sense, his thesis supports those who see cultural and political devolution as an end point (Scotland as a region of Britain, much like north-east England, for example), and not as a step on the path to Scottish independence.

Michael Gardiner, also a Scottish critic, develops many of the areas that Crawford neglects. He begins to address the English question, arguing that in recent years, what he terms 'the English problem' has received some attention by cultural critics aiming to find 'a national "voice" not subsumed in the UK' (*CRBD*, p. 146). Gardiner discovers signs of an emergent English culture not in literature, but in the rave music scene that emerged in the English countryside in the 1990s, a challenge, he argues, to the pastoral vision of the English countryside 'in official Anglo-British discourse' (*CRBD*, p. 118). Secondly, Gardiner's work attempts to move away from the Anglocentric British tradition of English Literature, instead re-centring the study of literature in its constituent nations. To this end, he argues that the political devolution achieved in 1999 is the 'British endgame' that will lead to the break-up of the union (*CRBD*, p. x). Crucially, he coins the term 'post-British', which he employs – in a similar sense to the conventional use of 'postcolonial' – to refer not only to the future break-up of the union, a temporal point of 'hard politics' not yet reached, but also to any writing that engages in imagining a Scottish, English or Welsh culture after the British nation-state has ceased to exist, even if such writing is produced before that historical point is reached (*CRBD*, p. x). Gardiner contends that this 'act of imagining' has begun a process of cultural devolution which anticipates and engenders its political counterpart. Part of this 'act of imagining' involves the recovery of national cultures that have been subordinated within the British union for centuries. These, he suggests, cannot simply be remembered by volition; they must be 'recovered' by re-contextualisation, a process which involves drawing attention both to post-British thought in each nation (a phenomenon which, thanks to Gardiner's definition, is as old as the union itself), and to the role the non-English (as well as the English) British nations played in the establishment and administration of Empire (*CRBD*, p. 21).

Gardiner's approach is bold, connecting cultural development to political change, and beginning to address the question of English national identity. It also complicates Scotland's relation to Britain, on the one hand resisting the 'easy' postcolonial reading by which some nationalists view Scotland simply as a victim of English imperialist aggression, while on the other drawing attention to postcolonialism's failure to recognise the 'transnational and margin-centred status of Britain itself' (*CRBD*, p. 20). However, as with Crawford, there are several areas in which Gardiner's work needs to be developed. Firstly, his wide cultural emphasis leaves comparatively little space for engagement with literature. Secondly, although he critiques the Anglocentrism of English Literature, he does not consider how the various traditions of literary criticism have created and sustained this bias. Finally, although the book is entitled *The Cultural Roots of British Devolution*, there is – again, as in Crawford's work – remarkably little mention of Wales. In fact, Gardiner discusses Wales only to summarise the reasons why the pressure for Welsh political devolution is not as great as it is in Scotland:

> *Plaid Cymru* (PC) has never exerted a fully pro-independence, post-British pressure, and nor do they today, concentrating on the Welsh Executive as a parliamentary pressure group. Wales still has very few separate civic institutions upon which to base a state. Arthurian and Tudor mythscapes have weighed heavily on Wales's sense of separateness, and the Welsh Renaissance, which pre-dated the Scottish one, had trouble collapsing culture and politics. (*CRBD*, p. 40)

Arthurian 'mythscapes' and the Welsh Renaissance will form part of a discussion of Welsh cultural identity, insofar as they concern my case study, but it is worth pointing out the brevity of these comments on Wales.

They show an unawareness of the long-lasting debates in Wales about Anglocentrism, and the re-centring of literary study, as well as a lack of sensitivity to the ways in which Wales's longer union with England, more vigorous indigenous language movement on the one hand, and more thorough Anglicisation on the other, have made the task of imagining a post-British Welsh culture even more complex than is the case with Scotland. The sheer complexity of the relation between culture and politics in Wales – indeed anywhere – should make us wary of 'collapsing' the distinction between them.

In spite of these drawbacks, the critical work of Crawford and Gardiner constitutes the most promising work to date within the field of devolutionary British literature. This book develops the work of these two critics by extending their Scotland-focused efforts to Wales. Rather than pursue Crawford's more limited aims, it follows Gardiner's ambitious efforts to re-centre literary study away from the Anglocentric British tradition of 'English Literature', and towards newly defined entities in Wales, Scotland and England. It aims to make good some of the areas on which Gardiner is silent, providing his wider cultural analysis with a more literary focus, and considering the role of the literary academy in the creation and maintenance of the discipline's Anglocentrism. In the paragraphs that follow, I aim to indicate, especially for readers unfamiliar with the scene, the complexity of the debate within Wales over literary devolution.

Gardiner suggests that the process of political independence for Scotland will force England to consider its own sense of nationhood, and renegotiate its relations to other nations in the union. In order to provide a cultural platform for political independence to take place, he argues for a critical approach to literature which re-contextualises writers, drawing attention to the way in which the political context of their time determines the parameters of the literary choices available to them. In this way, he is able to 'recover' Scottish writers for his 'post-British' reading, as well as to identify the Anglicising characteristics of those authors who have been historically accepted into the canon of English Literature. This method, implies Gardiner, not only unpicks Scotland's cultural ties to Britain since the eighteenth century; it also opens for discussion the relation between Scotland and imperialism – imperialism being central to the British project, and something to which all of its nations contributed..

A similar approach from a Welsh perspective would need to go back further in time, and address not only the centrality of imperialism to the British project, but also, since Tudor times, to the English nation. The Welsh historian Kenneth O. Morgan points out that while modern Scotland is the product of the Act of Union in 1707, modern Wales is 'the product of an act of conquest imposed on a defeated and fragmented people by Edward I over 400 years earlier' in the thirteenth century.[10] In 1536 and 1543, after two hundred years of occupation, following Henry VIII's break from Rome and the declared creation of the 'English Empire', 'Wales was assimilated into the English state and legal system', beginning a process that would lead to 'one Welsh institution after another [being] extinguished' and creating 'patterns of English or Anglo-Norman infil-tration' that are still reflected today.[11] Scotland, by contrast, was an estab-lished nation before its incorporation into the British union, and has since retained many of its national institutions, particularly in the educational, banking, and legal systems, although not – until its re-institution in 1999 – its own parliament. The process of the assimilation of Wales into the English state, following Henry VIII's declaration of the 'English Empire', thus arguably makes Wales the first English colony. The basic means by which Welsh assimilation was achieved – military victory, followed by the institutions of the colonising state assuming authority over, and usurping, those of the colonised – is a model that would be adopted in the later assimilation of Ireland and Scotland into an Anglicised Britain run from London, the seat of English government.

A similar approach from a Welsh perspective would also have to address the effects of nineteenth-century industrialisation on Wales, events which generated unprecedented historical change, but most significantly, pro-portionate to its size, demographic and linguistic upheaval unmatched by the experience of virtually any other European nation in that period. Some simple statistics begin to convey the enormity of the change undergone by Wales. At the beginning of the nineteenth century, the population of Wales was about half a million, equally spread across the country, of whom 80 per cent were employed in agriculture. The predominant language by far was Welsh and there were no urban centres. By 1914, the population had increased fivefold to two and a half million, half of whom spoke English, two-thirds of whom lived in the southern industrial areas of Glamorgan and Gwent, and three-quarters of whom lived in towns and cities (chief among which were Cardiff, Swansea, Merthyr and Newport). Of the people who left rural Wales, most went to the industrial areas of south-east Wales, although we should not forget that, by 1901, a quarter of the population of Carmarthenshire, in south-west Wales, lived in the industrial towns of Llanelli and Carmarthen, while a similar proportion of Merionethshire's population, in north Wales, lived in the industrial town of Blaenau Ffestiniog. A significant proportion of the rural population, too, left for the industrial areas of the English north-west, the English Midlands or London, while a further group migrated to Australasia or North America (an exodus which was not on the same scale as that from England, Scotland or Ireland). There were also unprecedented levels of immigration into Wales from Scotland, Ireland and England, as well as from other parts of Europe, a phenomenon that continued well into the second decade of the twentieth century (and which was abruptly reversed in the Depression years of the 1920s and 30s). During the first decade of the twentieth century, for example, 130,000 people arrived in south Wales, contributing to a level of immigration for the Welsh nation unsurpassed, in that decade, by anywhere other than the USA.[12]

These historical changes increased the complexity of the language question in Wales, in ways that are not repeated elsewhere in these islands. Unlike Scotland and Ireland, where Scots Gaelic and Irish Gaelic are spoken by 1 per cent of the respective populations, Welsh in the early twenty-first century is spoken by more than 20 per cent of people in Wales (a figure that is steadying after declining from about 50 per cent in 1901). The survival, if precarious, of the Welsh language – compared to others in the Celtic language family – has led to some historical differences between the modern literatures of Wales, Scotland and Ireland, particularly in the importance each nation ascribes to the indigenous language, and to the legitimacy of national expression in English. The complexity – and historical bitterness – of the language issue in Wales is little understood beyond its borders. As Tom Nairn, another Scottish critic, writing in November 1976 in the Welsh cultural magazine *Planet*, puts it: 'few Scots understand or sympathise with the anguishing dilemmas of the language problem here'.[13]

Nowhere are these 'anguishing dilemmas' more in evidence than in the public speeches of Saunders Lewis, the most prominent Welsh-language writer of the twentieth century, and co-founder of Plaid Genedlaethol Cymru, the Welsh Nationalist Party. In a lecture provocatively entitled 'Is there an Anglo-Welsh literature?', delivered to a University College, Cardiff audience in 1938, he advocates a monoglot Welsh society, declaring that there is no such thing as an Anglophone Welsh writer. Artists, he argues, represent society, and because there is no such thing as an organic, English-language, Welsh society with its own dialect, idiom and relation to the land, there cannot be a Welsh literature written in English.[14] Earlier on in the decade, he presided over Plaid's policy of de-industrialising Wales, and declared his ambition to 'annihilate English in Wales'.[15] In 1936, he famously took part in an arson attack on the newly

built RAF base on the Llŷn peninsula in the north-west, an overwhelmingly
Welsh-speaking region, claiming at his Caernarfon trial that 'for Wales,
the preservation of the Llŷn peninsula from this Anglicization is a matter
of life and death'.[16] His views (explored in more depth in Chapter Two)
broadly reflect the essentialist idea that to be Welsh, it is necessary to
speak Welsh, a position that of course problematises the identity of the
majority of people in Wales, most of whom live in the industrialised and
predominantly English-speaking valleys of south Wales. Such views have
not only generated an at times bitter linguistic divide within Welsh society;
they have also effectively disabled the nationalist movement in Wales by
historically preventing it from gaining the kind of support it might have
won among the English-speaking population of the industrial areas of
south Wales.

Unfortunately, such linguistic essentialism – while understandable as
an anguished response to the erosion of an indigenous language – has
remained a feature of Welsh culture through much of the twentieth century.
Saunders Lewis made another significant intervention in Welsh public life
in 1962 when, in his lecture 'Tynged yr Iaith' (The Fate of the Language),
he injected urgency and dynamism into the Welsh language movement,
predicting that, if nothing were done, Welsh would die out as a living
language by the beginning of the twenty-first century.[17] R. Tudur Jones
echoes Saunders Lewis, arguing that the Welsh language ('the supreme
mark of Welsh distinctiveness')[18] has a 'unique cultural thrill' that 'the
entire Welsh population' should 'share' (*DN*, p. 202). Acknowledging that
'this is not practically possible in this generation', Tudur Jones advocates
bilingualism as one of a series of public and education policies that will
bring it about 'in due course' (*DN*, p. 202). In 'The Welsh Language and
Religion', he expounds in similar terms on the true significance of
the Welsh language'.[19] Among 'monoglot English-speakers of Welsh
extraction whose parents or grandparents spoke Welsh', he argues that
English-speaking Welsh speakers who 'call themselves Welshmen . . .
lack the one distinctive qualification that gives the Welshman his cultural
uniqueness, namely command of the Welsh language'.[20]

    J. R. Jones, who in 1962 helped to found Cymdeithas yr Iaith Gymraeg
(the Welsh Language Society), shares similar views. He questions whether
meaningful dialogue can be held between those from the two linguistic
traditions: 'the split is deepening and the prejudices and hatreds which
are a consequence of it are worsening'.[21] Any 'bridge' between the two
sides must occur through the medium of Welsh (*NLD*, p. 144), in order
to avoid a situation in which Welsh continues to enjoy lesser status in

Wales, and in which it becomes merely a 'second-rate minority language' (*NLD*, p. 155). Jones rejects what he describes as 'negative and submissive craving for "dialogue" and "tolerance"' (*NLD*, p. 145), calling instead for activism that '*creates the conditions* for the restoration of Welsh to precedence in its own land' (*NLD*, p. 155).

The insistence by English-speaking inhabitants on their own Welshness has offered an understandable corrective to the linguistic essentialism demonstrated above. While much of this work has been carried out over the last fifty years by historians (Glanmor Williams, Gwyn A. Williams, Kenneth Morgan, John Davies, Dai Smith and Chris Williams, among others), literary scholars too have played their part in establishing the Welshness of the English-speaking culture that emerged in the south Wales valleys in the early twentieth century. While the battle to maintain Welsh-language communities and to extend Welsh-language culture continues (and faces new challenges in each generation), the kind of linguistic essentialism seen from the 1930s onwards is no longer the defining feature of Welsh culture.

Glyn Jones is one literary scholar who worked tirelessly in this field. The title of his 1968 publication, *The Dragon Has Two Tongues*, itself alludes to the fact that Wales is a nation in which both Welsh and English are spoken. Much of the book serves to distinguish English-language Welsh culture, mainly in the south Wales coalfield valleys, from English culture. It is a key text that successfully establishes Welsh writing in English as a legitimate and distinctive field of academic study. However, by today's standards, there are four areas in which Jones's book falls short: in its use of the terms 'Welsh' and 'Anglo-Welsh'; in its near-exclusive focus on the emergence of an Anglophone Welsh culture in the south Wales industrial valleys of the 1930s; in its reliance on auto-biographical experience to justify its claims; and in its exclusive focus on male authors.

Turning to the first of these areas, Jones's terminology unfortunately serves to undermine the Welshness of the English-speaking Welsh. Ever sensitive to 'Welsh-speaking *litterateurs*' for whom the appellation of 'Welsh' to English-speaking Welshmen 'appeared misleading, even pre-sumptuous', Jones 'reluctantly' develops different terms for writers from the two cultures: he calls English-language Welsh poets 'Anglo-Welsh', and Welsh-language poets 'Welsh, unqualified and unhyphenated'.[22] This is understandable in the context in which he was writing: in the aftermath of Saunders Lewis's 1962 predictions for the bleak future of Welsh-language culture, the formation of Cymdeithas yr Iaith Gymraeg, and the emergence of nationalist protest movements, it was important to build bridges between the two linguistic communities. However, Jones's terminology is not helpful in the way it implicitly qualifies the Welshness of those who speak English. His work is today best understood as a necessary stage on the journey of English-speaking Welsh culture to a position in which it can assert its right to speak for Wales, but one (now that this aim has been achieved) whose key terms are out of date.

The second and third weaknesses in Jones's approach – his near-exclusive focus on the emergence of an Anglophone Welsh culture in the south Wales valleys of the 1930s, and his reliance on autobiographical experience to justify his claims – are closely related. At one point, Jones calls Keidrych Rhys's journal *Wales*, founded in 1937, 'the first literary magazine of any standing, and standards, for Welshmen writing in English' (*DTT*, p. 34). This is a revealing comment: while the publication of Rhys's journal is certainly a major event in Welsh letters, its significance is distorted by Jones's self-conscious over-emphasis on the autobiographical. He declares: 'I find I can only write at any length and with understanding about the books of men with whom I have made personal contact, and for whom I feel, or have felt, sympathy' (*DTT*, p. 57). This tends to skew his analysis of English-language Welsh culture towards the south Wales valleys, and towards the 1930s. Of the six writers he considers in *The Dragon Has Two Tongues*, three – Gwyn Thomas, Jack Jones and Idris Davies – are from the industrial valleys of south Wales; one – Huw Menai – becomes a writer after moving there, and a fifth – Dylan Thomas – comes from Swansea. Only one of the writers, Caradoc Evans, from the Welsh-speaking, rural, south-west, remains outside the industrialised, predominantly English-speaking areas of south Wales. Jones himself is aware of this omission, pointing out the lack of any writer 'from the North Wales scene' (*DTT*, p. 59). He does acknowledge that Menai came from Caernarfon, where he was born, grew up and worked, and which he left at the age of eighteen to go south to the coalfield, but his analysis of Menai focuses entirely on his time in Merthyr Vale, south Wales (*DTT*, p. 144). Indeed, he writes that while Menai had known 'poverty' in north Wales, he only came across 'widespread industrial squalor', 'ruthless exploitation', 'strikes', 'lock-outs', 'victimization' and 'uncurbed economic banditry' when he came to the south, a statement that downplays the considerable north Walian experience of such phenomena (ibid.). Menai left the slate-mining area of Caernarfonshire in 1906, in the aftermath of one of the most bitter industrial disputes in Welsh history, described by Gwyn A. Williams as 'a class war whose sheer ferocity and tenacity were probably unique in Britain, certainly as harsh as the black year of 1926 in the South' (*DTT*, p. 200). Menai would therefore have been well-aware of the factors that Jones mentions.

Jones's study is limited not only by geography, but also by time: his focus on the 1930s. Most of the above-mentioned writers achieved recognition in the 1930s, but as recent work by Jane Aaron, Katie Gramich and M. Wynn Thomas in particular shows, there were plenty of English-language Welsh writers before this period. Jones indeed notes the existence of O. M. Edwards's 1890s journal, *Wales*, with its call for 'a literature that will be English in language but Welsh in spirit', but concludes that 'the dawn these modern-sounding words spoke of would appear to have been, in 1894, a false one' (*DTT*, p. 34, note 1). As the cautious wording of this footnote implies, Jones seems aware that this is a contentious issue: other periods and other English-language Welsh communities have also contributed to the tradition of Welsh writing in English. Turn-of-the-century journals like *Wales*, but also *Cymru Fydd* (*Young Wales*) and *Nationalist* all contain English-language literary material of 'standing and standards'. To label these as 'false dawns' on the basis of autobiographical experience reveals a bias towards the English-language culture of the south Wales valleys in the 1930s at the expense of other English-language communities within Wales at other times.

The fourth weakness in Jones's approach – the exclusive focus on 'Welsh*men* writing in English' (my italics) – could be excused as the unconscious use of a term (by which he in fact means 'Welsh men and women'), but it does reflect the fact that all six writers referred to in Jones's book are male (*DTT*, p. 34). This bias also occurs in some of the historical narratives to come out of the south Wales valleys in recent years: Gwyn A. Williams's otherwise brilliant tour-de-force, *When Was Wales*, published in 1985, is unfortunately marred by the occasional display of unreconstructed masculinity. At one point he refers to south Walian 'men [who], with most, if not all their women trailing dutifully behind, strutted like fighting cocks through an economy which was perhaps the most buoyant and expansive in Britain' (*WWWH*, p. 221). This compares to his description of the early 1980s, when, after the closure of much of Wales's traditional manufacturing base, 'the entire Welsh working population was beginning to take on the character of "women's work"' (*WWWH*, p. 298). The use of such terms may be defended on the grounds that they reflect the patriarchal culture from which they emerge (Williams's use of speech marks around 'women's work' suggests that he was drawing attention to the perception of non-manufacturing work within the culture, rather than endorsing the use of the term himself), but it is also worth pointing out that they are today unacceptable in a society which is attempting to move beyond these gender-based hierarchies.

Recent scholars have addressed the shortfall in each of these four areas. One of the strengths of Dai Smith's work since the 1980s, a major intervention in the field of Welsh letters, has been its assertion of the unhyphenated Welshness of the culture that emerged in Cardiff and the industrialised valleys of south-east Wales in the early twentieth century. Smith places himself in a tradition of historiography which, since Glanmor Williams's 1966 publication, *Merthyr Politics: the Making of a Working-Class Tradition*, has spoken 'directly of *industrial* South Wales', thereby countering the historically 'unbalanced' focus on Welsh rural history (*WW*, p. 7). Also helpful has been Smith's insistence on the absence of an 'unbroken community' in the history of any modern society, especially that of Wales (*WW*, p. 54), and on the eighteenth- and nineteenth-century invention of much of Welsh national culture (*WW*, p. 38). Smith writes of various Welsh traditions in this way – the symbol of the daffodil, Welsh costume, Dame Wales, the land of song and harpists, choral societies, and rugby – but he might have added to this list the translation into English of the Welsh literary tradition, which began in earnest with the work of Charlotte Guest and Thomas Stephens in the industrial centre of Merthyr in the mid-nineteenth century. Guest's *Mabinogion* and Stephens's *The Literature of the Kymry* are modern publications, cultural products of the nineteenth-century industrialisation and urbanisation of the south Wales valleys. Smith tends to downplay the importance of this English-language engagement with the cultural artefacts of a feudal Welsh culture. While he rightly points out that it is 'anachronistic to read our post-eighteenth century idea of nationality back into societies based on tribal loyalties' (*WW*, p. 42), he does not develop the idea that the modern-day reclaiming of this mythical Welsh culture can play a major role in the development of a modern sense of nationhood. Smith's relative silence on the avenues of enquiry opened up by this English-language reclamation of Wales's past is indicative of the principal shortfall in his work: like Glyn Jones before him, Smith's near-exclusive focus on the English-language communities of inter-war south Wales occurs at the expense of other communities within Wales. There is a diversity of Welsh-language culture which is hardly reflected in Smith's analysis. He rightly questions any sense of 'unbroken community' over centuries, but is in danger of painting the whole Welsh-language community with the same brush. For example, while he mentions that the industrialised valleys at the western end of the south Wales coalfield were Welsh-speaking, filled with immigrants from the depopulated rural Welsh hinterland, he does not develop the logical argument that, like their English-language counterparts in the eastern end of the coalfield, these western areas – the industrial district of the Swansea Valley, as well as communities around Ammanford and Carmarthen – constitute a new, modern society, founded on a break with the historical continuities of the past. The radical Welsh-language press in 1880s Caernarfon, to give another example, is hardly the organ for 'unbroken community' that Smith's analysis implies.

The final area in which Smith's work is occasionally found wanting, again like that of Glyn Jones, is in his reliance on autobiography. In *Wales! Wales?*, for example, his opening gambit is to title his first chapter 'A Welcome to Wales' and then to open with 'But a welcome to whose Wales? Mine of course!' (*WW*, p. 1), a hospitality matched only by Smith's love for the working-class culture of the Valleys to which he describes himself as 'irredeemably addicted' (*WW*, p. 3). However, Smith employs autobiography most notably in his book, *In the Frame: Memory and Society 1910 to 2010*, the opening lines of which are worth closer examination:

> This book is an alternative history of the past century in Wales. It is not a counter-factual history, nor revisionist history, just alternative. The viewpoint I use to recapture some of this unfolded history – almost two-thirds of which I have now lived through – is resolutely my own, and so it is necessarily askance, central, tangential, even close-up-and-personal, because squinting myopically can sometimes bring up the telling detail which is lost in a panoramic view.[23]

The emphasis from the opening line is on Smith's empiricism: the phrase 'it is not counter-factual' implies the existence of an empirically verifiable set of facts on which it is based, and carries echoes of Smith's criticism of Emyr Humphreys's 'buckl[ing] and bend[ing]' of historical 'detail' to meet a nationalist agenda (in Humphreys's 1983 text, *The Taliesin Tradition*) (*WW*, p. 167). Nonetheless, while Smith's approach may be 'factual', his contextualising of those 'detail[s]' also reveals something of his underlying concerns. Firstly, his use of the term 'Wales' co-opts the national descriptor for a book that is in fact more regional, focusing for the most part as it does on the industrial valleys in the south-east of the country. Secondly, there is a revealing ambiguity in his employment of a 'viewpoint ... resolutely my own', a phrase which, on the one hand, implies the humility of a personal account ('viewpoint' would seem to acknowledge the existence of other possible positions), and yet, on the other hand, suggests something more. By presenting a personal narrative while simultaneously claiming it as 'central', or using the device of auto-biography to present a story which he intends to be so much more than a personal account, Smith is having his cake and eating it. After Smith's lifetime of public service, this moment of self-indulgence is perfectly fine, but it is important to point out that, by using autobiography, Smith adopts a genre that allows him to bypass the usual due weighing of evidence associated with empirically based historical narrative, and present a more partial view. In a fragmented modern society, subject to so many dis-continuities through its history, and in which the national narrative is so contested, the use of autobiography serves the dual purposes of recording a culture that is constantly in flux, where lifestyles disappear with each generation (if not faster), and of forestalling the need to write beyond one's immediate subculture. As Barbara Prys-Williams writes in her study of the autobiographical genre in Wales: 'These are powerful personal constructions of a time and place. They should not, however, be mistaken for accurate historical record.'[24] Moreover, by focusing on 'memory' (rather than 'history'), Smith implies that he is giving a personal account, even though he was not alive for one-third of the period covered in the book, and was an adult for less than half. In the final analysis, there is little difference between his own approach and that for which he criticises Emyr Humphreys in *The Taliesin Tradition*: both writers' work reflects the difficulties inherent in conveying the 'reality' of the Welsh people, especially when the 'reality' in both linguistic traditions is subject to radical discontinuities through history. Humphreys elides the many changes that Welsh-language culture has undergone between its feudal past and its contemporary modernity, while Smith has to contend with the disappearance of the working-class Valleys culture in the last seventy years. Both writers are therefore selective in their use of so-called 'detail': Humphreys's account sweeps grandly over centuries, while presenting tenuous continuities, and Smith makes choices in terms of period, geography and autobiography, choices that are significant, as I have tried to show, in terms of what he excludes. Both, to quote Smith's critique of Humphreys, are presenting 'a future vision wrapped up in the legitimising clothes of the past, real or mythical: it scarcely matters' (*WW*, p. 43).

A critic who has done more than any other to develop the field of English-language Welsh literature, and to extend its parameters, is M. Wynn Thomas, whose seminal book, *Internal Difference: Literature*

in Twentieth-Century Wales (1992), engages in the hard task of documenting the relations and interactions between the cultures, literatures and
language-groups of Wales. His method of 'frank, provisional empiricism',
which patiently charts the interactions between writers in each linguistic
community across the regions of Wales, must be seen as a response-in-
kind to the matter-of-fact, evidence-based approach practised by cultural
historians (Dai Smith among others), but it must also be seen as an attempt
to counter the divisions made clear by the 'no' vote in the 1979 referendum
on devolution.[25] Coining his notion of 'internal discourse', Thomas explores
ways in which the two Welsh cultures have 'to some extent developed in
tandem, and share certain unnoticed common features that show them to
have been the products and producers of the same history' (*ID*, p. iv).
Alyce von Rothkirch and Daniel Williams have usefully characterised
his work as the effort to register 'tensions between competing visions of
"Wales" . . . whilst gesturing towards a critical approach that seeks to
foster a common ground beyond the bitter divisions'.[26] One of the drawbacks of *Internal Difference*, however, is that Thomas is 'chary of separat-
ing generalisations from the specific contexts which give them meaning',
a reluctance that causes him to characterise any 'systematic or schematic'
approach as a 'mistake' because it would be 'false to the elusive terms
on which literature itself actually functions' (*ID*, p. xiii). The result is a
series of powerful essays which, while they speak to the vital 'internal'
need to heal bitter linguistic divisions (by documenting the sheer range
of points of correspondence between many communities across the two
languages), necessarily lack the external impact that a systematic, theoretically informed, comparative approach might have. Nonetheless, Thomas's
emphasis on the 'internal' is a necessary stage; it brings closer the historical
moment when Welsh culture can overcome its divisions and define itself
against an external other.
    Another factor that brings such an historical moment closer has been
the success of the 1997 devolution referendum (not to mention the 2011
vote to extend the National Assembly's law-making powers). The existence
of a bilingual Assembly has led to an increased prominence for the Welsh
language. In many ways, the hope expressed in 1971 by cultural critic
Ned Thomas, that, given official status, Welsh would become a language
of modernity, with loosened ties to religious and rural ways of life, has
materialised.[27] Welsh is now the medium of instruction in many schools
in formerly English-speaking areas, and in some university courses. Bilingualism in all official literature is now the norm. Geraint Evans argues
that, as a result of the 'institutional changes' brought about by devolution,

'official forms and signs, legal proceedings, education, and above all broadcasting were beginning to give the language not just a legal status but a linguistic life in areas which were essential if survival was to be possible'.[28]

In 1999, two years after the vote on devolution in Wales, M. Wynn Thomas published *Corresponding Cultures: the Two Literatures of Wales*, in an atmosphere of hope and expectation. Its essays begin to engage with more theoretically informed approaches to Welsh literature, lines of enquiry that account for internal differences within Welsh culture by reference to external factors such as imperialism. 'Hidden Attachments', for example, suggests that Homi Bhabha's term 'hybridity' is a useful tool for 'those of us who acknowledge the validity of the different kinds of Welshness'.[29] The essay calls for 'new, subtle, ways of exploring the fluid relationship between cultures in Wales, with particular reference, for example, to liminal, or boundary states' (*CC*, p. 50). Thomas argues that there are 'innumerable' examples of how Welsh literature has been produced as a result of a 'cross-over from one language, and culture, to another', and argues that critics have 'scarcely begun . . . to examine the ways in which two cultures can be co-operative – can make history and make literature, at the same time and in the same place' (ibid.). Such a project, the essay continues, needs to consider factors including the 'common point of origin' of the Welsh-language renaissance and Welsh writing in English (ibid.); empirical consideration of 'translation, numbers of literary journals, so-called seepage [and] intertextuality' (*CC*, p. 52); ways in which each culture has portrayed the other as 'dark foil to its own virtues' (*CC*, p. 57); and the two cultures' 'shared social experience'. To embark on such a project would be 'to begin the process of making connections, finding associations, across the cultural divide that has been the making and undoing of modern Wales' (*CC*, p. 74). Thomas has shifted the debate in Wales away from internal divisions between 'monolithic' entities, towards a point at which the nation, its internal differences acknowledged, may be more significantly defined as a unified whole. These essays are therefore remarkable for what they reveal about how the terms of debate have changed: reflecting the new-found trust between the two linguistic communities, they insist upon the premise that both cultures are equally legitimately Welsh, and call for new ways of understanding recent divisions within the context of wider, external factors.

This is a call echoed in Thomas's introduction to the collection of essays edited by Tony Brown and Russell Stephens, *Nations and Relations: Writing across the British Isles* (2000). Here he argues that, 'in the light of the recent devolution of a degree of political power to the respective "national regions" of the United Kingdom', there is a need 'to reconfigure cultural relations through a realignment of thinking about writing the "Anglo-Celtic archipelago"'.[30] He calls for Anglophone Welsh culture to consider 'its relationship to other cultures, including those other constituent elements of the wider Anglophone (and traditionally Anglocentric) British culture' (*I*, p. iii). Such work, he goes on to argue, 'in order to be culturally productive . . . must involve a turn away from . . . the old Anglocentric ideology of Britishness' (ibid.). It must begin the task of establishing 'the cultural equivalent of a council of the islands' (ibid.). He also sounds a note of warning: until this happens, we will be unable to live 'intellectually and imaginatively, in a decentred world where England now takes its place in an intricate constellation of island cultures' (*I*, p. iv). While this strikes a slightly conservative tone – its use of the term 'decentred' reminiscent of Crawford's limited project (to which Thomas refers) – it nonetheless sets out the challenge for future work in the field of re-configuring cultural relations between the nations of these islands.

More recently still, critics have risen to M. Wynn Thomas's challenge in a range of different ways. The work of Jane Aaron, Katie Gramich and Kirsti Bohata, in particular, has countered the unreconstructed masculinity evident at an earlier phase of the Anglophone Welsh critical tradition. All three have recovered the work of Welsh women writers and have been supported in this enterprise by the publishing house, Honno. To single out one example, Gramich's most recent criticism of the Welsh-language author, Kate Roberts, building on critical work by Welsh-language col-leagues, has made her novels and short stories more widely available to an English-language readership.[31] Bohata has taken Thomas's use of Bhabha's 'discourse of hybridity' much further, developing the idea of postcolonial Wales.[32] This is a direction of travel indicated in the work of earlier critics, Raymond Garlick and Ned Thomas, who each made comparisons between Anglophone Welsh literature and that of other colonised nations, but in its thoroughness, and its application of post-colonialism's critical tools to the Welsh situation, Bohata's work marks a step change.

Adapting Bhabha for use within a devolutionary British context builds on a point made by both Gardiner and Daniel Williams, who, from a Scottish and Welsh perspective respectively, criticise the fact that 'even in the late 1990s, when devolution was taking apart the union, most post-colonial critics continued to ignore the national makeup of the world's most colonising state' (*CRBD*, p. 19). Gardiner indeed reserves his most pointed remarks for Bhabha, 'key chronicler of English Literature's "narration" of identities' and a critic who 'spent much of the 1990s discussing questions of transnationalism, cultural marginality, and break-up, without reference to the margin-centred status of Britain itself' (*CRBD*, p. 21). Williams, writing four years before Gardiner, is equally damning: 'whilst post-colonial critics have demonstrated an awareness of the dangers of homogenising "the East" in their writings, they are far less inclined to register the equally disabling tendency to homogenize "the West"'.[33] He points out that although it is important to acknowledge 'the central role that the Celtic peoples willingly played in Britain's imperial project', the West should not be totalised as 'the homogenous hegemonic centre of power', and he calls for more critical attention to be paid to the makeup of Britain as a colonising power, in order that the position of Wales and Scotland not be seen as coterminous with that of England.[34] Bohata does this effectively within a Welsh context. However, what she does not do – because Bhabha's critical terms do not offer the means to do so – is ground her postcolonialism in a materialist approach to culture in which imperialism is contextualised within an understanding of Western capitalism. This is a long-standing problem with postcolonialism in general, and one to which Benita Parry, Neil Lazarus and Crystal Bartolovich, among others, drew attention more than a decade ago.[35]

The failure to connect a transnational critical approach to a materialist understanding of society undermines many of the attempts to place the culture of colonised nations in a transnational context. Michael Cronin, for example, suggests that cosmopolitanism offers 'a conceptual framework for a way of thinking about the cultures of countries like Wales and Ireland that is potentially of interest [to those interested in] contemporary globalization theory'.[36] Identifying what he terms a macrocosmopolitanism, 'a tendency to locate the cosmopolitan moment in the construction of empires, in the development of large nation-states, [and] in the creation of supra-national organizations' (*GQ*, p. 188), he proposes an opposing concept of microcosmopolitanism, which he defines as 'cosmopolitanism not from above but from below' (ibid.). This enables him to see 'Irish set-dancing in a pub in rural Clare' as a practice not only 'deeply rooted in a locality' but also 'the fruit of the influence of French dancing-masters who came to Ireland at the end of the eighteenth century' (*GQ*, p. 195). Any local or national expression can therefore be seen as a transnational and cosmopolitan phenomenon. By bringing the same critical tools to bear on the literary registration of Welsh rural experience, Cronin argues that it will be possible to see it not as 'wistful *passéisme*' but as 'forward-looking, in its restoration of political complexity and cultural dynamism' (*GQ*, p. 196). However, his vision of a transnational level playing-field of interconnected cultures, manifested in local expression, is too idealist: it ignores the material basis through which power is unevenly divided between cultures, and through which literary expression is mediated, if not controlled.

In Wales, material factors since the Second World War have been crucial to the way that the literary field has developed. In particular, subsidy has enabled journals like *Poetry Wales*, *New Welsh Review* and *Planet* to flourish, while subventions operated through key agencies such as the Welsh Arts Council, the Welsh Books Council and the University of Wales Press have been essential to the publication of many books on Welsh subject matter. While John Harris calls for a diminishment in the dependence on grants, suggesting that 'state subsidy takes the dynamism out of publishing', his argument fails to recognise that forcing Welsh writers and critics to compete in a 'free' marketplace across Britain will lead to the non-publication of specialised texts that would fail a 'market' test.[37] Two seminal series of recent years – the seven-volume, University of Wales Press published *Guide to Welsh Literature*, and the Library of Wales series (which, after initially predominantly featuring male writers, in later years has included more female authors) – would be unthinkable, not only without the driving passion (often against institutional indifference) of committed individuals, but also without the system of state subsidy that underpins scholarly work in Wales. Also crucial have been the wide range of groundbreaking initiatives overseen by Meic Stephens in his capacity as Literature Director of the Welsh Arts Council, culminating in the publication of *The Companion to the Literature of Wales*, and the establishment by Tony Brown, under the auspices of the Association for Welsh Writing in English, of the journal, *Welsh Writing in English: a Yearbook of Critical Essays*. Any transnational analysis of the Welsh literary field cannot ignore this material and the institutional infrastructure that underpins it.

This book develops these trends in the Anglophone literary culture of Wales in two ways. Firstly, it builds on M. Wynn Thomas's work by demonstrating another point of correspondence between the two linguistic communities. Although Edward Thomas wrote in English, he did not come from the 1930s south Wales valleys. He was a Wales-identified, but London-born, writer whose point of contact with Welsh-language culture lay in the newly industrialised area around Ammanford and Pontardulais in south-west Wales at the end of the nineteenth, and beginning of the twentieth, centuries. Secondly, this study contributes to the recent trend in comparative approaches. It develops the case for adopting a 'world literary studies' approach to the Welsh condition, and, by employing this kind of theoretical framework, it draws attention to the economic inequalities that underpin the wider marginalisation of literature from Wales.

The emerging field of 'world literary studies', as Theo D'Haen remarks, has known 'spectacular' success in the new millennium, unmatched by any other approach to literary studies.[38] Originating in the late 1820s in the use of the phrase 'Weltliteratur' by German writer Johann Wolfgang von Goethe, and later taken up by his compatriots Karl Marx and Friedrich Engels in *The Communist Manifesto*, the term 'world literature' has, since its initial usage, suggested, on the one hand, a hoped-for form of 'transnational communication' among European and then 'world' intellectuals, and on the other hand, the more unwelcome commercialisation of the 'world of letters', and a growing distinction in the modern world between popular and high culture (*HWL*, p. 8). While the term 'world literature' never entirely disappeared in the intervening decades (re-emerging for example over the nineteenth century to mean a canon of global 'Great Books' and later occupying a significant place in US university curricula), it has nonetheless since largely been subsumed under a dominant concept of national literatures. It is only since the 1990s that globalisation has led to 'a wholly new approach to world literature' (*HWL*, p. 25). Critics preeminent in the emergent field of world literary studies have returned to the dichotomy within the definition – 'world literature' both as a form of communication across cultures, and as the product of a commercialised, globalising industry – in order to develop critical paradigms that enable literary texts to be considered in light of their role as sites that facilitate and negotiate the representation of one national culture to another, and in respect of their position within a transnational capitalist system.

Significant differences in emphasis between key practitioners of world literary studies are, unsurprisingly, already becoming clear. Since the terrorist attacks in New York in September 2001, there has been a renewed interest in the US in approaches to literature that generate understanding of other national cultures – broadly speaking, a harking-back to the first element in the definition of world literature. The emphasis on translation by critics including Emily Apter and David Damrosch may be seen in this context.[39] At the same time, another group of critics has emerged whose work focuses not on 'the intrinsic literary value of such or such a work, author, genre, or any such thing, but [on] examining the circulation of literary works, genres and authors within a transnational or even a

global context' (*HWL*, p. 96). The stress here on world literature as a
system echoes the second element in the definition of world literature
given earlier, and it is to this emerging tradition in world literary studies
that this study aims to contribute.

Franco Moretti and Pascale Casanova are key theorists in this area.
Moretti suggests that 'the literature around us now is unmistakeably a
planetary system' and that, as a result, the methods of comparative literary
enquiry (which developed out of, and were traditionally limited to, the
principal national literatures of Western Europe) 'will no longer suffice'.[40]
By broadening the field to include national literatures outside of this
narrow, conventional ambit, world literary studies offers, for compara-
tivists, the opportunity to escape the bounds of the main literary traditions
(French, Italian, German, Spanish and English). In doing so, it follows
postcolonial criticism by turning its attention to literature from once-
colonised nations. In particular, it offers a set of critical tools for analysing
the movement of literary forms from one culture to another, and it offers
the prospect of placing this movement within a materialist analysis of the
economic inequalities that underpin the literary field (something that
non-Marxist postcolonial critics have historically shied away from). It
also presents the critic with tools that may be used to do what Homi
Bhabha so conspicuously fails to do: uncover the workings of the literary
field within the constituent nations of Britain.

Both Casanova and Moretti identify a world literature system that
is, as Moretti puts it, 'profoundly unequal' and deeply 'embedded' in a
writer's literary decisions, especially regarding form.[41] However, there
are significant differences between their respective interpretations, and
it is the ideas of Casanova, which were originally set out in *La République
mondiale des lettres* (1999; English translation, *The World Republic of
Letters*, 2004), and augmented by a 2005 essay in *New Left Review*, that
have come to be acknowledged as 'the point of departure' for the emerging
field.[42] Although Moretti's ideas about the transnational movement of the
novel form are well developed, his theories about world literature are set
out in more sporadic form (articles in *New Left Review*, *Critical Inquiry*
and *Novel*, as well as the three essays that form *Graphs, Maps, Trees:
Abstract Models for Literary Study*). As Frances Ferguson has suggested
in her comparison of the two critics, Moretti's analysis is primarily abstract
and experimental: he is 'less interested' than Casanova 'in the systematic
and methodological features' of world literary space.[43] While his work
has been characterised as 'a schema' (*PLH*, p. 670), that of Casanova provides clear models and paradigms which demonstrate how, in Casanova's

view, national literatures are brought into being by the literary strategies adopted by individual writers working within a literary system that they know extends beyond national borders. And whereas Moretti's approach 'ends by producing a history of literature that experiences little outside pressure' (*PLH*, p. 676), Casanova's model brings the material infrastructure of the field – its publishing houses, critical journals, readerships and so on – more explicitly into the critic's remit. Casanova thus develops a number of tools for investigating the role of the institutions that emerge alongside a national literature, an area that I wish to explore. In the last analysis, for reasons that will become clear in my later examination of Casanova's ideas, it is her model – with its terms 'dominant' and 'dominated' – that seems the better suited to examining the power relations within world literature, while Moretti's notion of 'centres', 'peripheries' and 'semi-peripheries' establishes a spatial model that is better equipped for showing how literary forms travel geographically from one national literary tradition to another. For the purposes of this project, therefore, I have based my investigations on the paradigm offered by Casanova.

Casanova's model certainly claims to offer a set of theoretical propositions through which a writer from a dominated nation may be rescued from assimilation into the dominant culture, and recovered for a marginalised literary tradition. While in some ways the choice of Britain might seem limiting – after all, one of the aims of Casanova's theory is to structure literary space in such a way that it enables connections to be made between writers operating in geographically and historically diverse areas and times – my aim is to reveal some of the tensions and contradictions for a Wales-identified writer operating within an Anglocentric British space. Dominant within British literary space, as my later case study will show, is an ideology of Anglocentrism that privileges English (and non-English) writers who subscribe to it, or whose work can be received in such a way that does not challenge it. This ideology suppresses non-Anglocentric English writers, as well as non-Anglocentric writers from other, non-English, British nations. Casanova's model of international literary space proves useful for analysing British space, an area which after all contains, in literary terms, a group of contrasting nations that are, to varying extents, dominant or dominated. By exploring how her model might be applied to a writer operative within this single space, I hope to offer radical and surprising re-readings of a well-known author, to shed light on the construction of identities within Britain, and to expose the Anglo-centripetal forces at work. This is in line with Casanova's study, for, although she fails to mention Wales, she does imply that her ideas may be applicable to Britain. Firstly, in her 'Irish paradigm', Casanova shows how Irish authors writing between 1890 and 1930 developed strategies that enable them to escape from the cultural domination of Britain. Secondly, Casanova makes brief reference to Alasdair Gray, James Kelman and Tom Leonard, Glaswegian novelists whose use of vernacular, like that of Joyce in Ireland, successfully appropriates the English language for Scotland.[44]

Taking my cue from her, I look at one writer in depth to show how world literary studies can help reconfigure British literature by drawing attention to the Anglocentrism on which it is based, and by providing a mechanism through which marginalised traditions within Britain might be made more prominent. My chosen subject is Edward Thomas, born in 1878 in London to Welsh parents, who made a living as a prose writer and literary journalist for fifteen years (from 1900 to 1915), before enlisting in the British Army, in whose uniform he died on 9 April 1917. To date, his considerable critical reputation has rested predominantly on the posthumous Anglocentric reception of his poetry, but there is a substantial body of prose and literary journalism, hitherto largely overlooked, which this book will explore in order to challenge this established reading.

Although Thomas's Englishness has occasionally been contested by the Welsh, such challenges have never previously been more than desultory, and are relatively unconvincing. By contrast, this study sets out to demonstrate, for the first time, how profoundly Thomas's consciousness of a Welsh identity informed his aesthetic. Moreover, his is a case that opens up questions concerning the routine practice of appropriating writers who are not unambiguously English into an Anglocentric tradition of 'English Literature', a practice that critics from certain traditions within Britain have an interest in sustaining. There is ample archival evidence to support a number of transnational readings of Thomas's work, perspectives that show the narrowness of the dominant Anglocentric critical paradigm. He offers a wealth of material through which Casanova's theories can be investigated.

This book may therefore be considered as a contribution to three areas. Firstly, it examines the suitability of Casanova's theory of world literature to the task of recovering a writer for a dominated British nation; secondly, it makes a more specific intervention in the field of British literatures, revealing the contrasting ways in which Thomas's work has been viewed from within different national and critical traditions, and considering the implications for these of claiming him as a Welsh writer; thirdly, it intervenes in the field of Edward Thomas criticism by revealing, through an examination of his literary journalism and overlooked prose, radically new ways of reading his work.

In practical terms, the argument proceeds in the following way: Chapter One summarises the main precepts of Casanova's theory, before identifying several weaknesses in her argument, and modifying her model of international literary space accordingly. The rest of the book uses her adjusted theory to examine the case of Edward Thomas. Chapter Two considers his reception by critics writing respectively from within the Welsh, and from within the dominant Anglocentric, traditions. Chapter Three, building on the modifications to Casanova's model, attempts to position Anglophone Welsh literature within the political and economic arenas at the turn of the twentieth century. Thomas is positioned in relation to the key figures in these areas.

Chapters Four, Five and Six apply Casanova's 'Irish paradigm' to Thomas and Wales in order to reveal a radically different writer from the one critics are familiar with. Chapter Four argues that his prose, literary journalism and poetry are informed to a previously unsuspected degree by an interest in the Welsh cultural tradition. In Chapter Five, by considering literary journalism largely forgotten since its publication, I argue that Thomas draws attention within British literary space to the example of Ireland, and that he draws parallels between its situation and that of Wales. He also subverts the Anglocentrism of British literary space by helping to import French modernism – in the shape of Paul Verlaine's 'nuance' and Maurice Maeterlinck's symbolism – into London. Moreover, in the context of the aftermath of the Oscar Wilde trials, Thomas's positive reviews of gay writers may be seen as a defiance of the British authorities' interference in literature. Finally, Chapter Six draws on Ian Baucom's reflections on modes of identity in the British Empire to suggest that Thomas's work, and his poetry in particular, may be read as a critique of Englishness that is informed by his position as a Welsh writer. At the end of this chapter, by way of conclusion, I summarise my findings, and try to indicate the implications they seem to me to carry for the three areas (world literary studies, British literary studies and Edward Thomas studies) upon which they have the most direct bearing.

1

World Literary Studies and Britain

This chapter will briefly summarise Casanova's theory of world literary space, in so far as it is relevant to this book, and as it is laid out in her 2004 English-language publication *The World Republic of Letters*. Analysis of her project will then follow, identifying three unresolved contradictions in her work that can be used to challenge the premises on which her idea of international literary space is based: her notion of 'pure criticism', her under-used concept of 'literary capital' and her invention of an 'Irish paradigm'. The chapter will conclude with some modifications to Casanova's set of ideas, offering a revised model that will determine the approach taken in subsequent chapters. While the ensuing discussion might seem at one remove from Wales and from Edward Thomas, its aim in refining her theory is actually to produce a revisionist version on which the analysis of Welsh literary space can subsequently be confidently based.

The potential of Casanova's study is suggested by the outstanding reviews with which it was greeted on publication in left-wing and liberal intellectual journals in London and New York. Terry Eagleton called it 'a path-breaking study' and 'a milestone in the history of modern literary thought', while Louis Menand, with characteristic nonchalance, hailed a 'rather brilliant book'.[1] Perry Anderson, hailing Casanova's attempt 'to construct a model of the global inequalities of power between different national literatures', declared that 'whatever the outcome of ensuing criticisms or objections', her work is 'likely to have the same sort of liberating impact at large as [Edward] Said's *Orientalism*, with which it stands comparison'.[2] But how reliable a guide are such reviews to the usefulness of Casanova's theory for the task of recovering for Wales a writer usually assimilated to an Anglicised Britain?

Casanova's international literary space is ruthlessly competitive, composed of a series of linguistic-cultural areas within which there are national literary spaces. The power of each of these national literary spaces depends on its quantity of what Casanova calls 'literary capital': the status, prestige, and material infrastructure of its literature. A nation's literary capital depends on the age of its literature, the number of its national classics, the reputation of the language for literary production, the volume of works produced, the volume of translation into and out of the language, as well as the existence of a professional milieu, a cultivated public, an interested aristocracy or enlightened bourgeoisie, a specialised press, sought-after publishers, respected judges of talent, and celebrated writers (*WRL*, p. 15). Apart from these material factors, Casanova points out that literary capital is also an ethereal phenomenon: 'it rests on [the] judgements and reputations' of key agents within the literary field (*WRL*, p. 16).

All these factors mean that the national spaces that accumulate the most 'literary capital' are those with the oldest and most distinguished literary histories, and those whose historical economic pre-eminence has enabled them to build up the material, educational and cultural attributes to sustain it. A nation's 'literary capital', as Casanova defines it, is therefore relatively dependent on that nation's political history. Indeed, the nations with the most literary capital are the European nations which, through imperialism, 'by exporting their languages and institutions', have followed a policy of 'linguistic and cultural unification'; the result is a world literary space dominated by 'linguistic-cultural areas', each of which 'preserves a large measure of autonomy in relation to the others' (*WRL*, p. 117). Casanova identifies four of these areas, each with its own centre: Barcelona, the cultural capital for Spain and Latin-American nations; Berlin, the main city for German-speaking, northern European nations and non-Germanic central European countries formed after the break-up of the Austro-Hungarian Empire; Paris, central for authors from French-speaking Europe, Africa and Canada; and London and New York, which vie to be the centre of literary culture in the Anglophone world (with London, according to Casanova, coming out on top). In each of these centres, there is a relative literary autonomy, which Casanova defines as a literature that operates more or less independently of the national and political contexts in which it finds itself. Here, texts are judged according to formal literary standards believed by authorities in each centre to be disinterested and purely aesthetic. By far the most important of these literary centres – because, in attracting writers from beyond the Francophone sphere, it also functions as a world literary capital – is Paris.

One critic to attack this premise is Christopher Prendergast, who suggests that 'London and New York have "overtaken" Paris as the key metropolitan loci in the West'.[3] Casanova does acknowledge that today's literary world is in a 'transitional' phase, moving from Parisian dominance 'to a polycentric and plural world in which London and New York chiefly, but also to a lesser degree Rome, Barcelona, and Frankfurt, among other centers, contend with Paris for hegemony' (*WRL*, p. 164). However, it must be acknowledged that her understanding of 'polycentric' is, with the exception of New York, a Eurocentric one. Such it certainly seems to Debjani Ganguly, who accuses Casanova of operating a 'Euro-comparativist template', one which fails to account for literary centres that may today exist outside of Western Europe and North America, and which does not consider how the world of letters might look from, say, Beijing, Tehran, or Cairo, or even from 'local' places, remote from the literary centres, within Western Europe.[4] The need to modify Casanova's theory to account for the perspectives held by those away from Western literary centres, essential if her model is to be useful as far as Wales is concerned, is one of the areas that I consider later in this chapter as part of my own critique of her model.

Casanova narrates the historical development, from the sixteenth century onwards, of national literary spaces in Western Europe, a process that eventually led to the achievement in France, by the end of the nineteenth century, of what she calls an 'autonomous' literary field, a space in which literature could 'determine its own laws of operation', its writers free from the demands of the French national and political authorities (*WRL*, p. 37). The creation of 'literary autonomy' in France gave other countries concerned about cultural independence 'no alternative but to try to compete' (*WRL*, p. 70). National literary spaces based on this French model, in which 'literature' is the product of a classically educated elite, were developed in other Western European nations, including England. An effective challenge to the French model came from Prussian states, in particular from Johann Gottfried Herder, whose influence helped to bring about the second great stage in the formation of international literary space. From the mid-nineteenth century onwards, demands for national emancipation became closely connected to demands for linguistic emancipation, and to a new-found interest in the language and culture of the 'volk' or people. This second stage had a marked effect on those smaller European languages that had come close to disappearing under political domination, and those that were now only spoken by a peasant population. The role of the writer, grammarian, lexicographer and collector of folk tales was now of paramount importance in the construction of national identity. It is worth pointing out that Casanova's use of Herder as a basis for modern national identity is hardly new. For decades, critics have been debating the significance of Herder's concept of the 'volk' and its relation to the traditions of ballad collection, the anthologising of folk material and the development of national identity in Europe. What is new is the scale of Casanova's ambition. She places Herder in a historical narrative that stretches from sixteenth-century France through to what she identifies as a third great stage in the formation of international space: the post-World War Two (and ongoing) period of decolonisation. Here, 'the newly independent nations of Africa, Asia, and Latin America, obeying the same political and cultural mechanisms, [have] moved to assert linguistic and literary claims of their own' (*WRL*, p. 79).

The second and third stages have changed the structure of international literary space, effectively establishing an opposing pole of attraction to the pole of literary autonomy already established in the great literary centres. This opposition takes the form of a politico-national pole, which has emerged in each of the nations dominated by an external literary centre. According to Casanova, the role of the centre in respect of the nascent national literature is ambivalent. On the one hand, she argues that international centres export literary autonomy. In order to gain recognition at one of the centres (Casanova focuses particularly on writers who 'make it' in Paris), an author acquires the latest techniques of modernity, becomes 'consecrated' – or gains recognition – at the centre, and then returns to the dominated nation, importing what has been learnt. In this sense, Casanova argues that literary space is transnational. Not only does it have a structure based on centres and peripheries between which writers move, but the power of the centres encourages 'literary autonomy' in the nascent national literatures. International literary space is progressively unified along autonomous lines. On the other hand, as Casanova goes on to argue, this 'universalising' process is ambiguous. The centres of literary consecration

> reduce foreign works of literature to their own categories of perception, which they mistake for universal norms, while neglecting all the elements of historical, cultural, political, and especially literary context that make it possible to properly and fully appreciate such works. (*WRL*, p. 154)

In the very act of recognition at the centre, there is 'the ethnocentrism of the dominant authorities [and a] mechanism of annexation' (*WRL*, p. 154). However, in spite of their position, and their imprisonment in 'their own categories of perception', authorities at the literary centres nonetheless succeed in spreading 'autonomy' to writers from dominated nations within their sphere. In order to make it work in a Welsh context, this idea is challenged in my revision of Casanova's model, and will be dealt with later in this chapter.

The World Republic of Letters, at its heart, is an attempt to examine the range of solutions arrived at by writers from 'the literarily least endowed countries' in order to give 'meaning and justification to [their] works and aesthetic preferences' and to 'construct a "generative" model capable of reproducing the infinite series of such solutions on the basis of a limited number of literary, stylistic, and essentially political possibilities' (*WRL*, p. 177). To illustrate her model, Casanova sets out her 'Irish paradigm', a theoretical and practical framework that makes it possible to recreate and understand writers from dominated literary spaces, and give a comparative analysis of different historical situations and cultural contexts. It presents five consecutive stages through which writers from a dominated national literary space employ a range of strategies that enable them to achieve 'autonomy', both from a literary culture that is dominating their work, and from national-political demands within their own, nascent culture. For Casanova, Irish writers from 1890 to the mid-twentieth century provide a clear paradigm of this chronology, one that enables the critic to see a writer's choice of a particular literary strategy in the transnational context of the dominant, and the dominated, nations, and thereby to recognise, understand and recover the writer for the dominated nation. This also has the effect of undermining and questioning the narrow, single-nation foundations on which the literature of the *dominant* nation is constructed.

Its first stage centres on the well-known group of Anglo-Irish intellectuals that included W. B. Yeats, Lady Gregory, Edward Martyn, George Moore, George Russell, Padraic Colum, J. M. Synge and James Stephens, all of whom contributed in varying degrees to the project of 'manufactur[ing] a national literature out of oral practices, collecting, transcribing, translating, and rewriting Celtic tales and legends' (*WRL*, p. 305). This project succeeded both in presenting these popular legends through drama, and in evoking an idealised peasantry as a repository of national spirit, and 'supplying, in English, the foundations for a new national literature' (*WRL*, p. 307). A second stage involved the generation of interest in a national language – in the case of Ireland, Gaelic, achieved through the Gaelic League under the leadership of Douglas Hyde and Eoin MacNeill. This break with the English language was an attempt 'to put

an end to the linguistic and cultural ascendancy of the English colonizer'
(*WRL*, p. 307). It politicised a writer's choice of language, forcing him
to choose between 'proponents of Gaelic' (work that would be 'recognised
only in Ireland') and writing in the coloniser's tongue, English (which
offered the possibility of 'recognition in London literary circles and
beyond') (*WRL*, p. 310). Casanova suggests that an important development
from this stage occurred in the work of J. M. Synge who, faced with the
impossible choice between the extremes of a politicised Gaelic and a
coloniser's tongue, refused to choose.

Casanova's third stage involves 'the passage from neoromanticism –
the idealization and aestheticization of the peasantry, seen as incarnating
the essence of the popular "soul" – to realism – at first rural, then associated
with urban life and literary and political modernity' (*WRL*, p. 313). In the
case of Ireland, this was best exemplified in the urban realism of the
plays of Sean O'Casey. The next element in the development of a nascent
national literary space is the writer who rejects the nationalist requirements
of writing in her/his homeland in favour of exile in an external literary
capital, a stage personified for Casanova in the figure of George Bernard
Shaw. By moving to London and assimilating himself to British literary
space, he found 'a degree of aesthetic freedom and critical tolerance that
a small nation capital such as Dublin, torn between the centrifugal pull
of British literary space and internal self-affirmation, could not guarantee'
(*WRL*, p. 314). In recognising the contribution to Irish literary space of
writers like Shaw, who, by emigrating to England, have suffered 'accus-
ations of national betrayal' (ibid.), Casanova provides a model whereby
those writers who were previously thought to have deserted their nation,
contributing only to the literary history of their dominant neighbour, might
be recovered for the literary history of the dominated nation. Her work
in this area of course follows the (unacknowledged) lead of Irish critics
including Declan Kiberd, whose critical work has long created a space
in Irish literary history for such writers, including, in particular, Shaw.[5]

The final stage in the achievement of Irish literary space is exemplified
in the work of James Joyce who, 'exploiting all the literary projects,
experiments and debates of the late nineteenth century . . . invented and
proclaimed an almost absolute autonomy' (*WRL*, p. 315). Joyce's 'whole
literary work can be seen as a very subtle Irish re-appropriation of the
English language' (ibid.). He 'dislocated' English 'by incorporating in
it elements of every European language', 'by subverting the norms of
English propriety', and by 'making this subverted language of domination
[into] a quasi-foreign tongue' (ibid.). By refusing to choose between the

'English literary norms' of London and 'the aesthetic tenets of the nationalist' Dublin, he also 'disrupt[ed] the hierarchical relation between London and Dublin so that Ireland would be able to assume its rightful place in the literary world' (*WRL*, p. 316).

By incorporating these literary strategies into her 'Irish paradigm', Casanova presents them not as 'free' choices available to the writer, but as ones that are themselves grounded in the material and historical context of the emerging nation. Not only does this paradigm provide a way of looking at literature that avoids seeing 'each literary event, each work of literature [as] reducible to nothing other than itself' (*WRL*, p. 320); it also militates against the tendency to see each 'national particularism' as a unique manifestation, rather than as a characteristic it might share with other nations. The paradigm also involves a consideration of the different genres in which a writer works. Rather than simply accepting the existence of a set of genres – the novel, poetry and drama, for example – and focusing on one of them, the different stages of the 'Irish paradigm' draw attention to the ways in which genres become recognised as literature. Stage one, for example, which considers the *littérisation* of folk tales, their translation onto the stage, and ways in which they become more widely disseminated, involves the critical consideration of a wide range of forms of writing to which some critical approaches would not ascribe value, including collections of folk tales, popular anthologies and literary journalism.

There are, however, contradictions in Casanova's model of international literary space, which necessitate alterations to three of its aspects: her notion of 'literary autonomy', her concept of 'literary capital' and her 'Irish paradigm'. The three changes made here will enable the revised model to work better in Welsh literary space, and directly inform this study's critique of Edward Thomas. Firstly, Casanova's view of the 'literary autonomy' exemplified in the 'pure criticism' practised by authorities in the centre is, as we have seen, in the final analysis, a benevolent one. They succeed in selecting from those marginalised nations a few writers who 'make it' according to the detached, aesthetic criteria they favour. These chosen few are the ones who comprehend the true and unequal structure of world literary space, and who are able to exploit it in order to increase the autonomy of other writers from their own nation. They strategically target success in the literary centre as a way of 'subvert[ing] the dominant norms of their respective national fields' (*WRL*, p. 109). In other words, their success at the centre enables them to return to the dominated nation to challenge the national-political demands placed

on writers from a nascent national literary space. They manipulate the
centre's 'aesthetic models', its 'publishing networks', its 'critical functions',
and the prestige the centre bestows, in order to establish a freedom from
political and national demands on a writer's work (ibid.). This is the
'universalizing literary autonomy' which, Casanova claims, lies at the
heart of international literary space. It is difficult in such a system to
overestimate the importance of these centres to writers from the cultural
periphery: Casanova argues that 'every work' from such areas that 'aspires
to the status of literature' gains its status 'solely in relation to the consecrating authorities of the most autonomous places' (ibid.). 'In reality',
she declares, continuing her bold claim, 'the great heroes of literature
emerge only in association with the specific power of an autonomous and
international literary capital' (ibid.).

Nonetheless, this aspect of Casanova's model must be modified. 'Pure
criticism', through which consecrating authorities at a literary centre
recognise certain writers from dominated nations, does not have quite the
benevolent effects that Casanova depicts. Instead of allowing the dominated nation to enter the structure of worldwide literary space, it might
instead be seen as a tool for the dominant nation's appropriation of that
writer, one which has the opposite effect to that suggested by Casanova:
one which sustains the marginalisation of the dominated nation. It over-
estimates the interest of the centre in writers from a periphery, as well as
the desire of writers from a marginalised nation to gain recognition at the
centre. Moreover, it is unclear how such a writer's recognition by those
dominant powers leads to increased autonomy for the dominated nation.
Casanova's argument suggests that by achieving success, the writer is
recognised internationally as a representative of that nation – which gives
her/him the authority to resist national-political demands that the emerging
nation may try to impose, and which encourages other writers from that
space to develop the aesthetic and theoretical models s/he has imported
from the international 'bank' of autonomy based in the literary centre.
However, to argue that 'great heroes of literature emerge only in association with the specific power of an autonomous and international literary
capital', is to miss the relation between the work of literature and politics,
which often happens at the national level, as well as between the work
of literature and economics, which happens at the national, and also,
increasingly, in a globalising world, at the international level.

In the case of Welsh literary space, far from acting as a means of gener-
ating autonomy within Wales, and thereby providing a facility through
which writers can resist the national-political demands of being a Welsh

writer (as Casanova argues it does), 'pure criticism' actually functions
as an agent of Anglocentrism, its detached, aesthetic criteria serving
to marginalise any reading that places significance on the text's Welshness. Two recent examples of criticism of Henry Vaughan – a 2003 essay
by Belinda Humfrey and a 2008 piece by John Kerrigan – illustrate how
Casanova's notion of 'pure criticism' does not function as she suggests
in Welsh and British contexts. In her 2003 essay, 'Prelude to the Twentieth
Century', published in the seminal University of Wales Press series, *Guide
to Welsh Literature*, Humfrey aims to provide evidence of pre-twentieth-
century Welsh writing in English. Her approach, however, exemplifies
how a critical angle that emphasises a text's formal and aesthetic qualities, to the exclusion of any historical analysis – an example of Casanova's
'pure criticism' – sidelines the Welshness of any such writing. In Humfrey's
view, 'although there are Anglo-Welsh writers aplenty between the age
of Shakespeare and the advent of the First World War ... only two writers
can be described conscientiously as great Anglo-Welsh writers (and for
a small, sparsely-populated country, that is an achievement)'.[6] The two
writers concerned are Henry Vaughan and John Dyer, who are valued for
'producing poetry which is new, distinct and inimitable within the body
of English Literature' (*PTC*, p. 7).

There are several difficulties here. Humfrey's approach makes it clear
that she subscribes to the 'Great Writer' theory of literature, in which a
set of aesthetic criteria is applied to authors in order to see whether or
not they may be considered canonical within a widely-defined 'English
Literature'. There are several clues here to the aesthetic criteria Humfrey
applies: poetry must be 'new, distinct and inimitable', qualities that would
seem to favour the writer who can show her/his uniqueness and difference
from other practitioners in the wide field of English Literature – Casanova's
'internal reading' – rather than one with a different vision of her/his work.
Humfrey's next clause, 'within the body of English Literature', also
establishes a problematic context. If by 'English', she means the nation,
then by arguing that Welsh writers in English contribute to the literature
of England, she is immediately subordinating Wales to the status of an
English region. If, as seems to be the case, by 'English' she means literature
written in the English language, several issues arise. Are there not many
different national literatures written in English? Do the most widely recognised instances of these – such as American, Australian and Irish literatures
– also form part of 'the body of English Literature'? If so, is she suggesting
the redundancy of all the recent work establishing the existence of other
literatures in English? If these well-established other literatures in English

are indeed not a part of English Literature, on what grounds does she include Welsh writers in English within that umbrella term? Humfrey implies that a Welsh writer in English contributes, most importantly, to literature in the English language, and not to her/his own national literature. This approach is incongruous in a volume titled *Welsh Writing in English*.

Another issue that Humfrey overlooks is that of language. Certainly a Welsh writer in English is immediately conscious of using a medium that is not unproblematic: at least some Welsh people would regard it as, if not exactly foreign, then at least the language of a once-colonising power. By effectively demanding that the critic place value on the way a writer deals with the aesthetic matters that Humfrey believes to be important, rather than on other concerns regarding the relation of the author's language to the national literary space that his or her work will inhabit, Humfrey's critical approach necessarily favours writers who do not face these issues of language: that is to say, those for whom English is an unproblematic first language. In that sense the purely aesthetic criteria of her approach are a guise for Anglocentrism. While they greatly limit the number of eligible Welsh writers in English, they also make what these writers have to say about Welsh nationality of secondary importance to the aesthetic qualities their writing displays.

The result is that Humfrey can find only two writers she deems worthy of the adjective 'great', and in her analysis of their work, their nationality becomes incidental rather than a governing factor in the writing, and is even less a complicating factor in her understanding of 'English Literature'. For instance, even when she analyses Vaughan's use of Welsh forms in his poetry, she concludes that 'however Welsh his craft, it is Vaughan's "true" natural flow of English which contributes to making him outstanding' (*PTC*, p. 14). Given her critical priorities, the 'Welsh' aspects of Vaughan's work necessarily take second place to its 'English' qualities, in this case, a vaguely defined 'outstanding' quality to the way Vaughan uses the English language. Humfrey's assessment is a classic example of how approaching Welsh writing in English from the direction of its dehistoricised, aesthetic and formal qualities, without regard to the history of the text's production or reception, necessarily sidelines its Welsh characteristics.

John Kerrigan's 2008 work, *Archipelagic English*, shows that it is possible to approach Vaughan in a way that is sensitive to both Welsh and English identities. As far as Welsh writing in English is concerned, Kerrigan is aware that his approach intervenes in what he describes – rather simplistically – as 'disputes within Wales about the status of

Anglo-Welsh writing', in particular 'between those who hold that the Welsh language is the stem of the nation and those more pluralistic souls, often from the southern, more Anglophone areas, who see Anglo-Welsh literature as integral to the national heritage'.[7] Vaughan is, for Kerrigan, a key figure in this dispute because if his 'Welsh credentials' could be established, 'an indigenous, Anglo-Welsh tradition would have a very early and distinguished representative' (*AE*, p. 9). Kerrigan goes on to draw attention to 'the poet's background in bilingual Breckonshire', and shows how 'some of the most inward, loaded specificities of his writing, as well as larger aspects of his style and spirituality' are not simply aspects of his education in an English literary tradition, but 'spring from the predicament of Welsh Anglicanism during and after the civil wars of the 1640s' (ibid.). While Vaughan 'has been read by Anglo-American scholars as a mainstream Eng. Lit. figure', suggests Kerrigan, 'the arguments for reading [him] as "No Englishman" are strong' (ibid.).

The juxtaposition of Kerrigan and Humfrey clearly reveals the problem posed by Casanova's notion of a literary autonomy that is exported from the 'pure' critics at the literary centre to dominated nations. According to her model, it would be Humfrey who performs this function. It would be Humfrey whose critical approach maintains literary autonomy in Wales by judging texts according to a set of detached aesthetic criteria that provide Anglophone Welsh writers with a set of resources for countering the pressure to conform to a Welsh national-political agenda. Kerrigan, on the other hand, would presumably feature in Casanova's model as a critic who exists at the national pole of Welsh literary space, reclaiming a writer for the Welsh national tradition. But Casanova's belief in 'pure criticism' practised at the centre results in her failure to see how such an approach also makes it harder to connect the writer to her/his dominated nation. In this sense, Casanova's theory fails to see how a critical approach such as Humfrey's actually functions as the cultural arm of the colonial power, rather than providing Welsh writers with resources to secure the autonomy of their nation. It also appropriates a writer for a tradition of literature which, although it is supposedly international, is in fact, Anglo-centric. In contradistinction, it is Kerrigan's historically informed analysis that is sensitive both to the way that a word within the poem has implications for the portrayal of the nation, and to the way that conventional 'Anglo-American scholars' have appropriated Vaughan 'as a mainstream Eng. Lit. figure'. Kerrigan's approach, rather than Humfrey's, is able to recover Vaughan for the Welsh tradition, without neglecting the importance of the English tradition to his poetry's creation and reception. While

Casanova's theory purports to help writers from dominated nations understand the unequal structure of the literary space in which they find themselves, her notion of a 'universalizing literary autonomy' actually sustains and supports one of the mechanisms through which the dominant nation maintains its position.

Kerrigan, making the point vis-à-vis Vaughan's Welshness, effectively repeats the argument made by M. Wynn Thomas almost a decade earlier, without appearing to be aware of the substance of the earlier publication (which is given only passing reference in a footnote) – an oversight that, in the context of the argument he is making, can be best described as ironic.[8] This draws attention to another aspect of the unequal relation between the literary centre and a dominated nation. In a book written at Cambridge, and published by Oxford University Press (both institutions of the literary centre), Kerrigan, a Cambridge academic, can present, perhaps without knowledge, and effectively without acknowledgement, an argument that has already been made by a leading Welsh scholar in a highly regarded text published by the University of Wales Press. This reinforces the point that any analysis of the complex interactions between the literary centre and a dominated literary field such as Wales must take into account the economic bases of the literary infrastructure (in this case, how institutions, including its publishing houses, do not compete on a level playing field).

A nation's 'literary capital' is the second area of Casanova's model that requires alteration. Her use of the concept remains undeveloped. It is employed as a way of understanding how much literary power has been accrued at the linguistic-regional literary centres such as London and Paris, but not as a way of showing how a national centre develops. Having established her 'Irish paradigm', the obvious place in which to apply her notion of 'literary capital' would have been Dublin. In order to substantiate her paradigm, Casanova could have analysed the city over the course of her chosen period, 1890 to 1930, considering how the establishment of the Abbey Theatre, publishing houses, a specialised literary press and the literary credibility conferred by its respected critics, among other things, contributed to Ireland's burgeoning literary capital. No such analysis, though, is attempted. The concept therefore sits oddly with the rest of Casanova's analysis. By fully applying 'literary capital' only to the international literary centres, Casanova effectively suggests that national spaces – even when they achieve her 'autonomy' – do not develop a material infrastructure to rival that of the centres, and thus remain in important respects dominated. In this sense, she implies that Ireland's autonomy is purely a literary phenomenon, one that is not matched by any material infrastructure in Ireland. Rather, it is guaranteed by the autonomy of the international centres. It is as if literary resources could be redistributed more equally without a corresponding redistribution of the material resources upon which they depend. This is essentially an imperialist position, in that the cultural production of the nascent national space never loses its reliance on the material infrastructure of the established, often imperial, literary centre.

In this sense, Casanova's notion of a universalising literary autonomy gets in the way of her development of the concept of 'literary capital'. It does not require her properly to analyse the national political and economic fields in which the literary field is situated – why would she need to if, merely by returning from Paris to the dominated nation, fully armed with recognition and the latest aesthetic models, the writer brings autonomy to that nation? It also does not require her to consider the development of literary capital in the nation concerned. Analysing a dominated nation's literary capital would be an unnecessary critical activity because the nation's literary autonomy has nothing to do with its own literary capital. Rather, it is guaranteed by the universalising nature of a literary autonomy that spreads from the centre. But if we take just one aspect of Casanova's definition of 'literary capital', that of a 'cultivated public', it becomes clear that it operates differently in the literary centre to how it operates in the dominated nation. Casanova's use of the term suggests its ahistorical qualities, as if a 'cultivated public' could somehow be measured independently of the historical context in which it exists. However, in Wales and even in a literary centre such as London, it is a highly contested term.

The growth in adult literacy, achieved by the 1890s as a result of the Board schools built following the 1870 Education Act, might be said to contribute towards a 'cultivated public' in England and Wales. However, as Kate Jackson points out, 'literacy, as well as literature, is dynamic and contextual'.[9] She argues that, as a concept, it is 'very much enmeshed in the history and historiography of the years 1880–1910, when successive Education Acts and the expansion of the popular press focussed attention on the spread of the reading habit'.[10] The growth in literacy created a newly literate working-class and lower-middle-class readership which, thanks to the development of new mass printing technology, formed the target market for the London-based institutions of New Journalism, begun in 1896 in the form of Alfred Harmsworth's *Daily Mail*. However, the phenomenon of a 'reading public' becoming a 'target market' suggests another, more pejorative, interpretation of Casanova's term 'cultivated'.

Many critics have noted mixed reactions to the growth in literacy at this time. Mary Hammond, for example, refers to contemporary debate about these changes, citing an 1899 advertisement for the *Evening Standard*'s 'Library of Famous Literature' which divides 'the bookmen of the present' into 'two classes': 'those who deplore the enormous increase of books [and] those who welcome the increase'.[11] In such an economic and political context, it seems the 'public' was 'cultivated' in ways that Casanova's definition does not account for.

In Wales, the 1870 Education Act complicates the notion of a 'cultivated public' still further, through the Act's insistence that all children in Britain should be educated in the English language. In doing so, it built on the 1847 Blue Books *Report into the State of Education in Wales*, which attacked the language, morality and learning of the Welsh, and proposed the solution of an education in English.[12] Kirsti Bohata makes the connection between the 1847 'Blue Books' Report and Babington Macauley's infamous 1835 'Minute on Indian Education', which advocated the teaching of English Literature in India as a means of creating subjects 'Indian in blood and colour' but 'English in taste, in opinions, in morals and in intellect'.[13] 'Education policy in Wales', concludes Bohata, 'reflected a similar imperialist project' to that in India (*PR*, p. 133). She goes on to argue that for such pupils the resultant invisibility of Welsh language, history and literature in Welsh schools would lead to 'a problematic sense of dislocation – the result of identifying with the perspective of the Anglocentric hegemony [and thereby encouraging] a sense of the otherness and inferiority of the Welsh' (*PR*, p. 134). Bohata argues that the underlying premise of policies that educated the native population in English tastes and values was that colonial subjects were able to 'mimic but never exactly reproduce English values, and that their recognition of the perpetual gap between themselves and the "real thing" will ensure their subjection' (*PR*, p. 145). Given such a history, Casanova's decontextualised notion of a 'cultivated public' is clearly problematic. In this sense, 'literary capital' needs to be considered, not as a concept that somehow floats above history, but in the historical context of the dominated nation.

Like her notions of a 'universalizing literary autonomy' and 'literary capital', Casanova's 'Irish paradigm' also needs to be modified in some ways, an area to which this chapter now turns. Her theoretical and practical framework is presented as a way of making it possible to 'recreate and understand' writers from dominated literary spaces (*WRL*, p. 304). Although she prefaces the introduction of her paradigm with the admission that her scheme cannot hope to 'capture reality in all its complexity' (*WRL*, p. 303), she suggests the totality of her approach by arguing that the 'Irish para-digm' is a 'generative model . . . containing the full range of political and linguistic solutions, the whole gamut of positions from Shaw's assimilation to Joyce's exile' (*WRL*, p. 304). It enables the understanding of 'literary revolts in general (looking at both prior and later examples)', and provides 'a comprehensive analysis of quite different historical situations and cultural contexts' (ibid.).

In this sense, her theory aims to provide an essentialist theory that accounts for the range in historical experiences of different nations. A critique of such an approach is implied by Christopher Prendergast when he writes, of Casanova's work, that 'partial description is offered as *the* description', and by Debjani Ganguly when she argues that Casanova 'aims at nothing short of providing a comprehensive template to account for all aspects of international or world literary topography'.[14] Echoing these criticisms, I would argue that Casanova downplays the importance of what is unique in any nation's history. For example, she argues that the Irish experience was singular only in the speed with which its literary space emerged 'in the space of a few decades' and in 'certain secondary historical differences' (*WRL*, p. 304). Otherwise, she claims that the genesis of the structure of Irish literary space – its movement through the five stages – 'can be seen to be almost universal', while the position of any given national space within these chronological stages can be plotted at any given point in its history (*WRL*, p. 305). This is slightly disingenuous. Her relegation to the status of 'certain secondary historical differences' of any historical factors that might make the Irish situation unique, and her failure to provide any examples of these, reflects the lack of importance she attaches to the historical context within the individual nation. This in itself is hardly surprising: her model of international space places too much faith in the universalising effect of a writer who returns to her/his nation flush with the recognition and literary techniques s/he has won from the centre. Casanova's model does not require the critic to pay much attention to the historical circumstances of the nation itself, because, in the face of this 'universalising' structure, they are *necessarily* 'secondary'.

The critic, needless to say, should pay more attention than Casanova allows to the historical context of the individual nation. Doing so reveals that the 'genesis' of the structure of Irish literary space is not as 'universal' as Casanova hopes. A particular historical factor in one nation may prevent the chronological development of the structure as it occurred in Ireland. In the case of Wales, the fact that the indigenous language was spoken by a larger proportion of the population than was the case in Ireland thoroughly complicates stage two of Casanova's chronological 'Irish paradigm': the emergence of a literature in the indigenous language. At the beginning of the twentieth century, Gaelic (as the sole language) was spoken by 1 per cent of the Irish population, while Welsh was spoken by 50 per cent of the people in Wales. A literature written in the indigenous language has existed in Wales for well over a millennium. It might be argued that, in comparison with Ireland, the relative strength of the indigenous language in Wales made it much harder for Welsh writers in English to be accepted as Welsh, contributing to a polarised linguistic division that lasted for most of the twentieth century. Such a situation makes it hard for a Welsh equivalent of Synge, who refuses to make the choice between languages, to be recognised, and even harder for a Welsh Joyce to emerge. In other words, there is an assumed historical inevitability in Casanova's assertion that the 'Irish paradigm' is chronological, which may not be borne out by analysis. If it is true that historical circumstances are not secondary, and that they can intervene and affect the development of a national literary space, it also follows that it is not possible to plot the position of a national space within these chronological stages at any given point in its history. It may, for example, be the case that the different stages develop unevenly or simultaneously, and that historical factors unique to that nation cause the stages to occur at different times, or all at once, or not at all.

This is not to suggest that Casanova's 'Irish paradigm' is useless as a critical tool. Like her analysis of international literary space, it needs to be modified to incorporate an analysis of the historical context of the nation concerned. Her paradigm might be more usefully employed as a looser set of critical tools, one that does not presume the historical inevitability of the succession of one stage by another (which is to pre-suppose a chronology), but which might be better considered as a range of potentialities. Rather than reduce a writer's work to one of a historically determined set of stages, this idea allows for the possibility that a writer may contribute to the development of more than one potentiality (which may occur simultaneously). In the case of Ireland, such a loosening of Casanova's model would enable a writer like Yeats to be positioned not only in the first stage as a transcriber of Irish folk material (as Casanova positions him), but also, like Shaw, as a writer present in London, who subverts British space from within.

To draw together the points made in this chapter, it needs to be noted that there are several major drawbacks to Casanova's model. Firstly, as far as her notion of 'pure criticism' is concerned, Casanova's positioning of the 'consecrating authorities' of Paris, London and the other literary centres at the autonomous, international pole of world literary space exaggerates their role as guarantors of writers' freedoms in dominated nations, and fails to fully acknowledge its flipside: their position as agents of the dominant nation, and the current power structure. Her model also idealises the 'autonomising' and 'universalising' role played by writers who, on being consecrated by these central authorities, return to their dominated nation. Secondly, her notion of 'literary capital' is under-used: her 'universalizing literary autonomy' generates a contradiction that means Casanova sees the need to fully apply it only to the dominant literary centres, and not to the dominated nations. Thirdly, as far as her 'Irish paradigm' is concerned, by attaching more importance to the historical context of the individual nation, it may be the case that historical factors are not only of 'secondary' importance; they might also have a determining effect on the development of a national literary space. As a result, the consecutive chronology of the five-stage Irish paradigm is not as inevitable as Casanova argues. Indeed, it presupposes a chronology, which would be better replaced by the looser idea of a set of potentialities.

In spite of these major problems and omissions, I would like to suggest that there are many aspects of Casanova's model which are worth salvaging, albeit in an altered form. One of the model's strengths is its ambitious claim that there is a structure to international literature which privileges writers from certain nations, and disadvantages those from others (a phenomenon with which many writers from Wales can surely identify). Casanova is also right to make the case that a nation's enjoyment of literary dominance – its beneficial position within the international structure – is connected to a history of imperialism, conquest and capitalist accumulation. I suggest a revised model of analysis that incorporates the criticisms made above. My model would aim to keep the ambition of Casanova's: to find a way of incorporating the structure of international literary space into the literary analysis of texts by writers from dominated nations. Above all, it would lose her model's reliance on the notion of a 'universalizing literary autonomy' that spreads from the centre, and it would lose the contradictions produced by this reliance. Instead, it would return the politics and history of the dominated nation to centre stage.

Following this chapter's critique of 'pure criticism', my revised model will begin by considering how critics from within the dominated nation receive the writer concerned. Such an approach would necessarily be more sceptical about the benevolent effects of Casanova's concept of 'pure criticism', and more sensitive to the national and political context in which the critic is operating. It would also be important to examine how a writer from a dominated nation is recognised by the authorities in a literary centre, and whether or not his or her critical reception by these figures helps to develop the literary space of the dominated nation. Such an analysis would consider whether 'pure criticism', operated either from a literary centre or from within the nation concerned, marginalises the national significance of work by writers from dominated nations, thus sustaining the hegemony of the dominant nation. Chapter Two applies this aspect of my revised model. It introduces Edward Thomas in more depth, and analyses his critical reception on both sides of the English–Welsh border. In particular, it considers how Casanova's concept of 'pure criticism' applies within the British and Welsh literary spaces, and how it functions as a way of marginalising the Welshness of Thomas within the 'English Literature' canon, even though its criteria are supposedly neutral. Attention is also paid to the political agendas behind particular national traditions of Thomas criticism.

Following my critique of Casanova's under-used notion of 'literary capital', the revised model then considers the position of the nation's literature within the political and economic field at the time when the text is produced. This places the writer back within the dominated nation, and within the time in which he was writing. On the one hand, this would suggest immediate political and economic contexts that underpin literary decisions and in which his work may be read: for example, it might suggest why he chose to have his work published in London rather than Cardiff, or vice versa. By considering a nation's literary capital, and by comparing it to that of the relevant literary centre at a given point in history, it should be possible to gain some kind of insight into the opportunities available to the writer from the dominated nation, and the choices presented to him by the unequal position of nations within the international literary structure. Chapter Three develops these aspects of the revised model, examining the position of the literary field in both the political and economic contexts in Wales at the time Thomas was writing. By positioning the literary field in this way, I hope to suggest immediate political contexts to Thomas's work, and also to show how the material infrastructure of Welsh literature informs his literary decisions.

Finally, the revised model will employ Casanova's 'Irish paradigm' as a way of recovering writers for a dominated nation, but it will not insist on such a deterministic application of the paradigm. Employing the concept of potentialities rather than stages, history will be 'allowed in'; that is to say, the revised paradigm can account for the possibility that historical factors particular to that dominated nation might cause its literary space to develop in ways that rupture the chronological succession of stages presented by Casanova. Writers may therefore occupy positions in more than one point in a series of potentialities that might develop unevenly, if at all. Chapters Four, Five and Six develop these areas, considering Thomas's writing career and his publications through the perspective of a revised 'Irish paradigm', one which allows for the possibility that its stages do not unfold in the deterministic way that Casanova suggests, and which offers the chance of positioning Thomas in more than one of them: his *littérisation* of Welsh folk material and his subversion of Anglocentric British literary space from within.

This model, revised to better suit the Anglophone Welsh condition, nonetheless keeps the following advantages of Casanova's theory: its capacity to recognise, understand and recover for the dominated nation, the work of a writer formerly lost to it; its transnational basis, which offers the opportunity of undermining and questioning the single-nation foundations on which the literature of the *dominant* nation is constructed; its presentation of literary strategies, not as a free choice available to the writer, but as choices that are themselves grounded in the material and historical context of the emerging nation; the value it places on a range of forms and genres, thus helping to rescue from critical obscurity work such an anthology of folk tales, or literary journalism. The next chapter will begin to apply the revised paradigm to Edward Thomas.

2

The Reception of Edward Thomas

In the last chapter, I suggested three major modifications to Casanova's structure of world literature and proposed a critical approach that incorporates these changes. My revised model begins, firstly, by examining how critics from within the dominated nation receive the writer concerned, focusing a more sceptical eye on the benefits of 'pure criticism'. It goes on to consider how an author from a dominated nation is recognised by the authorities in a literary centre, and whether this reception develops the literary space of the dominated nation. Secondly, it makes use of the notion of 'literary capital' within the context of the dominated nation. It makes history more central to the literary analysis by positioning the nation's literature within its political and economic fields. Finally, it applies a less deterministic model of Casanova's 'Irish paradigm'; in the revised model it is acknowledged that historical factors peculiar to the dominated nation might cause its literary space to develop in ways that rupture the chronological succession of stages as presented by Casanova. The remainder of this book considers these matters by examining the case of Thomas. While Chapter Three addresses the second of my revisions, and Chapters Four, Five and Six examine the third, the present chapter will introduce Thomas before considering his work in the light of the first of these modifications: his reception either side of the English-Welsh border, and its relation to 'pure criticism'.

A writer with significant connections to Wales, and yet one who plied his trade mainly in the literary centre, London, Thomas has been critically assessed both in Wales and a wider British context. For reasons of space, it has not been possible to refer to every critic who has written about Thomas, but I have tried to address those who associate him with a particular national identity. Considering his Welsh reputation first, I argue that critics here, as a result of bitter linguistic division, have either emphasised a language-based identity from which Thomas is excluded, or, like Humfrey in the previous chapter, have adopted approaches which, although they might recognise Thomas's Welsh biography, are broadly based on a 'pure criticism' that marginalises the Welshness of Thomas's texts. This chapter then turns to Thomas's reception in Britain as a whole, arguing that in the space left by this failure of Welsh critics to recover Thomas for their literary tradition, there are historical periods during the twentieth century – after the First World War, at the beginning of the Second World War through to the 1950s, and with the resumption of the war in Ireland in the 1970s – when Thomas has been successfully appropriated for an Anglocentric British tradition.

Thomas's immediate family history, a story of economic migration and the loss of an indigenous language, reflects the upheaval caused by the nineteenth-century industrialisation of Wales, a process that caused population movement from Welsh-speaking rural regions into newly created, and predominantly English-speaking, urban areas. These were mainly, but not exclusively, in the south-east of Wales, but people also left for England, North America and Australasia, while there was also unprecedented immigration from England, Scotland and Ireland (but also from other parts of Europe) into these industrialised towns. Thomas's grandparents on his father's side were both Welsh speakers, originating, in the early-nineteenth century, in Gwent and West Glamorgan. They migrated to the newly industrialised area of Tredegar where the grandfather worked as a fitter. Their son, Thomas's father, Philip Henry Thomas, who was also a Welsh speaker, began his working life as a pupil-teacher in Tredegar before taking Civil Service exams, becoming a clerk at the Board of Trade, and moving to London, where he was active in the Liberal Party. Here he was later to become a friend of David Lloyd George, another Welsh expatriate, and even stood for election to parliament in 1918. Back in 1874, Philip Henry married Elizabeth Townsend, from Newport, south Wales, and in 1878 she gave birth to their first son, Edward. At an unknown date, Edward's paternal grandparents left Tredegar, crossing the English border to join a Welsh-speaking community in Swindon, Wiltshire, where the grandfather and one of his sons, Edward's uncle, worked on the railways (the Great Western mainline reached Swindon in 1872 and continued west into Wales thereafter). His paternal grandfather died before Thomas met him, but as a child he frequently travelled to Wiltshire to meet his Welsh-speaking grandmother. He also often travelled to Pontardulais and

Ammanford, a newly industrialised, Welsh-speaking area on the West Glamorgan-Carmarthenshire border, to stay with cousins or friends who included, as we shall see, his family relation, the Welsh-language poet, John Jenkins (whose bardic name was Gwili).[1]

Thomas's family tree illustrates how industrial development and the search for work determined successive generations' choices to head east until they left Wales altogether, a movement reflected in Thomas's later choice of pseudonym, Edward Eastaway (also the family name of one branch of his Glamorgan ancestors). They were not alone. John Davies reports that, by 1901, England had 265,000 Welsh-born inhabitants, a figure which would increase markedly if it took account of those, like Thomas, who considered themselves Welsh even though they were born outside Wales's borders.[2] Thomas represents the first generation of his family born outside Wales. He was also the first generation (on his father's side) not to have Welsh as his first language. His biographer, R. George Thomas (no relation) makes the point that although Edward lived and worked in England, from childhood onwards he had 'cherished the sense of belonging to another country'.[3] His friend Thomas Seccombe wrote, in a letter first published in *The Times Literary Supplement* on 16 April 1917, that he also 'sorrowed at times over the loss of his birthright in the Cambrian tongue'.[4] In these ways, Thomas found himself assimilated to a 'dominant' English language, and one generation removed from a 'dominated' Welsh one, by virtue of historical changes before he was born.

His formal education, however, was mostly English: grammar and private schools in London, followed by three years studying history at Oxford University from 1897. His tutor here was O. M. Edwards, one of the architects of the Welsh literary revival. From this period, he was also close to John Jenkins (hereafter referred to by his bardic name of Gwili) and Watkin Hezekiah Williams (referred to henceforth by his bardic name of Watcyn Wyn). These men were Welsh-language poets and successive principals at the Gwynfryn School in Ammanford, an institution at which members of Thomas's family were educated, and which is described by Huw Walters as a key centre for the education of Welsh poets and preachers in the late nineteenth and early twentieth centuries.[5] Thomas married Helen Noble in his final year at Oxford and had three children with her, Merfyn, Bronwen and Myfanwy, over the next ten years. Having failed, on graduating in 1900, to gain the degree class necessary to become a lecturer in north Wales, and having failed in his application to become a teacher in Cardiff, he became instead a London-based freelance reviewer for a number of literary journals and daily papers. By 1906, he had established himself in this profession, specialising in poetry reviews, but also writing commissioned books and his own non-commissioned sketches, almost all of which were published in London. Although his income from these jobs was insecure, in the sense that he was paid predominantly by review or book rather than regular salary, he nonetheless managed to earn over £250 a year from 1906 onwards, a remuneration double that of a teacher, and four times that of a labourer.

Thomas wrote or edited thirty-eight books between 1897 and 1917. Those considered in forthcoming chapters include the travel books *Beautiful Wales* (1905), *The South Country* (1909), *The Heart of England* (1909), *The Isle of Wight* (1911), *The Icknield Way* (1913), *The Country* (1913), *In Pursuit of Spring* (1914) and the essays 'Glamorgan' and 'Swansea Village'. They also include his books of short stories and sketches: *Horae Solitariae* (1902), *Rest and Unrest* (1910) and *Light and Twilight* (1911), and his retelling of Irish and Welsh folk material, *Celtic Stories* (1911). Also considered are some of Thomas's critical biographies: *Richard Jefferies: his Life and Work* (1909), *Maurice Maeterlinck* (1912), *George Borrow: the Man and his Books* (1912) and *Lafcadio Hearn* (1912), as well as the edited collections, *The Poems of John Dyer* (1903) and *The Pocket Book of Poems and Songs* (1907), and his single novel, *The Happy-Go-Lucky Morgans* (1913). An autobiographical piece, *The Childhood of Edward Thomas*, was published only in 1938, but written in 1913. In addition to these texts, Thomas wrote reviews and journalistic articles that appeared regularly in over twenty papers and literary journals between 1896 and 1915, some of which are referred to in this book. These prose works have often been seen as preparatory work for the later poetry, but this is somewhat misleading, for it was not seen this way at the time. Thanks to his reputation as a prose writer, his profile appeared in Britain in the *Bookman* in 1908, and in the popular magazine *T.P.'s Weekly* in 1913. This reputation had also crossed the Atlantic. Between 1904 and 1917, his prose works were reviewed on no fewer than nine occasions in the *New York Times*, where, in January 1913, his beginnings as a successful writer were the subject of a feature article.[6]

Although it forms the basis of his critical reputation, Thomas's poetic output is, by comparison with his prose, a tiny proportion of his writing. Having finished his first poem in November 1914, he wrote over half his work in this genre, seventy-five poems, during the next five months. Faced with the collapse of the literary marketplace in 1915, he enlisted in the British Army in July of that year. During the first eight months of 1916, there was another burst of activity in which he produced a further forty poems. The remainder of his 142-poem corpus was written in the second half of 1915, just after enlisting, and the last few months of 1916, before he left for France. In other words, four-fifths of his poetry comes from two six-month periods, and all of it was written in the twenty-six months between November 1914 and January 1917. At the end of January 1917, he was sent to France, where he was killed by a shell on 9 April 1917.

With the exception of two reviews in *The Welsh Outlook* and an article in *Tir Newydd* (New Land), literary journals in Wales hardly discussed Thomas.[7] One of the first writers from the Welsh-language tradition to comment on Thomas is Saunders Lewis, perhaps the most important Welsh-language public intellectual of the last century. In his historic lecture, 'Is there an Anglo-Welsh literature?', delivered in December 1938, Lewis points out that 'with rare exception English literary critics have never heard that there was, or is, a Welsh literature in a Welsh language'.[8] As a result of such ignorance, 'they do not call [Edward Thomas and W. H. Davies] Anglo-Welsh writers but simply Welsh' (*AWL*, p. 4). The implied danger is that Welsh-language literature cedes the perceived authority to speak for Wales to an English-language equivalent. The widespread mistaken recognition of Thomas as a 'Welsh' writer constitutes, in Lewis's eyes, a threat to the survival of the indigenous culture, and so the national descriptor is denied him. In the rest of the lecture, Lewis devotes considerable time to measuring the Anglophone writers of Wales like Thomas against their 'exemplary' counterparts in Ireland, setting out why, in his view, their work does not amount to an English-language Welsh literary tradition (*AWL*, p. 5). Firstly, Anglophone Welsh life, he claims, is based on an industrialism described as 'the destroyer of all nationhood' (unlike Ireland, which benefits from a national life that is 'peasant, uncommercialised and untouched by industrialism'); secondly, the English spoken in Wales is 'eminently the language of industrialism', not the 'speech of an organic community', and therefore lacks its own distinctive 'idiom' and 'folksong' (the English spoken in Ireland is 'rhythmically and emotionally and idiomatically separate' from that of England); thirdly, English-language Welsh writers, 'too clearly deraciné', do not write for Wales but for an English readership (whereas Irish writers are instead 'concerned with interpreting Ireland for herself', showing an especial interest in 'popularising . . . the work of Irish archaeologists and historians and literary researchers'); fourthly, Anglophone Welsh writers, unlike their Anglo-Irish equivalents, are not 'consciously and deliberately nationalist' (*AWL*, pp. 7–9).

These views are rooted in a polarising essentialism that sees modernity as an unwelcome import from England, and that idealises the 'organic', rural character of Celtic nations. Lewis remains silent on the industrial, metropolitan centres of Dublin and Belfast, as he does on the Welsh-language industrial communities in the Swansea Valley, around Amman-ford and Carmarthen, or around the slate quarries of Bethesda, Llanberis and Blaenau Ffestiniog. His conception, moreover, fails to allow for an industrial Anglophone Welsh society that might generate new forms of national identity, or uses of idiomatic English peculiar to an industrialised Wales. Lewis also grossly exaggerates the 'deraciné' quality of Anglo-phone Welsh writing. Research by Roland Mathias, a pioneer of Anglo-phone Welsh literary criticism, on Dylan Thomas (the example cited by Lewis) has drawn attention to his uses of tone, rhythm and idiom derived from the Welsh-speaking chapel culture of south-west Wales.[9] Indeed, more recent work by Jane Aaron and M. Wynn Thomas has found evidence for a distinctive Anglophone Welsh literary tradition that was well-established in the nineteenth century.[10] Lewis, however, misses the significance of historical correspondence between the two linguistic com-munities in Wales, pessimistically conceiving of Anglophone Welsh writers' doomed attempt 'to preserve . . . their inheritance against the levelling pressure of the cosmopolitan industrial machine' (*AWL*, p. 9). By adopting such a divisive line of argument, he does not have to entertain the complicating possibilities that a distinctive Welsh form of English might actually emerge from its exposure to Welsh culture and language, or that an Anglophone Welsh literary culture might be influenced by the work of '[Welsh-language] archaeologists and historians and literary researchers'.

Lewis's 1938 view of Edward Thomas is effectively determined by these preconceptions: he is portrayed as an Anglicised Welshman whose poetry is essentially the product of an English culture. There is no need, given Lewis's polarised conception of national identity in Wales, to explore ways in which Thomas's work might be thoroughly complicated and transformed by its author's exposure to Welsh literature and culture, or how he might be influenced by those working in the Welsh-language literary field (let alone examine the premises on which Welsh-language culture, in the mid-twentieth century, is considered the expression of an ongoing, 'organic' community). However, in spite of these limitations, what Lewis does, through his comparison of Irish and Welsh Anglophone literature, is to establish the premise that, for an English-language literature to be convincingly Welsh, its discourse needs to be distinctively inflected in ways that mark it out as the product of a culture that is not only different from that of England, but foreign to it. This is a key advance.

Tony Conran, an unjustifiably neglected critic and poet, writing almost half a century later, begins from the premise established by Saunders Lewis. Conran, however, is not only an outstanding practitioner of Welsh poetry in English, but also a strong advocate, in contrast to Lewis, of its legitimacy as a medium of Welsh national expression. He has a well-defined conception of Anglophone Welsh poetry, a tradition that differs from its English counterpart through 'inscription', or the deep embedding of Welsh-language literary forms, rhythms and tones in an English-language text. This conception effectively casts Anglophone Welsh litera-ture as the child of an older Welsh literary tradition, foreign to the English nation, rather than the means through which it would colonise and destroy an indigenous Welsh culture. Coming from a key critic within the tradition of Welsh writing in English, Conran's work is conciliatory, successfully reaching out to the Welsh-language community at a time of division.

Conran's 'inscription' provides a theoretical mechanism for reading the two literatures in linguistic correspondence. However, there are some ways in which Conran's work also subverts the Welshness of Anglophone Welsh literature. In his view, the writers' language is the consequence of the 'treason' of 'Welshmen who forsook their language' in the nineteenth century. The guilty here include 'teachers, the middle-class ladies with an eye to their family's advancement, and the workers confronted with over-whelming English and Irish immigration into their workplaces'.[11] Conran is uncompromising, proclaiming that 'the treason to the language is the sin of the fathers, visited in the shape of the Anglo-Welsh predicament onto the children to the third or fourth generation' (*F*, p. 3). This description of the Anglophone Welsh writer's 'predicament' helpfully anticipates hybridity, a more useful concept later developed by Homi Bhabha, but Conran's charge of 'treason' against those who 'forsook' the Welsh lan-guage is unfair. The shift to English was largely determined by economic, institutional and demographic factors that were beyond the power of these groups and individuals to alter. Not only does Conran suggest that they had more choice than they did; he implies that their English speech is the result of a crime against the nation. So, while Conran builds relations to the Welsh-language literary tradition, he does so at the cost of undermining the national legitimacy of Welsh authors who write in English. His work, in the period between the 1979 and 1997 devolution referenda, serves to remind us that the conditions for fully accepting Anglophone Welsh writing as a national literature had not yet arrived.

While 'inscription' provides a critical concept that might have been used to investigate Edward Thomas's use of Welsh literary forms, Conran instead positions Thomas outside the Anglophone Welsh literary tradition. Indeed, Thomas is named as the marker of a non-Welsh identity. Conran concedes that Thomas wrote a 'handful' of 'Anglo-Welsh' poems, along with 'a few poems that contain Anglo-Welsh elements, though hardly enough in themselves to dispute their provenance as English poems'.[12] Overall, however, he concludes that Thomas writes 'English poetry in the fullest sense', containing no 'strain' of Welshness (*TCS*, p. 54). Instead, his work is 'about England, [written] from an English point of view' and 'a development of the English literary tradition'. Crucially, 'it does not refer outside that tradition, either to Welsh or any other literature' (ibid.). Thomas's poetry, to sum up, is 'non-Welsh' (*TCS*, p. 57). All of these are claims that this study will dispute.

Conran goes on to argue that, while 'Thomas's work, when he died, was outside the orbit of Anglo-Welsh poetry as it existed then', it has, since the 1940s, 'proved so clear a guide and so potent an influence for the Anglo-Welsh that [Thomas] is now one of the poles round which we revolve' (*TCS*, p. 58). Thomas, indeed, is seen by 'certain sections of the Anglo-Welsh . . . as a kind of secular saint', which 'may have something to do with the fact that he is the only Welshman to "pass" (as they say of negroes) as a completely English poet without apparently losing contact with his homeland or severing his roots' (*TCS*, p. 62). Conran suggests that Anglophone Welsh poets can be divided 'along a scale according to the degree they subscribe to the Edward Thomas cult' (ibid.). Thomas is a figure of division for poets in Wales: those who do not see the distinctiveness of Anglophone Welsh poetry from its English equivalent make 'quite a large contribution to the cult' (*TCS*, p. 63). Indeed, Conran makes a poet's non-interest in Thomas's work a litmus-test of that poet's Welshness. Conran's comparison of the Anglicisation of the Welsh poet to the assimilation of African-Americans into white-dominated US society draws tenuous parallels between the two groups. However, in his portrayal of Thomas as a Welshman who effectively becomes English, he does not examine how his subject could also be considered as a member of the Welsh literary tradition. Instead, he is happy to allow Thomas to 'pass' as an English writer. This is a line of argument that Conran further develops in his next critical work, *Frontiers in Anglo-Welsh Poetry* (1997). In one of its essays, 'The Anglo-Welsh Vanishing Point: the Eastaway of Edward Thomas', he suggests that 'if Anglo-Welsh writing represents a pilgrim's progress towards the New Jerusalem of the blue-blooded English, then

Edward Thomas is the success story' (*F*, p. 30). He became, suggests Conran, an 'example' for 'Welshmen of the professional class in the 1940s and later', and especially for 'poets who were preparing to enter English culture and to leave behind them the constraints and the claustrophobia (as they increasingly saw it) of the *buchedd*, the Welsh way of life' (*F*, p. 41).

It is unlikely that Alun Lewis, who, in a 1941 issue of *Horizon*, reviewed one of the wartime reprints of Thomas's poetry, is among the writers that Conran has in mind here (Leslie Norris and Jeremy Hooker, as we will see, are more likely candidates). Thomas is clearly a strong influence on Lewis, as evidenced by poems that explicitly pay tribute to the earlier poet. However, the Anglophone Welsh identity that they shared remains unvoiced in the review, implicit only in its final sentence. Here, having written that Thomas 'loved England too well', Lewis returns to the poetry, as if the English tradition cannot fully account for what Thomas wrote: 'yet when all this is said, his poetry remains'.[13] This last line is full of possibilities, as if Lewis recognises that Thomas's work will not sit entirely within the English national literary tradition; indeed it is as if he recognises that what makes it 'poetry' emanates from something outside his love of England. R. S. Thomas's introduction to his 1964 selection of Edward Thomas's poems is in many ways similar to that of Lewis. Noting his 'Welsh parents' and his interest in 'Celtic tales and legends', the later poet identifies a 'vein of melancholy and dissatisfaction' which 'may have had a Welsh source'.[14] Otherwise, Edward Thomas's poems are discussed by R. S. Thomas only in relation to the English tradition of 'Georgian verse' and their depiction of 'English country life'.

In the late 1960s, another set of Welsh critics of Thomas emerges. While they do not employ definitions of Welsh identity that exclude Thomas, their critical approaches nevertheless fail to connect the Welshness they identify in his biography to their reading of his work. Unsurprisingly, given the tenuous position of Welsh writing in English between a more established English literature and a threatened Welsh-language equivalent, many of the critics at this time lack the tools and confidence to position Thomas within an English-language Welsh tradition. In the context of the language division, and the exclusivist definitions of Welshness put forward, as we have seen, by R. Tudur Jones and J. R. Jones, merely to assert Thomas's Welshness was a controversial critical act.

In 1967, Elis Jenkins published an article entitled 'Fiftieth Anniversary of the Death of Edward Thomas (1878–1917): Some of his Welsh Friends'. Through anecdotes from those who remembered Thomas's visits to the

Pontardulais, Ammanford and Swansea areas, the article begins to suggest the extent of his biographical connection to Wales.[15] A 1970 review by Welsh poet Leslie Norris develops this approach. Norris's own creative work, incidentally, acknowledges the influence of Thomas, who is the dedicatee of two poems, 'Ransoms' and 'A Glass Window', and who is described by Patrick McGuinness as 'the single most decisive presence in Norris's work'.[16] In his 1970 review, Norris explores Thomas's Welsh family background, his frequent visits, and the fact that he regarded himself as Welsh, pointing out that Thomas's first poem was called 'Eluned' (embedded in the text of *Beautiful Wales*), and that he wrote his book on the Cymrophile George Borrow while staying in Wales.[17]

In 'The Writings of Edward Thomas', Jeremy Hooker develops this biographical approach by establishing Wales as a key thematic concern of Thomas's work. The essay ignores the poetry, drawing instead on a wide range of prose material, including the short story, 'Home', from *Light and Twilight*, other short stories from *Rest and Unrest*, and later journalistic work like 'Swansea Village', as well as the novel *The Happy-Go-Lucky Morgans*. Themes such as 'boyhood', 'dreams', 'home' and 'imaginary country' are, for Hooker, 'keys', intimately linked to Wales, 'an important aspect of Thomas's imagination'.[18]

R. George Thomas claims his subject for the Welsh national tradition in his 1972 pamphlet on Edward Thomas for the *Writers of Wales* series. His work is unprecedented in its biographical knowledge. It draws attention to Thomas's 'frequent visits to South Wales and Monmouthshire and to the equally Welsh homes of his father's relations in Swindon'.[19] It mentions the 'Welshness' of Thomas's 'relations', and 'ancestors', as well as his 'early adolescent visits to his father's cousins at Pontardulais and the life-long friendship with Gwili', the Welsh-language poet whose relationship with Thomas will be discussed in Chapter Three (*ERG*, p. 69). It suggests that Thomas's Welshness is evident in the 'truly imaginative creation of Welsh characters' who emerged in short stories from *Rest and Unrest*, *Light and Twilight* and *Horae Solitariae*, and in his novel, *The Happy-Go-Lucky Morgans* (*ERG*, p. 71). His wartime essays, 'Glamorgan' and 'Swansea Village', are responsive, for R. George Thomas, to 'the double pull of industrial and rural Wales' (*ERG*, p. 71). He develops this knowledge into a full-length biography of Thomas, published in 1980, in which the biographical evidence for his subject's Welshness is detailed and extensive.

While all three critics – Norris, Hooker and R. George Thomas – make contested contributions merely by suggesting Thomas's Welshness, none of the three establishes the connection, beyond a thematic interest in

Wales, between a Welsh identity and the aesthetic concerns of Thomas's work. Norris, searching for 'an element of Welshness in Thomas's poetry', announces that 'if there is such a strain, I cannot recognise it'.[20] Instead, Norris places Thomas's poetry into an English tradition, pointing out what it owes to 'the principles that lay behind the *Lyrical Ballads*'.[21] In his essay on Thomas's poetry, Norris hints at a more meaningful way in which his subject's Welshness might inform his work: the sounds in 'As the Team's Head-Brass' 'remind us of the Welsh use of sound pattern and internal rhyming'.[22] However, his comment remains undeveloped, while description of Thomas's verse as 'warm, spare and alive' is reminiscent of the assessment of the prominent English critic of his day, F. R. Leavis (*LN*, p. 164). Norris himself links his line of enquiry to that of Leavis, quoting the Cambridge critic's summary of Thomas's ability to capture 'a representative modern sensibility', which is 'an achievement of a very rare order' (ibid.). His essay goes on simply to explore what this 'modern sensibility' might mean. In the end, he values Thomas for his poetry's 'exquisitely painful charting of man's essential loneliness' (*LN*, p. 172), for 'his unassuming voice, his plain diction, his infinitely sensitive forth-rightness and massive honesty', and for 'his technical skills and the high seriousness of his art' (*LN*, p. 178).

Norris's reliance on Leavis – a critic for whom the phrase 'English poetry' conflates English-language verse and ideas of Englishness – hinders any attempt to claim Thomas for a distinctive English-language Welsh tradition. In *New Bearings in English Poetry*, published in 1932, Leavis examines how Pound, Eliot, Hopkins and Yeats, among others, have contributed to 'English poetry', but his project hides a contradiction: all of these writers employ the English language, but each retains a loyalty or attachment to a non-English nation. While expressions of cultural nationalism are explicit in Leavis's long-standing interest in Englishness, it should be pointed out that they are also implicit in his more formalist analysis of these poets' work. The fact that Leavis writes of these authors without dwelling on their contributions to Anglophone literary traditions in the US, Ireland or Wales, instead focusing on each writer's contribution to 'English poetry', betrays the cultural nationalism implicit in his approach. This is equally true of Leavis's treatment of Thomas who, he writes, possesses 'a distinctly modern sensibility', defined as 'the record of a moment of relaxed and undirected consciousness'.[23] Thomas's poetry demonstrates 'the diction and movement . . . of quiet, ruminative speech' in which 'the outward scene is accessory to an inner theatre' (*NB*, p. 55). While Leavis makes passing reference to Thomas's 'English poetry', he

displays no interest in Thomas's prose, nor, of course, in Thomas's affiliation to Wales (*NB*, p. 55).

The pervasiveness of Leavisite methods of criticism in the half-century
after *New Bearings* is difficult to overstate. Eagleton, writing in 1983,
calls contemporary English literature students '"Leavisites" whether they
know it or not'.[24] The discipline has been 'irremediably altered by that
historic intervention', he argues; 'that current has entered the bloodstream
of English studies'.[25] One of the contexts that Eagleton misses is the
influence of Leavis even on critics with a primary interest in non-English
nations, and the way that his methods informed the approach of these
critics too. By applying Leavisite critical tools, Norris develops a line of
enquiry that could not be better designed to place the poet within an
English-language tradition, one in which the literary output of the poet
is to be judged according to supposedly disinterested, formal criteria (or
nebulous notions of how 'life-affirming' a poem might be) that attach no
value to the relation between text or author and the specific society in
which the work is produced and read. Such an approach makes it harder
for writers with complex relations to the English language to gain critical
recognition. The example suggests that even for critics who are committed
to literature from marginalised national traditions within Britain, the
dominant, Leavis-inspired tools of literary analysis 'entered the bloodstream' of the discipline's practitioners, prejudicing any attempt to make
the peripheral culture centre-stage to their critique.

Hooker, too, argues that English-language Welsh poets 'contribute' to
the English poetic tradition.[26] Describing 'debate' over Thomas's national
identity as 'sterile', Hooker announces that his poetry 'belongs . . . to a
tradition in English verse of dramatic lyric poetry to which Anglo-Welsh
poets have contributed a great deal', and in which 'the unique achievements of individual poets' are valued above all (*WET*, p. 64). 'Edward
Thomas', he goes on, in a critical line that echoes the Humfrey essay
mentioned earlier, 'belongs only to those who, without reservation, love
the English language' (*WET*, p. 64). Here, Hooker's 'tradition in English'
(to which Anglophone Welsh writers may belong) limits the role of a
Welsh writer in English to one of 'contributionism'. With this 'tradition
in English' (which seems to mean English-language literature), Hooker
avoids the question of Anglophone Welsh national literature, and conveniently omits to mention other Anglophone literatures, including the
Irish and American literary traditions, that were well-known at the time of
his article. While it must be acknowledged that Hooker's casual reference
to Wales as a 'region' is reasonable in 1970 (in the 1979 referendum on

devolution, a majority of the Welsh rejected the chance to establish a degree of political autonomy), his line of enquiry nonetheless shows how hard it has been to establish the distinctiveness (from English literature) of an Anglophone Welsh tradition. What is shocking, especially in 1970, in the midst of the language protests, is Hooker's conception of a Welsh writer who can 'without reservation, love the English language'. This demonstrates an ignorance of Welsh history, of English as the coloniser's tongue, of the 1847 'Blue Books', and the rise of the language movement in Wales at the time Hooker was writing. The relation of a Welsh writer to the English language is necessarily more complex than Hooker allows.

Like Hooker, R. George Thomas is concerned about Edward Thomas's status within the canon of English literature, despite his focus on Thomas's Welshness. His main concern is to present his subject as a poet worthy of a canonical position in English literature. Thomas's Welshness is characterised as a formative influence that becomes a thematic concern of his literary output, evident in the prose, which is characterised as minor, but it is hardly mentioned as far as the poetry is concerned. According to R. George Thomas, the poetry represents the epitome of Thomas's literary achievement, for which the years of writing prose were merely preparation. For example, Thomas's autobiography – written in late 1913 – was 'an inevitable next station on this progress towards unvarnished self-portrayal', a destination finally reached in the poetry that he began writing in 1914.[27] The notion of inevitability is, with hindsight, easy to apply, but hard to square with events as they unfolded. It also ignores the difficult question about the relation of self to poetry, and suppresses the issue of how that self can be portrayed in an 'unvarnished' way – whatever that means – through writing. The 'unvarnished self-portrayal' of the poetry is contrasted with what R. George Thomas describes as the 'tedious' task of writing commissioned books. It is difficult to support the clear distinctions that R. George Thomas draws: in effect, he makes the case that, after twenty years of writing commissioned and non-commissioned prose, as well as near-daily literary reviews for the papers, there survived in Thomas a pure 'unvarnished' self that is portrayed in his poetry. This metaphysical, unworldly self apparently lies beyond the reach of the world, and has no connection with Thomas's Welshness.

In 1978, *Poetry Wales* published a special issue dedicated to Edward Thomas. However, its then editor, John Powell Ward, immediately distances himself from the issue of identity. 'The vexed question of Thomas's Welshness', he argues, is 'necessarily of some interest to some of our readers but an irritant and bore to many others (perhaps also our readers)'.[28] His

declaration that Thomas 'seems a largely English person of Welsh parent-
age' is an attempt to end the matter and move on to a more fruitful – and
seemingly separate – discussion of the aesthetics of Thomas's poetry.
This suggests that for Powell Ward a writer's nationality has nothing to
do with his aesthetic, but when he goes on to suggest that Thomas's poetry
fills the 'gap' in 'the "English" line' between the Victorians and the Movement poets of the fifties, he seems blind to the contradictions in his position
– in particular to the national and linguistic connotations of 'the "English"
line'.[29]

In many ways, the most significant piece in the special issue, for the
wrong reasons, is a short essay by Joan Harding and Derwyn Jones,
'Edward Thomas and Wales', which takes a biographical approach; this
is an attempt to establish 'the actual facts of his connections, visits, and
publications about Wales', but, among other things, it puts Thomas's
interest in Wales down to the coincidence that 'in Clapham the Thomases
found themselves living next door to a Welsh family'.[30] Although the
authors acknowledge that more research needs to be carried out on the
matter, this approach betrays an inability to consider seriously Thomas's
Welshness. It mirrors the authors' refusal to allow Wales anything more
than a coincidental significance to his poetry:

> the point is surely not that Thomas in any way, conscious or unconscious,
> thought of Wales as this half-seen, elusive place, but that any person uprooted
> from a settled and very old community, even if he were born elsewhere,
> must experience some sense of absence, some entity he hears of and feels
> is to do with him yet is not within his reach. (*JHDJ*, p. 105)

The years after the unsuccessful 1979 devolution referendum do not
witness much development in the way that Welsh critics treat Thomas.
In 1987, Sally Roberts Jones enters the debate, making the now familiar
case for Thomas 'as a Welshman'.[31] Like her predecessors, however,
she does not develop a substantive connection, beyond the thematic,
between his Welshness and his written work. Thomas 'knew Glamorgan,
Carmarthenshire, Pembrokeshire and southern Cardiganshire in considerable detail', knowledge that can be seen in his essays 'Swansea
Village' and 'Glamorgan' (*ETW*, p. 79). She also traces odd references
to Wales in some poems – 'The Mountain Chapel', 'Roads', 'The Ash
Grove' and 'The Child on the Cliff' (*ETW*, p. 81). However, Thomas is
not responsible for 'technical innovation based on Welsh forms', nor do
poems that directly mention Wales necessarily make Thomas's poetry

distinctively Welsh (ibid.). Instead, Jones identifies two Welsh qualities in Thomas's work. The first is the 'accessibility' characteristic of a Welsh tradition that 'develops not through the scholar in his study or the University wit, but through the bard or story-teller . . . who must be accessible to the widest possible audience in order to survive' (*ETW*, p. 82). Jones notes the centrality of storytelling, reading aloud and character sketches to Thomas's prose work, including his autobiography *The Childhood of Edward Thomas* and his novel *The Happy-Go-Lucky Morgans* (ibid.). The second Welsh 'legacy' in Thomas's work lies in his 'sense of isolation, social and intellectual', which she traces to his sense of being a Welsh writer forced, by his dependence on the literary marketplace, to live in England (ibid.). In these circumstances, Jones argues, Wales became Thomas's 'unattainable "other country"' (*ETW*, p. 83). While she rightly points to the constraints of the literary marketplace at the time ('there was no possibility of Thomas's "returning" to Wales as a later generation of Anglo-Welsh writers could'), she does not explore how these constraints worked in practice, or the opportunities that did exist for publishing in Wales. This area of Jones's work remains undeveloped, but opens fruitful avenues for further enquiry.

These avenues are not pursued in Jeremy Hooker's 2004 essay on Thomas, 'Poetic Lands and Borderlands'. Here Thomas's Welshness is important only insofar as it contributes to the 'divided identity' that enables him to write poems which express 'nostalgia' and 'the temporary achievement of oneness'.[32] John Powell Ward's 2003 essay, 'Borderers and Borderline Cases', argues that 'any status [Thomas and others] may have as "border poets" has been partly overshadowed by their full stature as central figures in the full British tradition; and this is of course understandable enough'.[33] This is a revealing sentence, for even though Powell Ward identifies the phenomenon of border poetry, he views it through the prism of what he calls 'the full British tradition'. 'Our attention to these poets has to be incomplete', he argues, which implies that only by placing Thomas in a British context would his full status be realised.[34]

To recap so far: Thomas's work finds no secure home in the Welsh literary tradition, in spite of efforts since the late 1960s to establish a biographical basis for his Welshness. As we have seen, critics have mentioned a number of ways in which this identity is connected to Thomas's literary output, suggesting that his work shows Wales as a thematic concern, that it is informed by Welsh metres and folk material, and that its 'melancholy', sense of 'dissociation' and 'accessibility' originate in his Welshness. It is fair to point out that none of these lines of enquiry is thoroughly pursued. Instead, they remain marginal to critiques that value Thomas's 'contribution' to an English-language literature for which the Welshness of a given text is an incidental characteristic. In so far as they can be likened to Casanova's 'pure criticism' – in which texts are principally valued according to formal or aesthetic criteria divorced from their social and historical context – these approaches make it harder to establish Thomas within the Welsh literary tradition. According to Casanova's theory, in spite of their inability to see the obstacles faced by authors from 'dominated' nations, critics who practise 'pure criticism' nonetheless help a national literature to develop its autonomy. My research into Thomas's reception in Wales suggests a different conclusion: as with Belinda Humfrey's work, the criticism of Leslie Norris, Jeremy Hooker and R. George Thomas values Thomas's texts for characteristics that marginalise their Welshness. Their work, in this sense, serves to support the dominant Anglocentrism in British culture, making it difficult for critics in the Welsh tradition to establish the aesthetic grounds on which an Anglophone Welsh national literature may be read.

The reception of Thomas on the other side of the Welsh border, as we shall see, shows critics to be more confident in claiming his work – and his poetry in particular – for an Anglocentric British tradition. Thomas published only thirty-three poems in his lifetime, all of them under the pseudonym of Edward Eastaway, eighteen of them in *An Annual of New Poetry* (1917), edited by Gordon Bottomley. Although Thomas never saw the anthology, he lived long enough to see one unsigned review of it (written by John Cann Bailey) in *The Times Literary Supplement* of 29 March 1917, in which he is accused of employing a 'naturalism which the tremendous life of the last three years' – a euphemism for the war – 'has made an absurdity'.[35] Already, in this first criticism of Thomas's poetry, the immediate historical context in which the poems are read deeply affects their reception.

Thomas's first collection, *Poems*, was published on 10 October 1917, exactly six months after his death. In January 1919, *Last Poems* appeared, while *Collected Poems* was published in 1920. In Walter de la Mare's foreword to the *Collected*, the fact that Thomas died as a British soldier, and yet wrote poetry that is supposedly unconcerned with the war, is central to the ideology that lies behind his critical reception. Most of de la Mare's foreword is taken up with biographical comments that enable him to present a view of the immediate post-war historical context. He declares that Thomas 'was born to live and die a soldier'.[36] He refers to 'the sacrifice [in which Thomas] found an unusual serenity and satisfaction', and he links the act of reading the poems to the 'brave spirit that compelled him' to fight and die for his country. Thomas's death as a soldier is repeatedly associated with a particular way of reading the newly published poems:

> When, indeed, Edward Thomas was killed in Flanders, a mirror of England was shattered of so pure and true a crystal that a clearer and tenderer reflection of it can be found no other where than in these poems . . . England's roads and heaths and woods, its secret haunts and solitudes, its houses, its people – themselves resembling its thorns and juniper – its very flints and dusts, were his freedom and his peace. (*WDLM*, p. 249)

De la Mare declares that 'If one word could tell of his all, that word would be England' (ibid.). This clearly tries to read Thomas's posthumously published poetry in a way that legitimises the death of British soldiers in France. As we shall see, one of the characteristics of Thomas's reception within the Anglocentric tradition is the sensitivity of its critics to the political contexts in which they operate. Once the war ends, the critical reception of Thomas no longer refracts the need to sustain the war effort, but conveys attempts to retrospectively justify the extreme loss of life. In these changed circumstances, the 'naturalism' criticised as an 'absurdity' by the *TLS* reviewer becomes central to the ideology that underpins de la Mare's post-war criticism. Thomas's perceived refusal to engage with the war and his supposed focus instead on rural England are important to de la Mare's purposes, for they imply a continuation of the rural England, unchanged by war, for which all the sacrifice supposedly occurred. His approach Anglicises Thomas, implicitly conflating Britain, whose uniform Thomas wore when he died, with the rural England his poetry supposedly represents, a simplification which, of course, leaves no room for his Welshness.

The ideology that underpins the portrayal of Thomas the poet-soldier is evident in another publication of 1920, Robert Frost's poem 'To E.T.', published in April 1920 by *The Yale Review* and reprinted in the 1923 collection, *New Hampshire*. It is a poem that had a significant influence on subsequent interpretations of Thomas:

> I slumbered with your poems on my breast
> Spread open as I dropped them half-read through
> Like dove wings on a figure on a tomb
> To see, if in a dream they brought of you,

> I might not have the chance I missed in life
> Through some delay, and call you to your face
> First soldier, and then poet, and then both,
> Who died a soldier-poet of your race.[37]

These first two stanzas, like the foreword by de la Mare, link the acts of fighting and dying in wartime with the act of reading a poem. Frost's line 'soldier-poet of your race' is highly significant, the word 'soldier' softened and ennobled by its hyphenation with 'poet', while a writer who combines the two roles is presented as a worthy spokesman for his 'race'. The non-specificity of 'race' enables the poem to speak to members of an American readership, while only later readers, familiar with 'E. T.', would have made the connection to Britain. What is clear from this initial response is that – in contrast to the detached, aesthetic criticism Casanova's model leads us to expect from the institutions of a literary centre – the reception of Thomas's poetry outside Wales is highly conscious of the political and historical context in which it operates.

Thomas's posthumous connection with war is continued by another phase of Thomas publications from the late 1930s to the 1950s, a time when Britain, under different historical circumstances, again faced war with Germany. Between 1936 and 1949, Faber and Faber produced five reprints of Thomas's *Collected Poems*, while a series of biographical and critical works was also produced, including Robert P. Eckert's *Edward Thomas: A Biography and a Bibliography* (1937), *The Childhood of Edward Thomas* (1938), an autobiographical piece with a preface by his younger brother Julian, and Eleanor Farjeon's memoirs (1958).

Julian Thomas's preface to *The Childhood of Edward Thomas* ends with a sizeable quotation from one of Thomas's friends, E. S. P. Haynes, in which the ghost of the poet is invoked to encourage enlistment in another impending war. As with earlier texts, the connection is made between the beauty of the English countryside and Thomas's alleged readiness to die for it:

> Nearly six months after his death in April 1917 I sat watching a September sunset over Iken on the right bank of the River Alde in Suffolk. A line of firs stood black against the luminous reaches of the broad river and fading gold of the sky beyond. He and I had never seen this country together; but quite suddenly I felt that he was near at hand. Beauty alone had made life worth living for him even in the darkest hour; and now he seemed to be part of it all. It was indeed this beauty that he had died to save from the

hideous devastation of war. Nevertheless as the sun went down the con-
viction of his presence vanished with the light, and nothing but the sense
of loss and mortality remained.[38]

Haynes's narration links Thomas's death in war with the beauty of a
pastoral English scene. He implies that while Thomas's virtues as a poet
enabled him to perceive and express the beauty of the English countryside
better than ordinary mortals, his death as a soldier shows that his appreciation of that beauty was so heartfelt that he felt it worth joining the army
and dying for. The disappearance of Thomas's supernatural presence at
the end of the piece leaves the way clear for readers to step into his shoes.
It is impossible to separate the ideology underpinning Haynes's piece
from the year in which it was first published, 1938, when Britain, facing
another 'darkest hour', was again preparing for war.

Eckert's biographical approach also speaks to the political context of
the time in which it was written. Thomas's agony over whether or not to
enlist, for example, is simplified by Eckert in a way that ignores the social
and financial pressure to do so. Instead, he uses Thomas's eventual decision
as a vehicle for criticising 'the pacifist philosophy' of many in the late
1930s:

> although war seemed a part of the modern garishness he hated, noisier than
> the motors that roared along the roads of England and made life and tramping
> unbearable, he knew that the War must be ended, and ended victoriously.
> He recognised the flaw in the pacifist philosophy, and knew that the one
> remedy was victory.[39]

Eckert provides no evidence to support this interpretation of Thomas's
motives. Eckert's biography also downplays Thomas's Welshness. The
Thomases' decision to name their son Merfyn, for example, is romanticised
simply as Thomas's 'love for the melody of Welsh names' and his 'pride'
in his 'Welsh ancestry', while aspects of his Welshness – his relation to
the Welsh poet Gwili, for instance – are not even mentioned.[40]

While de la Mare in 1920 focuses on Thomas's death, part of an attempt
to persuade people that the slaughter in Flanders had been worthwhile, the
emphasis among critics of Thomas in the 1930s subtly shifts onto Thomas's
decision to enlist. In general, the 1930s texts seem to respond, with another
impending world war, to an unvoiced anxiety about the loyalties of the
British people, and their willingness to fight. In this war, unlike the last,
the Irish Free State was independent and neutral, and the relatively newly

formed Plaid Genedlaethol Cymru, the Welsh Nationalist Party, had adopted a non-cooperative policy, arguing that Welshmen's interests were not best served by fighting another war against Germany for protection of British imperialist interests. Behind Plaid's stance, which inspired an arson campaign against the RAF in the late 1930s, partly as a protest against aerial bombing, it is surely possible to hear both the neutrality of the Irish Free State, and the sense that the loss of Welsh lives, under the leadership of a Welsh prime minister in World War I, had been in vain. Eckert uses Thomas to attack this strain of pacifism in British politics. As a writer who may be perceived as an Anglicised Welshman – one who 'threw in his lot' with Britain – and as a 'soldier-poet' whose death in the First World War may be presented as meaningful, Thomas in the late 1930s sits at an interesting point in these wider debates and anxieties.

The British-Irish context may also partly explain the urgency with which de la Mare attempts, in 1920, to characterise Thomas's work as that of an English patriot. His comments occur four years after the 1916 Easter Rising, in the middle of the Irish War of Independence, at a time when many of the surviving British soldiers of World War I were returning from the continent only to be sent to another war in Ireland. Given the anxiety of Thomas critics in the 1930s over their readerships' wartime loyalties to an Anglicised Britain, it is not unreasonable to suppose that similar anxieties were at work in 1920 when nationalist forces were erupting in a different theatre on these islands.

The underlying anxiety about readers' loyalties to Britain is also present in Eleanor Farjeon's memoir, *Edward Thomas: the Last Four Years*, published in 1958. She recalls Thomas's answer to her question, 'Do you know what you are fighting for?'.[41] According to Farjeon, 'he stopped, and picked up a pinch of earth. "Literally, for this". He crumbled it between finger and thumb, and let it fall' (*LFY*, p. 154). This memory is used to reinforce the image of Thomas as an English soldier-poet, and is later connected to perhaps the most famous literary depiction of the English soldier, Shakespeare's *Henry V*:

> For love of the dust of his country [Thomas] cried 'God save England!' in 1915, as in 1415 he might have cried it at Agincourt. His hate-feelings were reserved for the Jingo Press and those who used its jargon in argument. (*LFY*, p. 180)

Here, Farjeon seems blind to her own use of jargon. Not only does her memoir foreclose any discussion of Thomas's Welshness, but in claiming that Thomas dies for 'love of the dust of his country', she resurrects the myth surrounding the patriotism of World War I soldiers evoked in the 'richer dust' and 'foreign field' of Rupert Brooke's sonnet 'The Soldier'.[42]

Farjeon's memoir inspires the worst kind of criticism of Thomas, one that recruits him for an English nationalism based on images of an unchanging countryside. Ralph Lawrence's 'Edward Thomas in Perspective' is a good example; here Lawrence declares 'without exaggeration' that 'no greater lover of England has existed than this London-born Welshman' before quoting Farjeon's anecdote of Thomas and the pinch of soil.[43] Lawrence asserts on the back of this anecdote that 'it was England herself whom he loved, with a passion as ardent as it was reticent' (*RLP*, p. 177). In an echo of de la Mare's 1920 foreword, Lawrence even mentions the things that 'never failed to beguile him': the 'mud, dust, pebbles, flints – the very substance of his English earth' (*RLP*, p. 178).

There is a third, later, British tradition of Thomas criticism that also reflects the political context in which it is written. A group of critics with links to Northern Ireland have, since the 1970s, seen Thomas's poetry as central to a revisionist canon that values traditional form at the expense of experimental modernism. While their critique thus engages with discussions taking place across the Anglo-American literary academy, their work on Thomas, as we shall see, also serves more regional political ends. Edna Longley places Thomas into an 'English line' which she opposes to modernism.[44] One critic, Peter Howarth, has identified the similarities between Longley's approach and that of Philip Larkin, whose 'reappraisals of Davies, de la Mare, Owen, Hardy and Thomas' constitute 'part of his aim to rewrite the history of modern poetry' in order to depict modernism not as 'a triumph over Georgian sentimental nostalgia, but "an aberration", whose foreign "culture-mongering" has lost poetry its audience'.[45]

While Larkin's work in this area is somewhat piecemeal, consisting mainly of reviews and forewords later collected in *Required Writing*, Longley is responsible for providing the backbone to this critical tradition. In *Poetry in the Wars*, she identifies an 'English' line in the poetry of Wordsworth and Clare, a lineage that extends down to Hardy and then to Larkin. Thomas, she contends, is the 'missing link between Hardy and Larkin' (*PW*, p. 113). The anti-modernist premise of her argument is evident in her suggestion that through Larkin and Thomas, 'a peculiarly indigenous quality has been preserved by their wariness about the Modernist invader' (*PW*, p. 118). In another essay Longley identifies 'Pound himself, rather than a Poundian future' as 'the enemy' – presumably this 'enemy' is also the 'modernist invader' against whom Thomas was earlier aligned (*PW*, p. 30). Thomas, she claims, harboured 'doubts' about Pound, while advocating the poetry of Hardy, Lawrence and Yeats (*PW*, p. 31). Frost and Thomas, meanwhile, offer an 'underestimated' alternative to the 'aggrandised' modernist couple of Pound and Eliot (*PW*, p. 22). Here, Frost's formally traditional poetry offers the prospect of a counter-point to the phenomenon of American modernism. In this 'poetry war', Thomas and Frost are 'natural allies', both making a stand against the modernism that 'partly originated in American and Irish rebellion against the English literary tradition which claimed Thomas's main allegiance' (*PW*, p. 32). Frost, it seems, is a different kind of American, one whose 'true or best self lingers near Thomas' (ibid.), and one whose 'English reputation', aided by Thomas, generated his later success in the States (*PW*, p. 23).

Longley does draw attention to 'Welsh horizons', which are allowed the role of 'complicating "Englishness"' (*PW*, p. 53). She also acknow-ledges an Irish literary scene to which 'Thomas's vision owes something' (*PW*, p. 56). However, this critical line, like that of its Welsh counterpart, remains undeveloped. Elsewhere, she writes that 'Thomas's "England" [bears] trace elements of Yeats's Ireland, Frost's New England, and bardic Wales'.[46] Although she concedes that the make-up of this nation is 'dialect-ical rather than unitary', the very idea of 'trace elements' within England subordinates the non-English nations, reducing their role to one of 'con-tributionism' (*GW*, p. 73). What, moreover, is meant by her 'bardic Wales'? Longley states that Thomas 'lov[es] English language and culture [and] accepts the logic of putting his life where his poetry is', a critique which, like the work of Frost and de la Mare before her, suggests that the poems should be read through the prism of Thomas's later death at the front (ibid.). It also blurs the distinction between the 'English language and culture' that his poetry is made to represent, and the British uniform he wore (ibid.).

In 'The Great War, History, and the English Lyric', published in 2005, Thomas is again portrayed as an anti-modernist war poet, a writer whose importance lies in the way his poetry demonstrates the continuance, through war and historical cataclysm, of traditional poetic form: 'poetry's mechanisms of tradition' are challenged, but ultimately strengthened, by the writer's experience of these events (*GW*, p. 66). The idea that new poetic forms might emerge out of historical experience, while others are rendered redundant, is not examined. This echoes the argument made two decades before in *Poetry in the Wars* in which Thomas is credited with 'develop[ing] specific qualities of English poetry itself', a role that makes him more widely 'important to the history of twentieth-century poetry in English' (*PW*, p. 47).

The most recent work by Longley demonstrates an increasing sensitivity to Thomas's interest in the Welsh and Irish literary traditions. Thomas's 'construction of England', she writes in 2007, 'was conditioned by his Welsh hinterland and influenced by the Irish revival'.[47] Once again, however, the Welshness is relegated to a 'hinterland', while the suggestion that it 'conditioned' a construction of England is not pursued. The 170 pages of 'Notes' to her 2008 *Annotated Collected Poems* (now rightly the standard edition of Thomas's poetry) display an unprecedented knowledge of the links between Thomas's poems, correspondence and prose, as well as possible allusions to the English literary tradition. These 'Notes' are also indicative of a greater openness to Thomas's Welshness. Certainly, Wales or visits to Wales are mentioned in her discussion of 'The Mountain Chapel', 'An Old Song I', 'An Old Song II', 'The Combe', 'Over the Hills', 'The Child on the Cliffs', 'Words', 'A Dream', 'This is no case', 'Rain', 'Roads', 'The Ash Grove', 'Home ("Fair was the morning")', 'The Watchers' and 'I never saw that land before'. Her 'Notes' also mention the anti-imperialism suggested in *The South Country*, as well as the September 1901 diary entry in which Thomas writes of his Welsh patriotism (both mentioned in the opening pages of this study). Longley even raises the idea that Thomas 'pursued a reading of "England" through Wales or Ireland'.[48] Again, however, this line of enquiry is not followed up. Instead, Wales is a place where Thomas 'spent childhood summer holidays' (*ELN*, p. 198), or a source of his Celticism (*ELN*, p. 284). Even the instances of Welsh influence that Longley identifies are never brought together. They remain isolated in her analysis of individual poems, collectively subordinate to her interest in a locally based version of Englishness: 'Thomas's Welsh and Western horizons make Wiltshire . . . rather than the Home Counties his spiritual epicentre' (*ELN*, p. 212).

Writing in 2008, Peter McDonald has offered his support for Longley's project. In a review of her edition of Thomas's *Annotated Collected Poems*, McDonald suggests that Thomas's poetry 'unsettle[s] those academic investors in Pound, Eliot and Anglo-American modernism', and prefigures 'real arguments still to be had' about 'the forms and genres of twentieth-century verse'.[49] In a further echo of Longley's anti-modernism, he writes that Thomas's work 'challenges dominant narratives about twentieth-century poetry'.[50] McDonald's equally anti-modernist line of enquiry reflects the one he took in his only full-length article on Thomas. Here, he opposes Thomas to Pound, arguing that the former's criticism is 'more

searching'.[51] This article is largely given over to a forensic examination
of how 'the poet's free will' and agency manifest themselves in Thomas's
'poetic technique',[52] a discussion which takes place without recourse to
the question of how wartime pressures to join up (not to mention his
Welsh biography or what Thomas referred to as his 'accidentally Cockney
nativity') affect the poet's agency. Elsewhere, McDonald has challenged
the tendency of some critics to 'universalise' and 'decontextualise' Northern
Irish writers in order to appropriate them into an English literary tradition.
He makes the case for a critical paradigm that enables the Northern Irish
context of writers to figure centrally in an appreciation of their work, not
as a 'model of some exemplary provincialism' but as (he hopes) 'the
central, and critically-defining location for poetry in the archipelago'.[53]
McDonald's criticism of the 'universalising' characteristic of much English
criticism, as well as his insistence on the centrality of traditions that have
been too easily labelled as 'provincial', is incisive and shares common
ground with this study. However, his attack on identity-based critical
approaches (after all, the main thrust of his study *Mistaken Identities*)
ends up insisting that the term '"British" need not be complicit with the
tendencies of identity and their ultimately deterministic discourse'.[54]
While this may one day become true, to assert that this is already the case
is to ignore how 'British' has been, and still is, highly operative in the
construction of identities across these islands in ways that are deterministic
as far as other identities (such as Welsh or Irish) are concerned.

The Northern Irish poet, Michael Longley, has published at least seven
poems that include explicit reference to Edward Thomas, and which, for
the most part, concern Thomas's experience as a British soldier during
the 1914–18 war. These references are often associated with depictions
of Longley's father's experiences at the front. In 'The Moustache', for
example, a photograph of 'Edward Thomas' in uniform serves to 'recall /
My father, aged twenty, in command of a company' nicknamed 'Longley's
Babies' (after their commanding officer).[55] The images of war thereby
associated with both men also link the front to more local political tensions.
Longley describes

> the Ulster division at the Somme
> Going over the top with 'Fuck the Pope!'
> 'No surrender!': a boy about to die,
> Screaming 'Give 'em one for the Shankhill!'[56]

This poem retells a foundation myth of British Ulster – its people's sacrifice for the British state in the First World War – and the association of Thomas with Longley's father draws the Welsh poet into this project. Longley has made use on more than one occasion of Thomas's 'War Diary', a journal (kept by Thomas of his time in Flanders) that intersperses brief notes of the fighting with observations of the surviving natural world in the trenches. One poem by Longley, 'Edward Thomas's War Diary', turns lines taken from the journal into a poem, while another, 'Mole', takes its epigraph from the same source.[57] McDonald too has written a poem, also entitled 'War Diary', which is based on this document.[58] The diary seems to touch a nerve for both poets, as if it provides evidence that Thomas's skills as a pastoral poet can survive the carnage (in ways that he did not), thus providing proof that the 'English poetic line' can engage with the worst horrors of history and war, and come out of the experience with its forms intact.

Many of these critics and poets have a significant biographical connection to Ireland, and especially to the divided city of Belfast. Indeed, Lucy Newlyn writes that 'nowhere is Thomas so much remembered, in connection with both world wars, as in contemporary Irish poetry', although she does not venture to suggest why.[59] Even Larkin, who tries to identify a non-modernist 'English' line, and depict modernism as a 'foreign aberration', spent crucial early years as a librarian at Queen's University in Belfast. Here, from September 1950 to March 1955, according to his biographer, he began to take an interest in Belfast politics.[60] His poem 'The March Past' demonstrates 'his burgeoning Orange sympathies'.[61] Edna Longley has been based, since the late 1960s, in Belfast, the home town of her husband, Michael. Her criticism's antinationalism (in an Irish context) is paralleled in her marginalisation of Thomas's Welshness. McDonald, who, like Michael Longley, grew up in Belfast, describes himself as 'a Belfast-born Presbyterian', an identity which, as we have seen, informs his critical interest in Northern Irish literature.[62] For many of these writers, Thomas is a poet whose decision to wear a British uniform is significant: it sustains a reading whereby his Welsh identity is pushed to the margins in the name of Anglocentric Britishness, or in the name of continuities of poetic form with which that identity is associated. This is a critical stance which both Anglicises Thomas for the kind of Britain that it depicts as under threat, and portrays him as a key figure in the restoration of an 'English line' to centre-stage in the history of twentieth-century English-language poetry.

In his 2006 collection, *District and Circle*, Seamus Heaney presents Thomas in a way that gently draws attention to his appropriation by this group of writers. He had already mentioned the 'sponsoring presence' of Thomas (not Joyce, he notes) in Michael Longley's poem 'The Linen Industry', suggesting enigmatically that this is 'sponsorship with just as much political significance as we want to assign it'.[63] Heaney's own poem, 'Edward Thomas on the Lagans Road', makes no mention of Thomas's association with the unionist sacrifice in the First World War; instead, Thomas, or his ghost, is imagined walking in Ireland, a place he did not visit, in the aftermath of the Second World War. This setting makes the connection between Thomas and Ireland, yet does so in a way that draws attention to its 'constructedness' and arbitrary appropriation by Northern Irish writers keen to associate Thomas with unionist sacrifice for Britain during the First World War. Heaney's depiction of Thomas returning from battle as a 'demobbed' soldier asks readers to question the way he is usually read through the prism of his death in that earlier battle. Moreover, the comparison of Thomas to 'one of the Evans brothers out of Leitrim' deliberately mists the 'national' glasses through which Thomas is usually envisioned.[64] By foregrounding the Evans brothers' origins in the neutral Irish Free State, Heaney draws attention to the Irish soldiers who fought with the Allies against Nazi Germany, a point that invokes the complex national allegiance of those who have historically worn the British Army uniform. These lines, which link the Irish 'Evans brothers' to an iconic British general, 'Monty', and battle in the 'desert', imply that – like these Irish soldiers – Thomas fought for a nation with which he had a more complex relation than that suggested by a straightforward reading of the uniform he wore.

Edna Longley's perspective on Thomas dominates his critical reception. Later critics, even those who take issue with Longley's anti-modernism, usually agree with her understanding of Thomas as an anti-modernist English poet. Andrew Motion, in particular, follows Longley's line of enquiry, depicting his subject as an English writer, and his work as an alternative to 'foreign' modernism. The 'relativism', employment of 'foreign languages' and 'international context' of Eliot's *The Waste Land* (as if none of these apply to Thomas) represent a modernism that is in contrast to the 'specifically English' context with which Thomas's poetry is concerned.[65] Motion has no time for serious consideration of Thomas's Welshness: his birth in London served to minimise any allegiance to Wales he might have had. Instead, Wales becomes little more than a holiday destination, a place with which he is 'flimsily' connected (*PET*,

p. 14). When discussing Thomas as 'Patriot and War Poet', Motion fails to even mention Wales. Instead, 'the ancient features of England . . . command [Thomas's] deepest admiration' and his 'keen love of England' dominates his poetic output (*PET*, p. 94). Yet again, Wales is marginalised in the thrust of an argument about England.

John Lucas, like Longley, discusses Thomas in the context of a wider study of 'English poetry' from 'Hardy to Hughes'. While he makes the point that 'Thomas never belonged', Wales is never mentioned, let alone explored, as a cause of this sense of 'unbelonging'.[66] Instead, Thomas is valued for his poetry's 'impassioned avowal of the continuity of an English tradition'.[67] Anthony Thwaite is another Longley-influenced critic. Writing in 1978, he supports her attempts to identify in Thomas the 'ancestry' of 'Philip Larkin and Ted Hughes, two of the best contemporary English poets'.[68] Thomas's poems, he argues 'have little to do' with Eliot and Pound, and 'yet they are quite centrally part of an English tradition that continues today' (*TCP*, p. 38). Thwaite discusses Thomas entirely in terms of England, oblivious to the irony in his statement that while 'his most characteristic subject-matter [is] the whole sense of rural England . . . only such a poet as his namesake, R. S. Thomas in rural Wales, can nowadays come unselfconsciously close to such concerns' (ibid.).

The Larkin-Longley-Motion positioning of Thomas has become so accepted as a commonplace that 'Edward Thomas' has become shorthand for the formally traditional poetry of a continuing English line, one that is directly opposed to modernism. In J. M. Coetzee's *Youth*, the narrator expresses despair at the pervasive influence of this tradition, as represented by the popularity of Edward Thomas:

> The British magazines are dominated by dismayingly modest little poems about everyday thoughts and experiences, poems that would not have raised an eyebrow half a century ago. What has happened to the ambitions of poets here in Britain? Have they not digested the news that Edward Thomas and his world are gone for ever? Have they not learned the lesson of Pound and Eliot, to say nothing of Baudelaire and Rimbaud, the Greek epigrammatists, the Chinese?[69]

Here, Coetzee, a writer essentially dismayed by the perceived anti-modernism of contemporary British poetry, nonetheless equates Thomas with such a tradition. By taking the 'British magazines' as an indiscriminate whole, he fails to recognise the different national traditions that make up Britain, but the use of Thomas as shorthand for a rejection of modernism shows how influential the Larkin-Longley-Motion 'take' on Thomas has been.

Anthony Easthope, writing from a modernist perspective equally hostile to a traditional English line, also nonetheless endorses the Longley reading of Thomas that places his work in opposition to modernism. He juxtaposes Eliot's *The Waste Land* with Thomas's 'Adlestrop', concluding that the latter is a good example of an English empiricist tradition that runs from Wordsworth through Hardy to Thomas:[70]

> Yes, I remember Adlestrop –
> The name, because one afternoon
> Of heat the express-train drew up there
> Unwontedly. It was late June.
>
> The steam hissed. Someone cleared his throat.
> No one left and no one came
> On the bare platform. What I saw
> Was Adlestrop – only the name
>
> And willows, willow-herb, and grass,
> And meadowsweet, and haycocks dry,
> No whit less still and lonely fair
> Than the high cloudlets in the sky.
>
> And for that minute a blackbird sang
> Close by, and round him, mistier,
> Farther and farther, all the birds
> Of Oxfordshire and Gloucestershire.[71]

Easthope's description echoes Longley who, in her essay 'Edward Thomas and Robert Frost', first labels Thomas an 'English empiricist' (*PW*, p. 44). Easthope contends that in 'Adlestrop' the speaker's voice is 'conventionally masculine', while its rhythm evokes the 'main English post-Renaissance [iambic] tradition' (*E*. p. 179). The speaker, who is 'coherent' and 'self-possessed', is 'a unified subject' who turns a moment of unexpected loss into a moment of 'imaginary plenitude' just like the speaker in Wordsworth's 'The Solitary Reaper' (*E*. p. 180). He undergoes a 'little crisis of subjectivity, as though meaning has dropped out of his world leaving him separated from it, facing only writing, a name, Adlestrop', before his experience of landscape is united with his own feelings, the correspondence between subject and object is restored, and he achieves

a moment of transcendent insight (ibid.). There are several points that
might be made in reply: firstly, the poem shares many of the characteristics of modernism that Easthope identifies in the work of Eliot.
For example, the empiricism he claims it displays is entirely contained
within the context of a dialogue with an unknown and silent other ('Yes,
I remember Adlestrop'). In this sense, it begins and ends in a subjectivity
that it does not escape. Furthermore, the separation from the world of
meaning, far from occurring in an isolated and momentary 'crisis of
subjectivity' is the speaker's prevailing mode of consciousness. Only
'unwontedly' and 'for that minute' does he find meaning in 'all the birds /
Of Oxfordshire and Gloucestershire'. This transcendent moment, moreover, might be described as mystical, but it is hardly 'empirical' in the
way that Easthope describes: it involves a loss of self, while the distinction
between subject and object becomes 'mistier'. Martin Dodsworth takes
issue with Easthope's interpretation on similar grounds, showing how the
poem concerns 'that collapsing of inner and outer worlds which Easthope
believes to characterize the Modernist poem', and disputing Thomas's
association with a 'cult of Englishness'.[72] He raises the interesting idea,
which he does not develop, that the 'mistiness' of the last stanza might
be related to Thomas's 'uncertainties about himself . . . related to his sense
of competing loyalties to England and to Wales'.[73]

Longley's work on Thomas, sustained over four decades, has proved
to be the key intervention, even for those critics who have argued against
her line. Stan Smith's 1986 monograph, which remains unsurpassed as
an attempt to integrate Thomas's Welshness into an understanding of his
work, identifies 'one major complication to the concept of Thomas as *the*
English poet: his Welshness'.[74] He identifies references in Thomas's poetry
to the English-language speech of Wales, Thomas's 1905 authorship of
Beautiful Wales, and the fact that his travel book, *The Heart of England*,
actually ends in Wales (*ET*, p. 13). He also balances discussion of the
poetry with the prose, referring to short stories set in Wales, and *The
Happy-Go-Lucky Morgans*, the novel Thomas set in the London Welsh
community. Smith also places emphasis on the Welshness of Thomas's
family history, as well as Thomas's own 'fretting about deracination' and
the 'sense of perpetual exile which pervades his poetry' (*ET*, p. 15). Smith
connects Thomas's confessed 'accidentally Cockney nativity' – the fact
that he is Welsh, yet born in London – to his 1908 description of new
Welsh towns as 'accidental mercantile and manufacturing congeries'
(ibid.), and goes on to trace the centrality of 'accidence' – by which he
means the given historical circumstances – to Thomas's work, arguing

that it explores the agency of the individual in history. This argument begins to suggest that Thomas's identity as an exiled Welshman is the key to understanding his writing. To this extent, Smith recognises the 'otherness' in Thomas's work more than any other critic, and even suggests that Thomas's Welshness contributes to his aesthetic. At this point, however, Smith retreats from the platform he has established. He does not develop his argument, focusing instead on how Thomas's explorations relate to an 'idea of England' (*ET*, p. 19). This is a missed opportunity. While Smith successfully refutes Motion's depiction of Thomas as the poet of an unchanging rural England, connecting him instead to a tradition of English radicalism, his monograph's main focus on England nonetheless sits uneasily with what he writes, in his opening chapter, about Thomas's Welshness. A similar emphasis on English national identity is evident in Smith's more recent work on Thomas.[75]

David Gervais, writing in 1993, also takes issue with Longley and Motion. He argues that it is 'intrinsically unconvincing that a slimmish volume of just two years' work could have constituted a bridge over half a century of English poetry as Motion and Edna Longley maintain'.[76] There is no single English line. Instead, in a meandering discussion, Gervais identifies several possible versions of Englishness in Thomas's work. These include 'a poetic language capable of drawing on the strength of vernacular English speech' (*LE*, p. 40), England as 'a retreat from the modern world' (*LE*, p. 44), and England as a nation 'partly hidden in time and only visible through memory' (*LE*, p. 48). Another defining characteristic of Thomas's Englishness is 'the fact that, English as the scene and situation are, England itself is not mentioned' (*LE*, p. 49). As this list suggests, while Gervais raises some interesting ideas, there is no sustained discussion of any one of them.

In *British Poetry in the Age of Modernism*, Peter Howarth also takes issue with the Larkin-inspired 'attempt to re-write the history of modern poetry, so that modernism becomes an aberration whose foreign-mongering has lost poetry an audience'.[77] This English tradition, he contends, is 'really a post-modernist assertion of the values of locality and limitation against modernist, polyglot internationalism (*BPAM*, p. 11). Howarth's approach focuses on British poets at the turn of the century, but rather than 'separate them off into some ex-post facto English tradition', he places them in the 'same context as their modernist counterparts: the historical situation of the early twentieth century, and their inheritance of post-Romantic poetics' (*BPAM*, p. 12). While he thereby avoids the idealised English tradition so beloved of Motion, he also avoids discussion of any other national tradition, or indeed the influence of nation in the making of the poetry. Instead 'Britain' remains an unexamined concept within the analysis, a geographical space conveniently wide enough to accommodate the modernist and non-modernist poets encompassed within his discussion of post-Romantic poetics. His analysis of Thomas's poetry rightly blurs the distinctions between the Georgian poetry that Thomas's work has often been taken to represent, and the modernist poetry to which it has been opposed. It also questions Thomas's fidelity to Wordsworthian ideas of 'emotion recollected in tranquillity'. Howarth's insights into Thomas's poetry are often brilliant, and by reading his poetry through the prism of an unpublished essay, 'Ecstasy', they convincingly show how his poems are 'radical reformulations of post-Romantic subjectivity' (*BPAM*, p. 106). Nonetheless, in discussing concepts such as 'placelessness' and 'displacement', Howarth does not make any allusion to Thomas's Welshness. For example, his analysis of 'The Ash Grove', a poem based on a Welsh folk song which it actually mentions, and a poem which Howarth argues depicts 'all happiness . . . in a state of suspension', does not make any connection to Wales (*BPAM*, p. 81).

Matthew Hollis's biography of Thomas also demonstrates an Anglo-centrism in its approach. Like other biographical or critical texts that mention in passing their subject's self-description as '5/8 Welsh' or 'mainly Welsh', Hollis's study proceeds to consider Thomas from an English perspective. Only one paragraph devotes serious attention to Thomas's Welshness, and then only to dismiss it as a Celtic heritage, part of Wales's 'almost mystical draw' which Thomas overcame in 1914 as he slowly grew into 'a conscious Englishman'.[78] While much new biographical material is aired for the first time in Hollis's otherwise excellent study, Thomas's sense of national allegiance is more complicated than Hollis's study allows.

One of the corollaries of the uncertain status of Thomas as a Welsh writer has been this confidence with which he has been appropriated by an Anglocentric British tradition. The fact that he died as a British soldier is the prism through which readers are encouraged to see his poems. This criticism is generally more politically engaged than Casanova's concept allows for. At the end of the First World War, again at the beginning of the Second World War and in the post-war years, Thomas's poetry is co-opted as a means of encouraging loyalty to an Anglicised Britain. Since the 1970s, his work has been appropriated by a group of writers with critical affinities to the Ulster unionist tradition, for whom he is a means of retelling the foundation myth of British Ulster identity – that of the Irish blood-sacrifice for the British in the First World War – or of reasserting the centrality of non-modernist, formally traditional poetry to the canon. Through the medium of Edna Longley's work, the critical premise behind this latter group has become central to the British reception of Thomas ever since, to the extent that many of the critics who disagree with Longley's conclusions nonetheless accept the assumptions on which her work is based. In the next four chapters, I hope to use the second and third aspects of my revised model of Casanova's theory (the notion of 'literary capital' and the 'Irish paradigm') to reclaim Thomas for the Welsh tradition, an intervention which, as I later conclude, has implications for each of the national critical traditions discussed in this chapter.

3

Welsh Literatures in their Political and Economic Contexts

In the last chapter, I addressed the first of my alterations to Casanova's model, arguing that critics of Thomas have failed to recover him for Anglophone Welsh literature, while others have successfully claimed him for an Anglocentric British tradition. My findings challenge the premise of Casanova's model that the 'pure criticism' of the authorities at the literary centres helps writers from dominated nations to gain recognition. Instead, they suggest a more complicated picture in which ostensibly 'pure criticism', carried out both within the dominated nation and from the literary centre, marginalises the importance of the nation to the way the text is read. In this chapter, I turn to the second of the modifications to Casanova's model: the need to make the 'literary capital' of the dominated nation – Wales – more central to the study, by setting its literature in relation to the political and economic contexts in which it is produced, and the need to place Thomas within these spaces. While what follows might seem – at least until the closing stages of the chapter – at one remove from a discussion of Thomas's work, it identifies the vital conditions of its construction.

Assessing the position of literature within the Welsh economic field in the last fifteen years of the nineteenth century and the first decade of the twentieth century, this chapter brings together research from a number of previously unconnected fields. It shows how the material infrastructure of Wales's Anglophone literature is dominated in economic terms by its larger neighbour, a fact that has consequences both for Anglophone Welsh writers, and for critical efforts to recover them. As far as the position of that literature within the political sphere is concerned, the chapter argues

that one of the pressing concerns of Welsh politics at this time is the land
question, and in particular the fears of the British establishment that the
agitation seen in Ireland would spread to Wales. The focus of these British
fears is the Welsh-language press, which was held responsible for gener-
ating anti-landlord feeling. There was a dispute between key Welsh literary
figures over the positioning of literature in relation to these political and
economic contexts, the implications of which are directly relevant to a
revisionist reading of Thomas, who can be placed in relation to the principal issues and figures in these battles. For instance, Thomas's work displays an interest in republicanism, and in Home Rule for the constituent
nations of Britain and Ireland. Thomas also has connections to key figures
in Welsh literary space at the time, most notably O. M. Edwards, but also
to the two Welsh-language poets with whom he was closely involved,
Gwili and Watcyn Wyn, both based at the Gwynfryn School in Ammanford, where Thomas was a frequent visitor. He also, as we shall see, wrote
fiction for the Cardiff-based journal, *Nationalist*. However, in order to
'join up' the implications of Thomas's association with these concerns
and figures, the chapter will spend some time setting out an interpretation
of the context.

　　Turning firstly to the economic context, work from both sides of the
Anglo-Welsh border demonstrates how, at the end of the nineteenth century
and beginning of the twentieth century, the literary infrastructure centred
in London dwarfed that of Wales. Ian Norrie, in his contribution to the
field, has little to write about Wales, showing instead how, in the nineteenth
century, 'publishing remained based chiefly in London and Edinburgh'
and how, by the century's end, many of the Scottish firms had transferred
their headquarters to London.[1] While comparisons between London and
Wales are fraught with difficulty, John Gross points out that, by 1900, there
were 400 separate publishing houses listed in the *London Directory*.[2] In
Wales, by contrast, the largest publishers tended, primarily, to be printers.
One study finds that at the end of the nineteenth century, in spite of much
development, there were only 'a few large printer-publishers': Gee of
Denbigh, Rees of Llandovery, Hughes of Wrexham, Humphreys of Caernarfon and Spurrell of Carmarthen.[3] Where figures are available, the
comparatively small size of these outfits is telling: Gee and Hughes, for
example, each employed fifty people and had 200 titles in print by the end
of the nineteenth century.[4] Spurrell in 1900 employed only thirteen people.[5]
Moreover, these firms operated in a wider British market. Scottish and
English publishers penetrated the Welsh market to the extent that they
produced many Welsh-language books, and even employed Welsh-

language compositors from the 1850s onwards (*TWP*, p. 179). Not all Welsh publishers actually printed their books in Wales. Hughes, for example, contracted out much of its printing, and 'went to considerable lengths' to hide the fact that London and Edinburgh-based printers produced the novels of the prominent nineteenth-century, Welsh-language novelist, Daniel Owen (*TWP*, p. 181). William Spurrell, meanwhile, learnt his trade in London, while his son, Walter, who took over the Carmarthen press in 1889, was influenced by wider British movements in publishing, in particular by William Morris's Kelmscott Press.[6] Within wider British studies of publishing, Wales receives scant attention. Norrie mentions Welsh publishing only once (a reference to the 1922 establishment of the University of Wales Press) and devotes only one paragraph of a chapter entitled 'Bookselling: Scottish, Welsh, Provincial' to the book trade in Wales. 'The Principality,' he argues, 'was not a prime bookselling area for the very good reason that, except in the south, it was sparsely populated, and in that industrial south there was massive unemployment' (*MPB*, p. 79). Another reason, not mentioned by Norrie, is Wales's historical status as a colony: the Welsh literary market was, for centuries, not allowed to develop because of policies emanating from London. Charles Parry points out that the 1557 Royal Charter that banned printing in Wales was effective until 1695.[7] Glyn Tegai Hughes makes the point that Wales's status as a stateless nation meant that, as late as the eighteenth century, the Welsh literary sphere still lacked 'major institutions to serve as growth points', while, 'alone of western European nations, Wales had no town of any real size until some way into the nineteenth century'.[8]

One of the consequences of these centuries of restricted development is that the changes which revolutionised the British marketplace at the turn of the twentieth century were less marked in Wales. An analysis of the British book and journal trade shows that it boomed at the end of the nineteenth century, while the growth in Wales is not as rapid as that of Britain as a whole, where 7,000 titles were published in 1900, rising to 10,914 in 1911, and 12,370 in 1913 (*MPB*, p. 20). Using figures compiled by Simon Eliot, Mary Ann Gillies records that, across Britain in 1880, a total of 1,835 journal and 1,033 magazine titles were published, and by 1900 these figures had increased to 2,471 and 2,328 respectively.[9] According-ing to Mary Hammond, novel production rose from 900 new titles a year in 1886 to 1,618 in 1914.[10] Paul Delany looks at employment figures to get an idea of this transformation in the printing market: he records that in 1871, 125,000 people worked in 'paper, printing and stationery', a figure that increased to 397,000 in 1911.[11]

The problem for the critic of Welsh literary space is that there are no reliable, comparable figures for the number of books published in Wales in the 1890s and the first decade of the twentieth century. The postcolonial critic Stephen Knight suggests that, as a result of the dearth of Wales-based publishers, Welsh writers in 1900 had little choice but to seek publication through London-based institutions.[12] While his argument does not allow for writers who willingly chose the more prestigious London-based outlets, even Knight is unable to provide figures that show how many books were published in Wales at the beginning of the twentieth century.[13] Hywel Teifi Edwards, whose study 'Victorian Stocktaking' aims to discover just this kind of information, relies on Victorian scholars John Rhŷs and David Brynmor-Jones who, writing in 1900, tell us that between 1801 and 1895, 11,613 'Welsh books, etc and those in some way or other relating to Wales' were published.[14] This indicates, hardly surprisingly, that the amount of literary material published in Wales at this time is dwarfed by that published in the rest of Britain. The number of people finding employment in printing in Wales supports this interpretation: compared to Delany's 1871 figure of 125,000 for the whole of Britain, in Wales in the same year, there were only 700, although this figure had increased to 2,000 by 1891, three-quarters of whom were employed in the industrialised areas of Glamorgan and Gwent.[15]

In the area of the turn-of-the-century specialised literary press, most of the available research has been carried out into Britain as a whole, with a consequent focus on London-based institutions. An exception is Scotland, where there is a thriving, independent Anglophone literary culture, especially in periodicals, well into the twentieth century. In London at this time, well-established magazines came under pressure to change along lines determined by the success of New Journalism, while new, more popular literary magazines appeared on the scene. For example, the *Pall Mall Gazette*, an establishment evening paper that offered 'solid articles on literature and topics of the day', changed in the 1880s under the editorship of W. T. Stead: it now contained more populist articles (*RFML*, p. 68). *Academy*, whose principal shareholders had been Oxford University academics, was bought in 1896 by an American tycoon for his daughter. She employed Lewis Hind as editor, a man whom Gross describes as 'a semi-popular journalist' under whom *Academy* 'irretrievably changed its character' (*RFML*, p. 213). At the more popular end of the spectrum of literary journals, a 'large, middle-brow public' read material provided by a new generation of 'mass-circulation mandarins' who provided literary magazines to cater for their tastes (*RFML*, p. 201). These include

William Robertson Nicholl, whose title, the *Bookman*, was launched in 1891 as a monthly for 'bookreaders, bookbuyers and booksellers' to sales of 15,000 (*RFML*, p. 202). New Journalism tycoons such as George Newnes launched, among other journals, *Tit-Bits* (1881), *The Strand Magazine* (1891) and *The Ladies Field* (1898), all of which contained literary material aimed at new readerships.[16] There was also *The Speaker*, from 1899, 'the leading paper of advanced Liberal intellectuals' (*RFML*, p. 221). H. W. Massingham's weekly *The Nation* was launched (eventually becoming part of the *New Statesman*), as was the *Saturday Westminster Gazette*. *The Times*, after failing with an offshoot *Literature*, successfully launched the *Times Literary Supplement* in 1902 (*RFML*, p. 227). Two notably more experimental literary journals also arrived on the scene, the *English Review* and *The New Age*, both of which were, for periods at the beginning of the twentieth century, critically important forums in which literary modernism was developed.

The Welsh market in literary journals reflects some of the wider British growth in this area in the final decades of the nineteenth century, although, once again, it is dwarfed by its magnitude. Accurate figures for the literary press are hard to find. John Davies suggests that in 1866, five Welsh-language quarterlies, twenty-five monthlies and eight weeklies had a combined circulation of 120,000, although this figure provides no detail and is hard to verify (*HW*, p. 404). The peak decade for the launch of new newspaper and periodical titles in Wales was the 1880s, when over a hundred titles were launched, of which eighty were English-language publications and twenty Welsh. The 1890s and 1900s saw similar numbers of launches: between eighty and ninety English-language titles, and ten to twenty Welsh.[17] Five Welsh-language papers were also produced in London and Liverpool over this time. These publications ranged in type, audience, circulation, regularity and, of course, success rate. A snapshot of the picture reveals that in 1891 there were 101 newspapers in Wales, of which four were dailies.[18]

The development of a specialised literary press in Wales does not occur on the same scale as it does in London. Aled Jones's declaration that, by 1897, 'the [Welsh] periodical press was a flourishing industry, spanning two languages and a wide range of political and religious opinion' needs to be put into context (*PPS*, p. 1). For example, the comparatively late development of urban areas made the establishment of a Wales-based literary press difficult: the main urban centres did not grow until the nineteenth century, and when they developed, they were overwhelmingly English-speaking, a factor that complicates their relation to the Welsh-language culture. Cardiff grew from a population of 1,800 in 1801 to 164,000 in 1901, Swansea doubled in population size between 1861 and 1891, and Merthyr Tydfil grew from 11,000 in 1811 to 58,000 in 1891, and 80,000 in 1911 (*PPS*, p. 91). Numerically speaking, a more just comparison might be made between Cardiff and Leeds (which had four times Cardiff's population in 1911) or Bristol (which had double its population), but even these industrial cities did not grow at the pace of the Welsh capital; nor were their situations complicated by the language question, or by Cardiff's status, claimed since 1873, as 'the metropolis of Wales' (*HW*, p. 472). In Cardiff, a specialised English-language literary press did emerge, but there is so little research into this area that it is difficult to gain anything other than a snapshot of individual periodicals. O. M. Edwards, Thomas's history tutor at Oxford, launched the journal *Wales* in 1894, as a complement to its Welsh-language equivalent, *Cymru*. It began well with 3,700 subscribers in its launch year, but had only 1,100 by the end of 1897.[19] These figures, however, do not tell us about the volume of the English-language Welsh literary periodical market as a whole, although they do indicate its relative size.

The specialised Welsh-language press faced even greater problems than its English-language equivalent. As a result of the nineteenth-century movement from Welsh-speaking rural areas to predominantly English-speaking urban or industrial ones, it held a 'structurally disadvantaged' position 'in relation to the English-language press'.[20] Hywel Teifi Edwards argues that at the end of the nineteenth century, Wales still lacked 'the progressive works of literary criticism that . . . would be proof that [Welsh-language] literature in Wales was truly a serious cultural undertaking' (*VS*, p. 228). He points, however, to three literary periodicals, the quarterly *Y Traethodydd* (The Essayist) published by Thomas Gee in Denbigh, *Y Beirniad* (The Critic), edited by John Morris-Jones, and *Y Geninen* (The Leek), all of which nonetheless provided 'a valuable context for the appraisal of Welsh literature' (*VS*, p. 228). Sales of *Y Traethodydd*, which claimed to be 'the highest court in the realm of Welsh literature', were only 1,500 per issue.[21] O. M. Edwards's Welsh-language journal *Cymru* had a print run in its launch year of 5,000 (*PPS*, p. 97). It remained relatively successful, still retaining over 3,000 subscribers six years later in 1897 (*B*, p. 202). Others were limited to a more local readership. *Cwrs y Byd* (The Course of the World), for example, a radical monthly advocating trade unionism, land reform and political separatism, was popular at the end of the nineteenth century only in the tin-plating and mining area of east Carmarthenshire and west Glamorgan, an area with which our case study, Thomas, was familiar.[22] Many of the figures involved in this industry, including Gee, Morris-Jones and Edwards, are also important figures in the political context of Welsh literature, and will be discussed later in this chapter.

Any Wales-based paper or journal aiming for national coverage had to contend with the linguistic and demographic effects of colonisation and industrialisation, as well as a rail network whose development, argues John Davies, was principally 'a matter of connecting different regions of the country with populous areas of England' (*HW*, p. 397). Writers were aware of these issues at the time: J. O. Jones, editor of the *Merthyr Times*, writing in 1895, defends the Welsh press from those who compare it unfavourably with its London equivalent. He points out that a London daily has a potential readership of 5 million within a relatively small geographic area, which gives it 'immense circulation and a practically inexhaustible source of advertisements . . . secured at the minimum of expense'.[23] In Cardiff, by contrast, 'the population is only 150,000, and the advertisements must be collected, at considerable outlay, from sources farther afield' (*NAW*, p. 280). Welsh wealth, he points out, derived from heavy, extraction-based industries that did not need to advertise, a factor that further limited potential revenue (ibid.). He also comments on the railway system that connects Wales to English urban areas, leaving connections between north and south Wales 'so inadequate that a Northern paper has no chance of working up a circulation in South Wales, and vice versa' (*NAW*, p. 281). Road and rail networks connected, as they still do, the south of Wales to London; mid-Wales to the English west Midlands, and the north of Wales to the Liverpool/Manchester area. The A470, the 270-km road linking the north and south of Wales, was designated only in 1972, before which all major roads ran from east to west, while there is no efficient north-south rail connection. These factors indicate the difficulties in establishing a Welsh daily newspaper with national coverage – historically, they have been based in either the south or the north; they also begin to explain why, in the twentieth century, London-based newspapers were able to make significant inroads into the English-speaking market in the south of Wales.

While these problems were faced by Wales-based journals, both Welsh-language and English-language alike, the difficulties in establishing Welsh-language periodicals and papers were more significant, mainly due to the demographic changes caused by industrialisation. Welsh-language publications served a population which, at the beginning of the twentieth century, constituted almost one million people. However, the distribution of this population meant that any Welsh-language publication needed to reach a far-flung readership (without an adequate transport system to do so) and, unlike its English-language equivalent, could not count on a readership from any single significant urban centre. For example, although more than 80 per cent of people in Caernarfon (in the north-west) spoke Welsh, there were numerically more Welsh speakers in Cardiff (in the south-east), even though the city was predominantly English-speaking. Given this social geography, it was (and is) historically difficult to fund a periodical through advertising. The recent success of Welsh-language journals, incidentally, would be difficult to imagine without the system of state subsidy that emerged after the Second World War, and which has been consolidated since devolution, a system that diminishes reliance on the 'free' marketplace. Significant as well have been the new forms of on-line publication that diminish the need for physical distribution networks. Even so, finding employment in the field within Wales is notoriously difficult: writing as late as 1968 of the Welsh-language literary scene, Glyn Jones questioned whether 'there is at the moment in Wales a single full-time professional Welsh-language literary man'.[24]

In London, the existence of a developed literary infrastructure spawned new developments that were not possible in Wales at the turn of the century. On a daily basis, London-based publishers competed against each other in the London press by advertising their lists of books. For example, page 3 of the *Daily Chronicle* from 3 December 1909, a typical literary page in a broadsheet daily, contains advertisements for 'Methuen's Popular Novels', 'Messrs Methuen's New Books', 'Mr Heinemann's New Books', 'Popular Six Shilling novels' (published by Stanley Paul), 'A. & C. Black's New Books' and 'Macmillan's Books for Presents'. In Wales, there were no literary publishers of comparable size or prestige. Those who were large enough to do so advertised their lists in the Wales-based press. Gee of Denbigh, for example, placed twice-weekly lists in *Baner*, a paper that he, of course, owned, but the scale and spread of its readership was not on a par with its London-based competitors. Moreover, as Philip Henry Jones records, by the beginning of the twentieth century, even the largest Welsh publishers had concluded that 'they were too small to risk launching new products' (*TWP*, p. 183).

Another material difference between the London and the Welsh literary scenes lies in their use of literary reviewers. Each London paper and journal employed several professional literary reviewers. Journalists and production staff were all paid a regular salary or wage. Established free-lancers (like Thomas) earned between £250 and £400 a year. In contrast,

Aled Jones makes the point that, even at the beginning of the twentieth century, most of the production and reportage that went into Welsh papers and periodicals remained unpaid (*PPS*, p. 33). J. O. Jones argued in 1895 that 'there is not a single Welsh paper that gives anything like adequate reviews of books' (*NAW*, p. 282). Most papers publish 'scores of reviews of books which they have never seen' while 'publishers deem it almost useless to send out review copies' (*NAW*, p. 283). In Wales, the top-selling daily, the Cardiff-based *Western Mail*, which went from circulation figures of 12,000 in 1883 to 100,000 by 1890, launched a monthly literature supplement in February 1896 and, in the same decade, an eight-page 'Ladies' Own Supplement', which contained a fiction section. Nonetheless, compared to the London scene, with its numerous specialised literary journals, its literary review pages in the dailies, and its relation to a well-established publishing industry, the connections between the press and publishing industries were undeveloped. The level of professionalisation that marked the field in London had not yet occurred in Wales. Making a living from literary journalism was therefore impossible in Wales, compared to the opportunities available in London at the time.

Given this situation, many journalists and writers, even those most associated with the Welsh nationalist cause, crossed the borders of language and nation. Thomas John Hughes, for example, was editor of the nationalist organ, *Cymru Fydd*, and sub-editor for the Cardiff-based Liberal paper, the *South Wales Daily News* (the *Western Mail*'s main rival), as well as Welsh correspondent for the London-based *Daily News*, and the *Manchester Guardian* (*PPS*, p. 41). O. M. Edwards too crossed the language divide as editor of *Cymru* and *Wales*, and the national divide, publishing travel narratives with Wales-based presses, and acting as commissioning editor for the *Welsh Library Series*, published in London by J. M. Dent.

Welsh literature, therefore, was precariously positioned in the economic field. Its historical status inhibited the development of a publishing industry, as well as the development of institutions that would support its own literature. The language divide and urban-rural population spread caused by British industrial policy further complicated the issue of a national literature. Moreover, the transport system made quick and efficient national distribution extremely difficult, and eventually opened different Welsh regions to domination by journalistic and literary institutions based in England, all of which were structurally more advantaged than their Welsh neighbours in terms of the proximity of large readerships, effective distribution networks, the single-language market, and the availability of advertisers. While the institutions of an Anglocentric British literary space were clearly established, those of a comparable Welsh space were either non-existent or in their infancy. Moreover, they faced considerable disadvantages as a result of the industrial, linguistic and demographic changes wrought by colonialism, and the 'free' market in which they were made to operate.

Welsh writers of the time must be seen in this context of the huge imbalance in the relative status of the British and Welsh literary fields. In particular, the historical constrictions placed on the development of Welsh literary space mean that there should be a place in modern Welsh literary history for those who pursued their writing career in London, while any decision to cross back over the national border and contribute to a Welsh literary journal or paper might be seen as a significant statement of national allegiance. The critic should remain sensitive to these economic conditions, and make it possible for a writer, past or present, who pursues a career outside of Welsh geographical space to be recovered for the literary history of the nation. Before considering if, and how Thomas, can be related to a Welsh literary space thus positioned in the economic field, attention needs next to be paid to the position of Welsh literature in the political field.

In what follows, I argue that Welsh political life at the turn of the century should be seen in the context of wider British politics, in particular in the attempts to link the campaign for Irish land reform and Home Rule with similar campaigns in Wales, and the fears of the British authorities in Wales that what was happening in Ireland would spread to Wales. It was in this context that a debate over the position of Welsh literature took place between key figures in Welsh culture. Establishment figures like John Morris-Jones distanced the national literature from modernity and from what was happening in the Welsh-language press, and called for a return to the use of medieval Welsh forms and morally suitable subject matter, while others, such as David Adams (hereafter referred to by his bardic name, Hawen), Gwili and Thomas Marchant Williams, argued that literature should engage with the issues of the day, and challenge the strictness of inherited forms. Our case study, Thomas, can be positioned in relation to these debates.

The 1880s was a decade in which many of the institutions of Welsh civic society became established: the National Eisteddfod 'took familiar shape in 1880'; the *Cymmrodorion* 'emerged as a national cultural society from 1872 . . .; the network of county schools thickened [and] University Colleges at Cardiff and Bangor were opened in the early 1880s' (*WWWH*,

p. 231). Kenneth O. Morgan suggests that, from this decade onwards, the nationalist movement in Ireland was 'an inspiring example' to many Welsh people.[25] John Davies concurs, arguing that from 1868 until the First World War, 'the example of Ireland was to be important to Wales' (*HW*, p. 421). The possibility of the kind of nationalist movement seen in Ireland spreading to Wales became real in February 1886, when Michael Davitt, Irish nationalist leader and founder of the Irish Land League, spoke at Blaenau Ffestiniog, north Wales, sharing a Land League platform with Welsh Home Rule Liberal MPs Tom Ellis and David Lloyd George. According to John Davies, Davitt 'received a warm welcome' there and at Tonypandy, south Wales, where he also spoke (*HW*, p. 441). The meeting occurred at a time when land ownership and reform was one of the most contentious issues in Welsh politics, and when the success of Davitt's campaign in Ireland led to calls for similar legislation in Wales (*HW*, p. 433).

The Welsh Land League was founded by Thomas Gee, republican Denbigh printer, publisher of *Y Traethodydd* (The Essayist) and proprietor of the pioneering Welsh-language paper *Baner ac Amserau Cymru* (The Banner and Times of Wales). *Baner ac Amserau Cymru*, or *Y Faner* as it was known, unlike other Welsh newspapers, did not print a syndicated London letter, translated from the English dailies, but employed its own Welsh-speaking correspondent in London, enabling it to present London news from a Welsh perspective, and to build bridges to the expatriate Welsh-language community in London. It is described by John Davies as 'the principal scourge of the landlords in Wales' (*HW*, p. 399). In 1887, Gee's Land League merged with the Anti-Tithe Leagues, which had emerged in many rural counties to form a front in what Aled Jones describes as 'a popular revolt against landlordism and an alien church' (*PPS*, p. 168). The new organisation garnered support for Welsh Home Rule and organised protests across rural Wales in which there were violent clashes between police and rural inhabitants. In June 1887, for example, eighty-four people, including thirty-five policemen, were injured in one such battle at Mochdre (*HW*, p. 440). According to Gwyn A. Williams, 'soldiers had to escort English auctioneers of distrained property into Welsh villages' (*WWWH*, p. 228). Aled Jones argues that 'it was out of these struggles that Young Wales and the *Cymru Fydd* (Young Wales) movement emerged' in the late 1880s (*PPS*, p. 169). This nationalist movement, according to K. O. Morgan, was similar to those on the continent, and initially depended on émigré communities in London and Liverpool for its support, before becoming widespread in Wales during the 1890s (*WBP*, p. 105). M. Wynn Thomas describes Cymru Fydd's English-language journal, *Young Wales*, which was launched in 1895, as 'the official organ of a very powerful movement taking its inspiration from such key nineteenth century nation-building programs as had been promoted by Young Italy and Young Ireland'.[26]

Thomas's judgement is borne out by an analysis of *Young Wales*, the first editorial of which, written by J. Hugh Edwards in 1895, declares that 'the Welsh people are fully entitled to the status and dignity of a true nation'.[27] Edwards draws attention to 'this new spirit of Nationalism which is now taking to itself a definite form by the name of the Cymru Fydd league', and goes on to outline the movement's aims: 'to re-organise our political forces and to federate existing agencies' and to 'establish a union between the literary and the political forces of our country' in order to obtain 'a national system of self-government for Wales'. He draws an explicit connection to Young Italy and Young Ireland, and suggests that 'in like manner Young Wales finds its raison d'être in the advent of that wave of national sentiment to this – our native land'.[28] Subsequent issues maintain the connection to nationalist movements in Ireland and Italy. The June 1895 issue contains a letter to the journal editor by Welsh Nationalist and Liberal MP Tom Ellis, good friend of O. M. Edwards, in which he argues for 'administrative autonomy . . . along the line desired by Ireland', a goal that he believes 'we are rapidly approaching'.[29] Another issue contains the anonymously penned, 'Thoughts from Mazzini', a series of quotations from the Italian to inspire Welsh nationalism.[30]

In the September 1895 issue of *Young Wales*, W. Llewelyn Williams wrote a sarcastic piece about John Bull, which links the issue of land reform to English colonialism throughout the British Isles: 'it is his benevolent mission in the world to turn the poor bodies who may have been born Welshmen, or Irishmen, or Scotchmen, into fair imitations of Englishmen'.[31] He continues: 'In spite of his repeated failures and the general muddle he is in, John Bull still believes that it is his mission to Anglicise the whole earth' (*OFF*, p. 197). Wales 'would have none of his Church, she said, and she would put up no longer with the intolerable rule of his landlord garrison' (*OFF*, p. 196).

As this article implies, since the late 1880s there had been a hardening of political positions on the issue of land reform. On the one side, in December 1886, a group of north Wales landowners formed the North Wales Property Defence Association under the chairmanship of Lord Penrhyn, while a similar organisation was formed in the south, the Land-owners' Association of South Wales and Monmouthshire. On the other side, Lloyd George set up *Udgorn Rhyddid* (The Clarion of Liberty) in Pwllheli in 1886 in order to campaign for land reform. In 1892, Lloyd

George and W. J. Parry established the Welsh National Newspaper Company in Caernarfon, which published *Y Genedl Gymreig* (The Welsh Nation), *The North Wales Observer* and *Y Werin* (The People) in order to try to broaden the land campaign and lobby the Liberal party to support its cause.

A confidential policy document by the North Wales Property Defence Association, 'Remarks on the Welsh Press', published in 1888 (and reproduced in Aled Jones's *Press, Politics and Society*), blames the Welsh-language press for spreading radical ideas about land ownership:

> It is most important at the present time that serious attention should be called to the dangerous and insidious teachings of the Welsh press, that is, the papers published in the Welsh language. The majority of these papers are, and have been, for a long time poisoning the minds of the ignorant Welsh people with the most Revolutionary, Socialistic, and Communistic doctrines it is possible to imagine, often written not only in most violent, but even in profane language; often as revolutionary and disloyal as anything in the Irish press, and rather more communistic, exciting the people against all those who possess any kind of property, and inflaming the worst passions by all sorts of exaggerated misstatements, such as that 300 years ago all the land belonged to the people, and that they have been robbed of it by landowners. (Cited in *PPS*, p. 171)

At another point the policy document refers specifically to the issue of land agitation:

> The result of all this is, that a class hatred and war against property is being stirred up, which, if not properly coped with and counteracted, will, at a much earlier date than is now apparent, land us in Wales in a similar state of things to what has, unfortunately existed in Ireland for some time. (Cited in *PPS*, p. 172)

The document expresses the fear that 'the Welsh press are also advocating and getting up a cry for a species of Home Rule for Wales, and the entire exclusion of Englishmen from all official appointments'. It again raises the spectre that the Irish situation would spread to Wales as a result of the press reviving 'the long buried cry of "Wales for the Welsh", and in other ways to follow the example of the Irish Nationalists' (ibid.). The document reveals the extent to which the situation in Ireland was a determining factor in the British establishment's discussion of how to govern Wales. John Davies reports that the Conservative leadership at the time believed that 'the unrest prevalent in the Irish countryside was spreading to Wales' (*HW*, p. 440).

The movement to 'cope with and counteract' the Welsh Radical press was orchestrated by James Vincent, grandson of the Dean of Bangor, educated at Winchester and Oxford, secretary of the Landowners Association of South Wales and Monmouthshire, and advisor to Lord Penrhyn. In an article in *The Times* on 27 September 1887, he draws attention to the issue. Readers, he suggests, are 'alarmed at the language used' both in 'Indian native journals' and Irish papers, and 'justly' shocked by 'the violence and the frank brutality' of the latter (cited in *PPS*, p. 173). Worse, 'they have remained hitherto in blissful ignorance of the fact that within 200 miles of London are published newspapers at least as bold and virulent as those of Calcutta or of Dublin' (ibid.). Significantly, by making the connection between the Welsh press and that of Ireland and India he provides evidence to support the case, relevant today, for Wales being perceived as a colonised nation.

Jones traces how, following the *Times* article, the issue of the Welsh Radical press seeped into the consciousness of the British establishment. It was discussed at the Conservative Party conference in Caernarfon in 1888. In 1889, the Church appointed John Owen as Dean of St Asaph's in order to keep an eye on the Welsh-language press. Other writers investigated the matter in the British press, and the land issue became important enough to warrant the establishment in 1893 of a Royal Commission on Land in Wales, a classic establishment tactic for kicking the issue into the long grass. As Dai Smith reports, the Commission held 1,086 interviews over three years, of which only twenty-one were actually with agricultural labourers.[32] Aled Jones shows how Vincent fed questions and gave advice to members of the North Wales Property Defence Association who were being interviewed at this Commission. According to Jones, the aim of Lord Kenyon and Vincent at the Commission was 'to get Gee in particular to admit to having libelled in his papers various landowners and agents' (*PPS*, p. 175). In this they failed, although the threat of libel did curtail the freedom of the Welsh press, as the following June 1891 letter from the editor of the Liberal paper *Y Celt* (The Celt) to one of his correspondents shows:

> If we publish your letter we will place you and ourselves in the dangers of libel law. The Tories in this district have men appointed to look over the Welsh newspapers in search of a chance to bring them before a court of law. This is one of the weapons they use these days to prevent freedom of opinion. (Cited in *PPS*, p. 176)

The pivotal role played by the Welsh-language press in the issue of land reform, a key plank of the nationalists' agenda, is suggested by the way that different branches in London's Cymru Fydd, including those in Finsbury, Hackney and Paddington, were named after prominent Welsh journalists.

In the September 1895 issue of *Young Wales*, W. Llewelyn Williams shows the extent to which the issue of land reform had permeated the English-language Welsh press. He alludes to the attempts by the land-owners to portray the land question as an issue exacerbated by political agitators: 'Young Wales, they said, had been led astray by wicked agitators and political dissenters, like Thomas Gee'. He concludes, however, that 'Young Wales was only crying out in English what Old Wales had cried out in Welsh; that the land question was the natural consequence of John [Bull]'s folly in the sixteenth century when, in the majesty of his might, he substituted his own senseless system of land tenure for the equitable system which prevailed among the Welsh people' (*OFF*, 196). The October 1895 issue features an article, 'National Self-Government for Wales', by Lloyd George, in which he calls for 'Home Rule all round' as the last possible chance of providing a solution that would be acceptable to the growing nationalist movement in Wales.[33] By this stage, a significant and powerful impetus for the Welsh cause had built up. The North Wales Liberal Federation amalgamated with the Cymru Fydd league behind a nationalist agenda, under the leadership of Lloyd George.

A crucial meeting, called in January 1896 in Newport, south Wales, aimed to bring the south Wales Liberals into the new alliance. At a meeting that Lloyd George afterwards claimed had been deliberately packed with unionists, representatives of the Cardiff and Newport Liberals told Lloyd George that south Wales 'will never submit to the domination of Welsh ideas', thus ending the hope that Wales could be politically united behind a nationalist agenda to be secured through the parliamentary Liberal party (*HW*, p. 453). K. O. Morgan argues that from this occasion on, 'the prospect of national unity vanished' (*WBP*, p. 163). The critic Dafydd Johnston characterises this historical moment as the end of a 'naïve optimism', but Stephen Knight, writing in 2004, describes it as 'a costly failure, at a time when Ireland was shaping a strong anti-colonial position'.[34] While the Cardiff-based *Western Mail* celebrated the division, Lloyd George wrote a piece in *Y Faner* in which he asked whether 'the mass of the Welsh nation [was] willing to be dominated by a coalition of English capitalists who have come to Wales, not to benefit the people, but to make their fortune?'.[35] If this was Wales's 'Parnell moment', then the difference between what happened in Wales and Ireland could not be more stark. Unlike in Ireland, where the nationalists turned their attention to non-parliamentary means of achieving their goals, in Wales the movement went underground to emerge several decades later as Plaid Cymru, a more focused parliamentary movement (on the whole), while Liberal leaders like Lloyd George settled for the more limited party programme of minor land reform and the disestablishment of the Anglican church in Wales, instead of Home Rule. Nonetheless, our knowledge of what happened subsequently should not lead us to forget the powerful movement for Welsh Home Rule that almost came to fruition.

The character of Welsh politics at this time had consequences for Welsh literature. Welsh writers did not contribute to the nationalist political movement in the way that their Irish counterparts did. Johnston describes how the Welsh literary revival was dominated by Emrys ap Iwan ('Robert Ambrose Jones') whose prose, reacting against the number of English idioms that had crept into the Welsh language over the nineteenth century, aimed to achieve a purer Welsh language (*LR*, p. 4). Other key figures included John Morris-Jones, first Professor of Welsh at the University of North Wales in Bangor (from 1894), and Sir John Rhŷs, Professor of Celtic at Oxford (from 1877), Morris-Jones's tutor, and later Principal of Jesus College. Both were former members, along with W. Llewelyn Williams and O. M. Edwards, among others, of Cymdeithas Dafydd ap Gwilym (The Oxford University Welsh Society). Like Emrys ap Iwan, Morris-Jones aimed 'to rid the language of the corruption which had taken root since the eighteenth century' (*LR*, p. 7). Morris-Jones did so through various means: he spent meetings of 'the Dafydd' in the late 1880s standardising the orthography of the language, and he disseminated his findings through articles in *Cymru* (Wales) and *Y Beirniad* (The Critic), a quarterly journal that he edited from 1911 to 1920.[36] He also published *Welsh Orthography* (1893) and *A Welsh Grammar* (1913), 'his definitive account of the trad-itional literary language' (*LR*, p. 7), as well as using his position as judge in the Chair competition at the Eisteddfod to insist that poets 'follow the example set by the medieval bards, both in metrical practices and in use of language' (*LR*, p. 7).

The achievement of this group of scholars was seminal. They were part of a powerful, anti-colonial cultural initiative that, by connecting modern Wales with a largely unexplored 'golden age' of medieval poetry, laid the grounds for a new, creatively enabling pride in Welsh-language literary achievement. In doing so, they constructed a 'continuous' vision of Welsh cultural development which, however questionable, helped to invent a strong, anti-colonial literary tradition. They contributed directly to the explosion of talent that constituted the early twentieth-century Welsh-language literary renaissance. The influence of Morris-Jones on this literary revival is evident in T. Gwynn Jones's 1902 *awdl*, 'Ymadawiad Arthur' ('The Passing of Arthur'), a poem that put Morris-Jones's medievalism into practice, and which, by winning the Eisteddfod Chair that year, ensured that Morris-Jones put his 'stamp' on the competition.[37] His influence is also evident in the achievement of later writers, including Kate Roberts (taught by Morris-Jones at Bangor), whose 'increased resources of vocabulary and idiom' stem from her exposure to the medieval classics that he promoted (*JMJ*, p. 80). Towards the end of his career, he made what Allan James describes as his 'most celebrated' contribution to Welsh letters by publishing *Cerdd Dafod* (1925); this was a detailed classification of Welsh prosody, one that has continued to inform the 'flowerings' of Welsh poetry through the twentieth century, and a critical text that proved beyond doubt that, in the words of T. Gwynn Jones, the Welsh language could be 'used for the purpose of [literary-critical] scholarship' (*JMJ*, p. 36). However, while Morris-Jones did much for Welsh letters, his influential position also highlights the ambivalent role played by the literary revival. It certainly drew attention to Welsh-language literature, yet also functioned as a reactionary force by insisting on standards of 'purity' that originated in medieval times. The Welsh language could exist by itself, independent of English, but only, it was argued, by returning to the language of the pre-modern past. Indeed, the codification of Welsh metrics achieved by Morris-Jones argued for a return to pre-eighteenth century rules and subject matter, which effectively consigned literary Welsh to a pre-Enlightenment state, rendering it less effective as a means of achieving nationalist aims, or accepting modernity.

As holder of the first Chair of Celtic Studies at Oxford, a position established in 1877 and described as a 'turning point in the development of Welsh scholarship', Sir John Rhŷs was also responsible for many of the seminal developments in Welsh letters described above.[38] However, as with Morris-Jones, there is an ambiguity in his achievement. Rhŷs reviewed the Welsh press, declaring that 'the shoddy Welsh which prevails in many of the newspapers published in Welsh' was actively undermining 'the supremacy of literary Welsh' (*PPS*, p. 196). Given the political context in which the Welsh-language press operated at this time, this intervention suggests Rhŷs's affinity with the British authorities and the aristocratic landowners against the vernacular Welsh used by the radical press. Indeed, these figures in the Welsh literary revival, with their insistence on the purity of a 'literary Welsh' and explicitly opposed to the language used in newspapers, not only blunt any national-political purpose that the literary revival might have had, but, in their opposition of the 'literary' and the 'vernacular', echoing the establishment's condemnation of the 'virulent' vernacular press, also serve to position the weight of the literary revival firmly behind a conservative, unionist political agenda.

The Welsh literary revival, however, was not the united movement that Johnston implies. O. M. Edwards, another Oxford-based scholar, was, according to Hazel Davies, 'arguably the greatest Welsh-language cultural figure at the turn of the century' (*TUL*, p. 335). His travel narrative, *Tro yn Llydaw* (A Journey in Brittany), published in 1889, described by Davies as being 'as much about Wales as it is about Brittany', sets up a parallel between the French treatment of Bretons and the English treatment of the Welsh:

> As the English sought to Anglicize Wales and as Welsh children were deprived of their language and history, so did France seek to wipe out the Breton language by insisting that French was the language of all the schools in Brittany and that French culture should replace the indigenous culture of the country. (*B*, p. 200)

Although Edwards's (and Morris-Jones's) later support for the World War I recruitment drives shows his support for unionism, here his work demonstrates parallels between oppressed Celtic nations in a way that begins to establish the colonised status of Wales, and begins to find affinities with other nations. Renowned as one of the literary apostles of the Welsh nationalist movement, Edwards had been joint editor of the nationalist magazine *Cymru Fydd* from 1889 to 1890, prior to the founding of his own journals. Edwards, moreover, is, at times, critical of the literary purists led by Morris-Jones and Rhŷs, 'the champions of the strict rules of *cynghanedd*', who are responsible for 'the bloated, clumsy and unnatural style of the present age' and the 'artificiality of Welsh prose and verse'.[39]

Other writers of the time supported Edwards's criticisms of the literary purists. In an article in *Y Geninen* (The Leek) in 1899, Gwili supported proposals put forward by Hawen to modernise the Eisteddfod tradition; Hawen argued that literature should engage with the issues of the day, and challenge the strictness of inherited forms. As we shall see, that support is significant to this case study, given Gwili's friendship with Thomas. Hawen argued for an end to the tradition by which poems submitted for the Eisteddfod competitions had to be written on a morally suitable subject matter, in one of a number of particular Welsh poetic forms. Correspondingly, he suggested an end to the puritan moral standpoint by which poems were judged, suggesting that poets be allowed to address any subject matter, and not be judged on strictly formal criteria (*VS*, p. 215). 'For Hawen', argues Hywel Teifi Edwards, 'there could be no modern poetry without bringing Welsh culture into energizing contact with modern thought, no matter how "dangerous" the consequences might be for a literature long rooted in orthodoxies' (*VS*, p. 216). He makes the point that Hawen, like Gwili, 'in opposition to Morris-Jones, was far less prescriptive in his approach to poetry', achieving support for his position particularly among other young poets (ibid.). Huw Walters concurs with this analysis of Gwili's position, drawing attention to Gwili's criticism of Morris-Jones for attempting to set laws that hinder the poet's muse.[40]

The launch of *Cymru* in 1891 was O. M. Edwards's attempt to begin 'a completely new kind of Welsh periodical' that drew contributions from the ordinary people of Wales (*B*, p. 201). Its motto was *'I godi 'r hen wlad yn ei hôl'* ('To raise the old country to her former glory') and, according to Hazel Davies, it succeeded in raising consciousness among Welsh people of Welsh history, hymns, folk songs, *penillion telyn* (stanzas for the harp) and nursery rhymes (*B*, p. 202). The launch of an English-language equivalent, *Wales*, in 1894, was an equally momentous event. In the introduction to its inaugural issue, Edwards proclaims 'a literature that will be English in language and Welsh in spirit', an announcement that represents what one critic describes as a significant, and early, definition of Anglophone Welsh literature.[41] It echoes Douglas Hyde's hopes, in an Irish context, for 'the de-Anglicising of our people', and Yeats's efforts to create 'a national tradition, a national literature, which shall be nonetheless Irish in spirit from being English in language'.[42]

Edwards is also involved in holding the recently established University of Wales to Welsh account. In 1895 in *Wales*, he charged its Senate, then only two years old, with doing 'everything in its power to prevent the study of Welsh history and Welsh literature in Wales', a charge he repeated in 1905 in *Cymru*.[43] It was only after the First World War that this situation changed: the University of Wales Press began in 1922, Welsh departments were founded in the immediate post-war years, and *Y Llenor* (The Writer), the semi-official journal of the University's Welsh departments, was launched in 1922. This had the effect, argues T. Robin Chapman, of professionalising Welsh literary criticism, and leading to a 'corresponding decline in the prestige of the Eisteddfod' and the power of culturally conservative critics like Morris-Jones.[44] One of the pioneering Welsh lecturers of the post-war era was Gwili, based at Cardiff, who, like Edwards prior to the war, had been involved in attempts to moderate the strictness of the 'literary' standards then being established by Morris-Jones.

Edwards's call for a literature 'English in language and Welsh in spirit' is taken up in the first decade of the twentieth century by the journal *Nationalist*, in which there is evidence of the same debate between a Morris-Jones camp, and the reformers, over where to place Welsh literature in relation to the politics of the time. The journal, relatively neglected by recent critics of the period, lasted from 1907 to 1912 and was edited by Thomas Marchant Williams, nicknamed 'the acid drop' for the caustic and satiric nature of his views on Welsh political and religious leaders.[45] His journal included literary work by key Anglophone Welsh writers of the day, including H. Idris Bell, Ernest Rhys, J. O. Francis and, as we shall see, Edward Thomas. Recent work by Allan James has rightly pointed to the vitriolic and personal nature of Marchant Williams's attacks on Morris-Jones, in which he accused the Bangor professor of maintaining a malign influence through his work as poet, teacher and grammarian, and of undermining the legitimacy of the Eisteddfod judges.[46] Indeed, it might be argued that the perseverance of these attacks undermined the declared aim of the journal's editor, set out in its inaugural issue in March 1907, to foster 'among the Welsh people of all sects and of all parties a true national spirit' and to promote 'the advancement of every cause and every movement that tend to make the sons and daughters of Wales proud of the Land of their Fathers'.[47] Nonetheless, the opening issues also established a clear position in relation to the debate between Morris-Jones and the vernacular Welsh press. 'Our Point of View', also written by Marchant Williams, summarises, in translation, an article from the reformist Welsh literary quarterly, *Y Geninen* (The Leek), applauding its description of Morris-Jones's 'fatal shortcomings as an authority on style and poetry', a line of attack which is pursued again in the tenth issue of the journal, published in December 1907.[48] Here, the 'Reviews' section contains an anonymous four-and-a-half page demolition of Morris-Jones's *Caniadau* (Songs):

> The Professor's sense of style is very defective. Not one of these thirty lyrics can justly be said to be, in point of style or poetic thought, in the least degree superior to the conventional verse of the local newspaper . . . In all

sincerity, we urge him to give up the manufacture of vituperative verse, and devote himself steadily to grubbing in grammar.[49]

The pointed comparison of Morris-Jones's own poetry to the language of the local newspaper tackles head-on the attempts by Rhŷs and Morris-Jones to position the Welsh literary field in opposition to the vernacular language used by journalists. The journal is unrelenting in its pursuit of Morris-Jones: in May 1908, the anonymous author of 'Reviews: *Y Traethodydd*' strongly disagrees with a reviewer who had written positively of Morris-Jones's work.[50] In 'Our Point of View' in the April 1908 issue, the editor launched an attack on James Vincent, a British establishment figure active in Welsh politics and journalism, and the main player, as we have seen, behind the landowners' two-decades-long attempt to prevent Irish agitation spreading to Wales:

> We part company, for the present, with the priggish Mr Vincent, and in doing so, we again fall back upon some of his own choice words and phrases: 'The views expressed by him show a fundamental misapprehension of the Welsh character; they are narrow, virulent, wanting in sense of humour, and astounding in vanity to a degree calculated to stir the derision of the Welsh, and the indignation of the sober-minded Englishmen'.[51]

These attacks on those who thwarted either a more nationalist Welsh politics or a reformed Welsh literature are matched by efforts to support those who campaign for change in both the political and literary fields. The June 1907 issue contains an anonymously written favourable review, 'Reviews: *Y Geninen*', of two articles by the Eisteddfod reformers Hawen and Gwili, which had appeared in a recent issue of the Welsh-language literary journal, *Y Geninen*.[52] In addition to keeping its readers abreast of what was happening in the Welsh-language literary press, the journal launched numerous literary translation competitions from one language into the other, celebrated 'national' Welsh events, and carried feature articles on prominent Welsh national figures from both the literary and political spheres. The brief life of *Nationalist*, and the attacks by Marchant Williams on Morris-Jones, are important because they show that the standardising of the language initiated by the Bangor professor, the classification of Welsh prosody, and the strict interpretation of medieval forms in the modern period, all of which have since had a significant impact on Welsh literature and its position within society, were contested at the time by some key figures of a nationalist persuasion. The episode serves as a reminder that narratives of Welsh literary history have always been challenged. In this revisionist interpretation of events at the turn of the twentieth century, Edward Thomas has a role.

Thomas has surprising and critically unexplored connections to many of the key figures, institutions and issues in Welsh literary space discussed above. Readers familiar with the Anglocentric readings of Thomas might be surprised to see any connection with Michael Davitt. Thomas's auto-biography, *The Childhood of Edward Thomas*, written in 1913 and pub-lished only in 1938, nonetheless contains accounts of his Sunday evening visits to the Washington Music Hall in Battersea, south-west London, to hear radical speakers including John Burns, the dockers' leader, and Keir Hardie of the Independent Labour Party.[53] He recalls one visit when he saw Davitt 'standing by an iron pillar, dark, straight, and austere with his armless sleeve dangling'. Davitt, like Burns, is described as 'glorious, great, and good'. 'I think I knew', writes Thomas, 'that he had then just come out of prison, and this probably helped him to a place in my mind with the Pathfinder and Milton's Satan' (*CET*, p. 105).

The association between Davitt, the Pathfinder, a character from James Fenimore Cooper's 1840 novel of the same name, and Milton's Satan is not explained, but all three are the protagonists, the ones who drive on the plot, in their respective spheres or works. All three are moral characters, driven by a sense of justice and a dislike of monarchical and imperialist power. The pathfinder, Natty Bampoo, is, according to observations made by Cooper, an 'example of what a just-minded and pure man might be'.[54] He is, Cooper claims, 'untempted by unruly or ambitious desires', char-acteristics that Kay Seymour House attributes in the novel to the imperialist British and French.[55] Milton's Satan, as opposed to the biblical Satan, is a figure who feels guilt knowing that his actions in tricking Eve will have consequences for innocent people. Like Cooper's pathfinder, and of course Davitt, he is an advocate of republican principles, arguing that he and the angels are 'self-begot, self-raised', and not dependent on the authority of God or monarchy. In an Irish context, 'Sinn Féin', meaning 'by ourselves', echoes this idea.

Of this formative time, Thomas writes, 'Poetry was nothing to me compared with Home Rule. Or rather Home Rule took the place of Poetry, and was really an equivalent in so far as it lifted me to vaguely magnificent ideas of good and evil' (*CET*, p. 105). This, from Thomas's autobiography, was written in 1913, after twelve years of poetry reviewing, and one year before Thomas started producing his own poetry. In that year, the issue had come to the fore yet again ('Home Rule All Round' had first been

suggested in 1886), with the British parliament voting on the matter, and
the two sides in Ulster arming themselves for civil war. The connection,
nonetheless, is vaguely phrased, as if Thomas is pointing readers who
wish to understand his interest in poetry towards Home Rule, but leaving
the details unexplained, or as if he senses a subconscious connection but
cannot fully account for it. In a scene towards the end of *The Happy-Go-
Lucky Morgans*, published in 1913, one of the characters calls for 'Home
Rule for Ireland', a call that turns into one for 'Home Rule all round',
and then ends with everyone singing the Welsh national anthem.[56] This
scene will be discussed at greater length in Chapter Six. 'Home Rule for
Ireland' was a burning political issue throughout Thomas's 1880s childhood and, in 1895, Lloyd George won a House of Commons vote in
favour of the principle of 'Home Rule All Round'. The issue resurfaced
in the pre-war years when Thomas was writing his autobiography and
his novel. From 1910 to 1914, the Welsh MP E. T. John campaigned to
secure Home Rule for Wales, introducing a bill to this effect in March
1914 – a bill which, like its equivalent for Ireland, was lost with the
beginning of World War I. The mention of Welsh Home Rule in two books
written in 1913 is an intervention in the contemporary debate, as well as
a recollection of formative events in the 1880s and 90s.

   Thomas's own republicanism is suggested by a scene in *Beautiful
Wales*. The narrator, a barely disguised Thomas, visits 'a new public-house,
the worst of the buildings in the place, because the most impudent ... It
glittered and stank and was called "The Prince of Wales"'.[57] Inside, there
is a 'harper, who was doing his best with "God bless the Prince of Wales"'.
A visitor, in 'a voice which might have cut glass', mistakes this song for
the Welsh national anthem, 'whereupon, with sublime, gentle anger the
harper played and sang the National Anthem of Wales' (*BW*, p. 158). The
narrator continues, 'Slowly we emptied the house of all its Englishmen
by encouraging him to play the airs which the harp had known through
all its life' (*BW*, p. 159). He reports how at first 'the harper hesitated
between the English tunes that were most in favour at "The Prince of
Wales" and those songs for which the harp was made'. Eventually, 'we
praised the Welsh airs and though he seemed to ignore us, he played
nothing else' (*BW*, p. 161). The scene is a riposte to what John Davies
describes as the vilification of the Welsh nation in some English circles,
following the political rise of Lloyd George through the 1890s and early
1900s (*HW*, p. 469). The extract implies that these tensions are sometimes
expressed through folksong, and Davies indeed reports that, six years
later, some members of the aristocracy hissed at a band playing the Welsh

song 'Men of Harlech' at the 1911 Caernarfon investiture of the new Prince of Wales (*HW*, p. 469).

Another way in which Thomas fits into this economic and political context is through his connection to O. M. Edwards, his history tutor at Oxford from 1897 to 1900. Edwards had planned for Thomas to get a post teaching at an unidentified higher education institution in north Wales (presumably the University of North Wales in Bangor) once he graduated, but following his failure to achieve a first class degree, Edwards informed him that he had no position to offer him (*ETAP*, p. 91). Nonetheless, further correspondence between the two suggests the importance of Wales to Thomas's subsequent choice of career. A letter from Thomas to Edwards dated 31 July 1900 asks Edwards about the possibility of 'a schoolmaster-ship in Wales' (*TUL*, p. 340). Another written almost a month later declares that Wales 'seems to contain something essential to me, in spite of my accidentally cockney nativity' and asks for Edwards's help in securing 'an interview or anything else you might have to suggest' (*TUL*, p. 341). A letter dated 24 November 1900, written after Thomas had secured 'a little work' at London-based papers 'the *Chronicle*, *Literature* and the *World*', informed Edwards that he had applied for a teaching job at an Intermediate School in Cardiff. Judging from a letter dated 12 February 1901 in which Thomas writes that he 'had almost given up hope, even of a schoolmastership', it seems his application was unsuccessful. In this letter, Thomas asks his former tutor for 'any introduction which might bring reviewing' (*TUL*, p. 342). The following year, Thomas accepted Edwards's offer of the chance 'to prepare a volume of John Dyer [the English-language Welsh poet], on the terms you mention' (*TUL*, p. 344). This was one of the *Welsh Library Series*, published in London by J. M. Dent, and edited by Edwards. In this series of letters to Edwards, Thomas also reveals that he has been reading Daniel Owen's novel *Rhys Lewis* in Welsh, as well as *The Mabinogion* (ibid.).

The connections to Edwards do not stop there. A letter dated 25 December 1901 is lavish in its praise of O. M. Edwards's *Wales*: 'That such a critic and historian as myself should admire the book would not concern you, but I am sure that because I am Welsh you would be glad to know how much I love the book' (*TUL*, p. 343). This straightforward self-identification as a Welshman is missing from any critical work on Thomas on either side of the border. The letter goes on to express Thomas's 'regret' that, in moving to Kent, he had 'moved farther away from Wales'. It also reveals Thomas's hopes for his journalism: 'it compelled me to wish that my small activities were usefully connected to Wales'. To this end, Thomas asks Edwards 'to suggest any kind of work which I could do far away from libraries, to help you and the Welsh cause'. He asks whether Edwards can suggest a Welsh Grammar in order to 'learn Welsh', and whether 'even before I am thoroughly acquainted with Welsh, I could be of any service'. Finally, he asks Edwards's permission to dedicate to him his forthcoming book of essays, *Horae Solitariae*, which he describes as 'bound to Wales, because my visits to Wales have been in an obscure fashion their inspiration' (*TUL*, p. 343).

Thomas's private correspondence anticipates his laudatory review of Edwards's *Wales* in the *Academy* on 8 February 1902. In his review, Thomas describes how 'his country is known to its own people as Cymru, the land of brothers, and to the world as Wales, the land of strangers', a reference to the way the naming of the nation by outsiders has stuck ('Wales' derives from '*wealh*', an Anglo-Saxon word meaning 'foreigner').[58] He notes that 'the strange element in Welsh history from foreign incursion and inward disunion is so large', and praises Edwards's efforts as 'a subtle history of the patriotism that arose from these unpromising roots'. He divides that history into two phases: 'the period of the princes, during which the whole of Wales was never once united, in spite of the centripetal force which lay in the ideals of many distinguished princes, and in the ceaseless English attacks', and a second, more recent, phase:

> the period of the peasants, when, after the loss of many of its laws and all its superficial independence, the country developed the unique sense of nationality which is mirrored in its glorious literature, even today substantially untranslated, and perhaps untranslatable. (*R*, vol. 3, p. 6)

'Inward disunion' and 'foreign incursion' as 'roots' of an unlikely patriotism invite comparison with the experience of Ireland, implying indeed that Thomas endorsed Edwards's presentation of Wales as a colonised nation. The notion of a second phase of history, a 'period of the peasants', in which a sense of Welsh nationality was developed through its indigenous literature, also suggests affinities with Ireland, and Casanova's analysis of Yeats's evocation of an idealised peasantry as a repository of national spirit. The review ends by mentioning the patriotism that exists 'in younger poets, like Gwili, and in older poets, like Watcyn Wyn', the two contemporary Welsh-language poets with whom Thomas was closely acquainted, and proclaims that 'the Welshman cannot but look back on that early age to which the historian has naturally given so much of his space, and ask, "if Arthur will come again?"'. The piece concludes with the rousing declaration that '[the Welshman's] future is full of his past and that was full of ideals' (*R*, vol. 3, p. 6). This is an attempt to present Arthur in familiar ways as a patriotic figure who will come again to rescue the Welsh nation from its enslavement. It contrasts with Thomas's critique, elsewhere, of British alternatives, and his endorsement of the way Irish writers figuratively express their own sense of patriotism: Irish poets, he suggests, 'sing of Ireland herself with an intimate reality often missing from English patriotic poetry, where Britannia is a frigid personification' (*R*, vol. 5, p. 75). Given the wider British-Irish political context in which Welsh politics is being played out, it is significant that, like his admiration for Davitt, it is from Ireland that the example to follow comes.

Thomas's review of Edwards's *Wales* mentions Watcyn Wyn, a poet who won the Eisteddfod Crown in 1881 and the Bardic Chair in 1885. Wyn, as we have seen, was principal of the Gwynfryn School in Ammanford, an institution whose foundation in 1880 coincided with the development of Ammanford as a thriving commercial town (Ammanford became the regional centre of the new coal and tin-plate industries). The school had a national reputation as a centre for Welsh-language education, and as a hothouse for the training of poets and preachers, reaching the zenith of its cultural significance between the last decade of the nineteenth century and the first decade of the twentieth (*CP*, p. 148). Watcyn Wyn enjoyed Wales-wide recognition, as a teacher, poet, lecturer and Eisteddfod performer, a reputation also gained by Gwili from 1901 onwards (*CP*, p. 148). The school taught *cynghanedd*, the rules of Welsh poetic metre, and encouraged its boarders, as well as local day pupils, to take part in local and national Eisteddfodau. Its alumni included W. Llewelyn Williams, regular contributor, as we have seen, to *Young Wales* and one of the founders of Cymdeithas Dafydd ap Gwilym (Oxford University's Welsh Society), not to mention the Barry branch of Cymru Fydd. As a Liberal MP, he was also the parliamentary contact approached by Thomas in a successful attempt to get a Civil List pension for fellow Welsh writer, W. H. Davies.

Thomas's association with this institution has never been explored. He knew Watcyn Wyn from his frequent visits to the area, sometimes to stay with his father's family (some of whom were now employed in the tin-plating industry) and, from 1897, from his visits to his relation Gwili. *Beautiful Wales* contains translations of Watcyn Wyn's versions of two Welsh folk songs, 'The Maid of Llandebie' and 'The Maids of Carmarthenshire' (*BW*, p. 134).[59] Thomas's three younger brothers, Reggie, Julian and Oscar, at times attended the Gwynfryn School while another, Ernest, under the pseudonym Merlin, won a prize for illustration at the 1900 National Eisteddfod. Thomas's interest in Welsh folk material, discussed in Chapter Four, coincided with Watcyn Wyn's own interest in this field, and also suggests connection with a network that included O. M. Edwards. Watcyn Wyn published versions of 'Llyn y Fan Fach' ('Story of the Lake') and 'Llyn Llech Owen' ('The Lake of Owen's Stone') – both, as we shall see, also referred to by Thomas – in O. M. Edwards's journal, *Cymru*.

The other Welsh-language poet mentioned in Thomas's review of Edwards's *Wales* is Gwili, who, having begun as a pupil at the Gwynfryn School, won the National Eisteddfod free metres competition in 1901. He became a teacher at the same institution in 1897, then left (as did W. Llewelyn Williams) for study at Oxford University, before returning, on Watcyn Wyn's death in 1908, as the school's principal (*CP*, p. 172). He was later to become a lecturer in Welsh at University College, Cardiff, as well as editor of *Seren Cymru* (The Star of Wales). According to R. George Thomas, the friendship between Thomas and Gwili began in 1897 and lasted until Thomas's death (*ETAP*, p. 215). E. Cefni Jones provides more colour, describing how the two met, along with the Welsh-language poet Ben Bowen, on one of Thomas's frequent visits to Amman-ford, and quickly became regular walking companions and literary correspondents.[60] The dedication of Thomas's biography, *Lafcadio Hearn*, to Gwili suggests the latter's importance to Thomas. Firstly, as teachers of Welsh poetic practice, Gwili and Watcyn Wyn were key to Thomas's own development as a writer and poet familiar with the Welsh-language tradition (as the next chapter will show). In this context, Thomas's association with Gwili, and also Edwards – both of them, as we have seen, key figures within the modernising camp of the Welsh revival – suggests his affinity with their project. Secondly, as Huw Walters's work has shown, Gwili was responsible for a Walt Whitman and Edward Carpenter cult in the Amman valley, a phenomenon that lasted from 1909 to 1920 (*CP*, p. 255); as we shall see in Chapter Five, this interest in Whitman and Carpenter was also shared by Thomas.

Gwili's 1920 elegy for Thomas, which could be seen as the first Welsh reception of Thomas, has received no critical comment by those writing about Thomas from within an Anglocentric critical tradition, and only one brief aside – by Tony Conran – from within the Welsh tradition. E. Cefni Jones mentions Gwili's heartbreak at learning of the wartime death of Thomas, but does not go on to discuss the wider significance of his elegy to him.[61] 'Edward Eastaway', referring to Thomas's pseudonym, is the most prominent poem in Gwili's English-language collection,

Poems. Unlike the pieces written by two of Thomas's friends in the English tradition – de la Mare's foreword, and Frost's 'To E. T.', both published in the same year – Gwili's poem presents Thomas in an unmistakeably Welsh context. It places Thomas in a succession of English-language Welsh poets including the 'nursling bard of Grongar Hill' – a reference to John Dyer, whose poetry Thomas introduced for Edwards's *Welsh Library Series* – and the seventeenth-century prose stylist, Jeremy Taylor, whom Thomas himself mentions in his 1902 sketch 'Inns and Books'.⁶²
Gwili's poem is also startling for its association of Thomas with Welsh place names: with 'Carreg Cennen', a site of Welsh resistance to English rule, with 'the cave / Of Llygad Llwchwr, and Cwrt Bryn y Beirdd', as well as Llandyfân, Derwydd, and Glyn Hir.⁶³

The speaker addresses Thomas, writing, albeit in a Romantic and archaic style, of the two men walking near 'Llyn Llech Owen' ('the Lake of Owen's Stone') in Carmarthenshire. He recalls how its

> legend led thy dreaming spirit far
> To some grey Past, where thou again couldst see
> The heedless horseman gallop fiercely home,
> And the well drown the moorland with its spate. (*GP*, p. 93)

This is a local reference to Owain Glyndŵr, who, having watered his horse at a local well, forgot to reseal it, and awoke to find the surrounding moorland flooding. Glyndŵr is 'the national hero of Wales' who, at the beginning of the fifteenth century, tried to 'free the Welsh people from the slavery of their English enemies', later becoming 'a powerful inspiration to Welsh patriots, especially to the advocates of political nationalism in modern times' (*NCLW*, p. 548). The connection of Thomas to Glyndŵr might seem surprising to those readers used to reading him as an English poet but, in *Beautiful Wales*, Thomas himself alludes to the Welsh hero, describing

> a man who watered his horse at a well and forgot to cover it with the stone, and riding away, saw the water swelling over the land from the well, and galloped back to stop it, and saw the lake thus created and bounded by the track of his horse's hooves. (*BW*, p. 21)

This is a reference to the same local legend of Glyndŵr at Llyn Llech Owen that Gwili mentions in his elegy. Nonetheless, Gwili goes further than Thomas. His reference to how Eastaway's 'song burst out of silence',

'the depths' of his 'mysterious spirit' becoming 'unsealed', suggests that
Thomas's turn to poetry in 1914 had its origins in his vision of Glyndŵr
in the Welsh landscape. Glyndŵr is not the only leader of an oppressed
people to whom Gwili likens Thomas. His poem continues:

> And again I cross through sedges, and the gorse
> Burns like the bush of Horeb unconsumed. (*GP*, p. 93)

This is a reference of course to Moses who, discovering that he was an
Israelite and not the son of an Egyptian pharaoh, returns from exile to
lead his people to their promised land. Gwili here moves the burning bush
of *Exodus* from Sinai to a Welsh moor, equating the situation of the Welsh
people with the slavery of the Israelites under the Egyptians, and implying
that Thomas, undergoing a shift in his national loyalty, is a Moses-figure
for the Welsh. Significantly, Moses spent most of his life in exile and died
before he reached the land promised for his people. The idea of Thomas
turning to Wales in adult life is suggested later in the poem when the
speaker records how, 'London cares' having made his 'Celtic blood / Run
slow', Thomas looked for his 'mother Wales / Full suddenly' (*GP*, p. 94).
The idea of a sudden, and later, interest in Wales is suggested by an August
1899 entry in Thomas's notebook:

> Day by day grows my passion for Wales. It is like a homesickness but
> stronger than any homesickness I ever felt – stronger than any passion.
> Wales indeed is my soul's native land, if the soul can be said to have a *patria*
> – or rather a *matria*.[64]

Aside from these connections to key figures in Welsh literary space,
Thomas also contributes to Welsh literary institutions. Dependent for a
living on his income from writing from 1900 until he enlisted in the British
army in 1915, he wrote mainly for the London-based papers, for which
writing reviews was well remunerated. These included the *Daily Chronicle*,
where he succeeded Lionel Johnson as poetry reviewer in 1902 (this
remained his principal source of work), as well as *Academy*, *The Speaker*,
World, the *Bookman*, the *Daily Mail*, the *Morning Post*, the *English Review*
and *New Age*, among others. One letter to Gordon Bottomley suggests his
financial dependence on the institutions of New Journalism, and laments
his need to 'hang about the skirts of the ½d. Press'.[65] As my analysis of
the position of the literature within the economic sphere suggests, however,
the fact that most of Thomas's journalistic work was carried out for

London-based institutions should not be read as a straightforward statement of his national allegiance.

Given the utter imbalance between the literary infrastructure centred
in London, and that based in Wales, it is surely significant that Thomas
also published on the Welsh side of the border. Indeed, one of the strongest
pieces of evidence for Thomas having looked for his 'mother Wales' has,
in fact, been entirely overlooked hitherto. No previous writer on his work
– not even among those most keen to claim him for Wales – has noticed
that he wrote for the Cardiff-based literary journal, *Nationalist*. Thomas
published two sketches in this journal: his short-story, 'The Patriot', which
appeared in the October 1909 issue, and his sketch, 'At a Cottage Door',
which was printed in January 1910. 'The Patriot' opens and closes with
the scene of 'a young soldier [who] lay dying in a foreign land' (*P*, p. 38).
The last moments of this man's life are juxtaposed with memories of
his first trip to Wales, from London, where he lives in exile. As my introduction mentions, the piece ends with the soldier realising, just before he
dies, that 'his country [is] not the country he had fought for' (*P*, p. 43).
Not only does the story anticipate Thomas's death as a British soldier eight
years later; it also offers a corrective to the critical traditions, discussed
in the previous chapter, which have attached so much significance to his
death in a British uniform. In this respect, it also anticipates W. B. Yeats's
poem 'An Irish Airman Foresees His Death', written in 1918 and published
a year later, which presents similar views from an Irish perspective.[66]

The other sketch, 'At a Cottage Door', published in *Nationalist* in 1909,
is devoted to an urban description rather than the countryside implied by
its title:

> On pleasant days the smell of the sea, modified by the docks, mingled with
> the acrid smell and taste of smoke from the smelting of copper and the
> burning of carcasses for manure; but at night either smell was drowned by
> that of fried fish.[67]

While Thomas here demonstrates an ability to write about urban scenes,
the sketch begins to place them in a context of national identity. Indeed,
the unnamed Welsh industrial port, a barely disguised Swansea, is
described in romantic terms that are juxtaposed against more realist
depictions of the spread of modernity:

> The wires of telegraph, telephone, and electric light ran amongst and over
> antique stone and timber work . . . Here and there an old house had been

pulled down, and its place hidden by a temporary wooden fence, stuck over with advertisements in black and white, crimson and blue, of drugs, infant foods, political meetings, auction sales, corsets, men's clothes, theatres. (14)

While there are elements of Thomas's idealisation of the unchanging peasant – Catherine Anne Jones, its only named character, 'talked nothing but Welsh' (10), and lived in a cottage that looked down from the mountain-side over the city – the story captures the transformation of rural south Wales into an urban metropolis, and the paraphernalia that went along with that change. It is also conscious of modernity's uneven arrival: the 'wires of telegraph, telephone, and electric light' are contrasted to the 'antique stone and timber work', while the English-speaking characters who populate the new urban centre exist in the same space as the Welsh-speaking cottager on the hillside.

In conclusion, then, setting out an interpretation of the political and economic contexts in which Anglophone Welsh literature operated at the turn of the twentieth century has led directly to discoveries that prove crucial to a revisionist reading of Thomas. It has also established a way of reading 'from the margins' which provides a justification for placing more weight on Welsh aspects of his work that Anglocentric readings have passed over. These include the significance of the patriotic pieces in *Nationalist*, along with Thomas's association with Watcyn Wyn, Gwili and O. M. Edwards, key reforming figures at the time, and even his liking for Davitt, the Irish nationalist leader. The next chapter develops this line of argument, pursuing Welsh cultural references in Thomas's work through its use of Casanova's revised 'Irish paradigm'.

4

Edward Thomas and the Welsh Cultural Tradition

In the previous chapter, I set turn-of-the-century Welsh literature in its economic and political spheres, a modification to Casanova's model that I proposed at the end of Chapter One. This enabled me to locate Thomas in relation to some of the key Welsh literary and political figures and issues of the period. Without such an analysis of the local historical context, many of Thomas's connections to Welsh journals and figures would not have been uncovered. In this chapter, I examine further the literary manifestation of Thomas's Welshness by considering his work through stage one of Casanova's 'Irish paradigm' – the *littérisation* of folk material (a category that includes folklore, legend and folk or popular poetry), its translation, and wide dissemination as the literature of the 'people'. This chapter argues that such an activity occupies some of Thomas's work as a reviewer, and plays a significant part in his published prose and poetry. I should point out that, in an effort to show the importance of Welsh influences on Thomas's work, the chapter also refers to Welsh-language cultural matter of a very different order, variously related to the great *barddas* (strict-metre poetry) tradition, ancient Welsh historiography, the *Mabinogion* and medieval poetry. Tracing the references to all this material across Thomas's poetry and prose, I show that they are more central to Thomas's project than critics have hitherto understood.

As a result of Thomas's prose material having been so little attended to, and because I want to establish the extent of his interest in Welsh cultural material, passages from it are described in some detail. There is an element of repetition in what Thomas does (partly due to the range of genres and audiences for whom he writes), so there is inevitably some cross-referencing in what follows. The chapter begins by showing how Thomas's concern for Welsh folklore and literary material informs his review work, his novel, sketches and travel narratives, and even emerges in his literary biographies. It argues that in his book on George Borrow, Thomas almost boasts about his knowledge of the manuscript sources of Welsh legend and ancient historiography, and that he addresses the subject matter directly in his own interpretations of key Welsh myths (from the *Mabinogion*) in *Celtic Stories*. The chapter concludes by showing how his interest in these Welsh cultural traditions also informs his poetry.

In his 1906 commissioned publication, *The Heart of England* (a journey in search of England's 'heart' whose destination proves to be Wales), Thomas quotes from the Scottish ballad, 'The Death of Parcy Reed', 'God send the land deliverance / Frae every reaving, riding Scot!', before wondering:

> whether the great work done in the last century and a half towards the recovery of old ballads in their integrity will have any effect beyond the entertainment of a few scientific men and lovers of what is ancient, now that the first effects upon Wordsworth and his contemporaries have died away. Can it possibly give a vigorous impulse to a new school of poetry that shall treat the life of our time and what in past times has most meaning for us freshly as those ballads did the life of their time? It is possible; and it is surely impossible that such examples of simple, realistic narrative shall be quite in vain.[1]

Here, Thomas is interested in how the folk tradition can be used to illuminate the 'life of our time', and he sets his own work in the context of the recovery of the ballad tradition by eighteenth- and nineteenth-century antiquarians and collectors.

Thomas's interest in the *littérisation* of native Welsh sources follows that of O. M. Edwards, whose journal, *Cymru*, as we have seen, aimed to raise consciousness of Welsh history, as well as of the nation's folk and singing traditions. It also called for the creation of 'a literature that will be English in language and Welsh in spirit'. As we have seen, Edwards is an important influence on Thomas at the beginning of his writing career. The 1901 correspondence with Edwards at once asserts his identity – 'I am Welsh' – and his aim 'to help you and the Welsh cause' (*TUL*, p. 343). Helping 'the Welsh cause' explicitly takes the form of his writing, whether in some of his literary journalism – the 'wish' that his 'small activities' could be 'usefully connected to Wales' – or in complete books (*TUL*, p. 343).

The opportunities for raising awareness of the Welsh folk tradition through his position as a literary journalist in Fleet Street were infrequent, but when they occurred, they show Thomas's concern that it should reach a wider audience. On 16 December 1907, he reviewed Jenkyn Thomas's *Welsh Faery Book* for the *Daily Chronicle*:

> Mr Jenkyn Thomas's book comes in answer to a real need. There was no Welsh fairy book before, except Sir John Rhys's *Celtic Folklore: Welsh and Manx*, and that is far too expensive to be widely circulated. (*R*, vol. 4, p. 41)

The same concern that Welsh folk matter be made more available is evident in his review of Marie Trevelyan's *Folk-Lore and Folk-Stories of Wales* in the *Daily Chronicle* of 15 August 1909. The review expresses regret that Welsh folk material, which is 'of great significance', is not more 'easily obtainable' (*R*, vol. 4, p. 120). Trevelyan's book, since it 'does not seriously overlap any other', is praised as 'to all intents and purposes a new book'. Thomas, by 1907, is writing from a position of knowledge. Five years earlier, he had received from Edwards a copy of Charlotte Guest's groundbreaking translation of the *Mabinogion*. His correspondence in subsequent years displays a growing knowledge of Welsh literary material. A letter to Gordon Bottomley reads:

> There is I believe a good deal that Welsh is the only key to: many tales of the princes and their women, for example, in the 'chronicles of the princes'. *The Mabinogion* is the only readable translation of Welsh and even the unreadable – like the *Four Ancient Books of Wales* are few. (*LGB*, p. 214)

His 1909 diary records that he was reading the *Mabinogion* on 10 and 11 March of that year, and unidentified 'Welsh folklore' every day from 1 to 15 August.[2] A letter to his literary agent, Frank Cazenove, dated 8 December 1907, proposes a project for 'an anthology of Welsh writers' to include

> Geoffrey of Monmouth, Gerald of Wales, the *Mabinogion*, the medieval Welsh poets and romances, some fairy tales, 3 or 4 of greatest religious poets (Herbert, Vaughan, Traherne), some great preachers, theologians.[3]

The book did not materialise, but it gives an indication of the extent of Thomas's familiarity with folk and literary material. Perhaps most significantly, it suggests, as early as 1907, a vision of Welsh letters that incorporates writers from both linguistic traditions. A further indication of the depth of his knowledge is suggested by his familiarity with the range of 'translations from Dafydd' (Dafydd ap Gwilym, the medieval Welsh poet), and his criticism of Evelyn Lewes in the *Daily News* on 24 April 1914 for what he sees as her overly poetic interpretation of ap Gwilym's work; he advises her to read instead 'the prose versions published by Mr Idris Bell in the Welsh *Nationalist*' (*R*, vol. 6, p. 122). Thomas is also familiar with Taliesin, the sixth-century Welsh poet, a translation of one of whose poems appears in Thomas's 1907 anthology *Pocket Book of Poems and Songs for the Open Air*. His review work reveals a knowledge of the extant original sources:

> Those who cared for these things had to go to Sir John Rhys, to Giraldus, the Iolo MSS, to him who tells the Story of Cwellyn Lake, to Elias Owen, Wirt Sykes and others. In the popular collections, there is hardly a Welsh tale to be found. (*R*, vol. 4, p. 41)

The 'Iolo MSS', to which references occur elsewhere in Thomas's prose, are the collected papers of the remarkable antiquarian, scholar, poet – and forger of medieval literary poems – and self-educated stone mason, Iolo Morganwg (1747–1826), who is presented in *The Happy-Go-Lucky Morgans*. Here, he is depicted favourably as a supporter of the French Revolution, and acquaintance both of the English radical, Tom Paine, and the American founding father, Benjamin Franklin. Iolo is praised as a man who 'hated kings' (*HGLM*, p. 105), and who 'never forgot the bardic triad, "Man, Liberty and Light"' (*HGLM*, p. 109), recognising its spirit 'in the French Revolution', and almost leaving for America 'to fly from the numerous injuries he had received from the laws of this land' (*HGLM*, p. 110). At one point Iolo is 'worthy to be immortalised in stained glass' (*HGLM*, p. 103); at the next, his name 'will outlive most stained glass, for one of the finest collections of Welsh history, genealogies, fables, tales, poetry, etc, all in old manuscripts, was made by him, and was named after him in its published form –"Iolo Manuscripts"' (*HGLM*, p. 104). He is depicted as a poverty-stricken Welsh character who will not touch the 'dirty money' England offers him. In spite of his poverty, he refuses offers of financial help from family members whose money originated in the slave plantations of Jamaica: 'he would not even administer their property when it was left to him', while 'the sound of the bells at Bristol celebrating the rejection of Wilberforce's Anti-Slavery Bill drove him straight out of

the city' (*HGLM*, p. 111). At another point, one of the characters in the
novel receives, like Iolo, an ash stick cut at Craig-y-Ddinas, before relating
the story – also found in *Beautiful Wales* (p. 125) – of how Iolo travels
from London back to the cave at Craig-y-Ddinas where King Arthur and
his knights wait to free Britain from the Saxons (*HGLM*, p. 86).

There is another reference to the 'Iolo manuscript' in *Beautiful Wales*.
The title *Beautiful Wales* was chosen by the publisher A. & C. Black, who
commissioned from Thomas the text to accompany Robert Fowler's
romantic pictures of north Wales. Thomas's text, however, subverts the
publisher's intentions. It is not a travel guide, and it does not focus on
the landscapes of Snowdonia that most English readers associated with
'romantic' Wales. Instead, it employs a series of anecdotes and cultural
allusions to inform English readers of the otherness of Wales. R. George
Thomas describes Thomas's disappointment with the final book, but notes
'the carefully detailed research into Welsh history, and contemporary
Welsh culture and society, that preceded his final manuscript' (*ETAP*,
p. 121). At one point, the narrator, coming to a 'strange farmhouse' where
'the farmer sang to me from the Welsh hymn book and from a collection
of old Welsh songs', discusses the 'Iolo manuscript' with 'a fierce-
thoughted, mild-eyed young minister' (*BW*, p. 190). Here, Iolo is described
as 'poet, great discoverer of manuscripts and splendid human being, . . .
lover of liberty and of the Revolution in France' (*BW*, p. 96). As one of
a group of Iolo scholars, Cathyrn Charnell-White demonstrates that, over
the course of his career, Iolo 'construct[ed] an innovative Welsh national
identity'.[4] She shows that he appropriated late eighteenth-century ideas
of bardism as a way of 'reconfigur[ing] the [prevailing] Anglocentric
notion of "barbarous Wales, civilized England"', writing to an English-
speaking readership in order to subvert their preconceptions in this respect.[5]
As we shall see, Thomas's interest indicates a concern for a similar kind
of cultural reconfiguration.

Beautiful Wales contains a fictional Welsh poet, Morgan Rhys, who
loves, 'alone of mortal things', the 'liberty and integrity of Wales' (*BW*,
p. 96) Like Rhys, the narrator is also a Welsh patriot: 'I do not easily
believe in patriotism', he declares, 'in times of peace or war, except as a
party cry, or the result of intoxication or an article in a newspaper, unless
I am in Wales' (*BW*, p. 174). The narrator describes a '*noson lawen*' ('a
merry evening'), a night of stories and song around the fire, in which the
talk is of Welsh heroes: 'Llewelyn the Great, or Llewelyn the Last, or
Arthur, or Kilhwch, or Owen Glyndwr, or the most recent'. Each is referred
to as a 'prophet' with whom those present are 'utterly at one' (*BW*, p. 49).

The word 'prophet' is significant, implying a future date at which an independent Wales will be achieved. The idea that Arthur will return again to rescue the Welsh from their imprisonment, referred to in Thomas's review of O. M. Edwards's *Wales*, is repeated: 'as the poet has said, "Folly would it be to say that Arthur has a grave"' (*BW*, p. 50). As these examples suggest, there are political connotations to this use of Welsh folk material. The references to Arthur and other national heroes are common features of writing associated with the Cymru Fydd movement. In the shape of Iolo and Welsh national 'prophets', Thomas raises awareness of semi-historical, semi-mythical figures who serve 'the Welsh cause'. In many cases, however, his texts make extensive or passing reference to Welsh cultural materials. While this does not necessarily make a political point, it does raise the literary status of the previously subordinated native tradition in the way that Casanova describes.

In *Beautiful Wales*, the narrator likens his inability to recall the details of days spent walking across the Welsh mountains to that of 'a child who, in the Welsh story, went to the land of the fairies, and could only say that he had been listening to sweet airs, when he returned after a long stay' (*BW*, p. 164). The 'Welsh story' is that of Elidir, a folk legend from Gower first recorded by Gerald of Wales, in which a young boy out playing is led away by the Tylwyth Teg (literally translated as 'the fair or magic folk') to a magical fairy land. Caught attempting to bring something back from there, he is made to forget all he knows of it. The Tylwyth Teg are mentioned elsewhere in *Beautiful Wales*, when they 'exchanged people's children with their own' (*BW*, p. 129), while the story of Elidir is more fully related later in the book (*BW*, p. 181). The Tylwyth Teg are associated in Welsh folk culture with the lake of Llyn y Fan Fach, which is also mentioned in *Beautiful Wales*, and is within walking distance of where Thomas's family lived in Ammanford; it is a place about which Watcyn Wyn had also written.

Llyn y Fan Fach is the setting for another legend of the Tylwyth Teg, that of the Speckled Cow of Hiraethog, also related in *Beautiful Wales*, in which one of the Tylwyth Teg daughters agrees to marry a farmer's son 'on the condition that he should not give her three causeless blows; if he did she would disappear' (*BW*, p. 170). Having been hit three times and having returned to the land of the Tylwyth Teg, the wife, by now also a mother, nevertheless appears to her sons one final time in order to reveal to them the medicinal qualities of plants. The sons go on, as Thomas's narrator informs us, to head a familial line of 'good physicians', treating 'Rhys Gryg of South Wales', 'the last of their descendents . . . buried in

1739 at Myddfai church' (*BW*, p. 172). The 'Physicians of Myddfai' is a well-known Welsh legend with its origins in history, and is preserved in a series of medical texts from the medieval period. *The New Companion to the Literature of Wales*, which links the phenomenon of 'educated, professional families' passing medical knowledge from one generation to the next to 'similar examples' in Scotland and Ireland, reports that 'the gravestones of the last of their line, David Jones (d. 1719) and John Jones (d. 1739)', are still to be seen in the church at Myddfai (*NCLW*, p. 520). Thomas's knowledge of Welsh folk history may have come from his reading of the eighteenth-century Welsh antiquarian Lewis Morris, whose letters mention the Physicians of Myddfai, or from John Pughe's 1861 translation of *The Physicians of Myddfai*, edited by John Williams.

There are numerous further references to Welsh folk and literary material in *Beautiful Wales*: there is a translation of the song 'Claf Abercuawg' (*BW*, p. 39), 'Eluned' (*BW*, p. 82), and the music and words to Watcyn Wyn's versions of 'The Maid of Llandybie' and 'The Maids of Carmarthenshire' (*BW*, p. 134). There is also a translation of a Taliesin poem from the classic *barddas* tradition (*BW*, p. 87), and the book begins by referring to 'the songs of the Eos Ceiriog' (the nightingale), alias the poet Huw Morus (*BW*, p. 5). Finally, there is a reference to the legend of Cantre'r Gwaelod (The Lowland Hundred), a Welsh version of the drowned city myth, in which the sea, in this case Cardigan Bay, 'now covers a country that was once populous and fair and rich', containing 'sixteen fortified towns superior to all the towns and cities in Wales' (*BW*, p. 51).

Allusions to Welsh folk tradition, and its practice, also litter Thomas's sketches. In 'Exiles at Play', part of *Horae Solitariae* (in which most of the sketches have some reference to Wales), the narrator listens 'to Welsh songs, devised sweetly about the streams and hills of the very place where we lay', while in 'Recollections of November', another sketch from that text, he reads 'the lines on November by a Welsh poet of four or five centuries back' (an allusion not to folk material, but to medieval Welsh poetry), and imagines 'the delicious evenings the old Welsh spent, exchanging by the fireside proverbs and tales'.[6] In the sketch, 'Isoud with the White Hands', he refers to 'that sweet saint, Dwynwen of Wales', the patron saint of lovers, and relates the story by which she achieved this status (*HS*, p. 185).

A 1909 letter to Bottomley reads, 'One or two stories I worked at did not turn out badly. I used some old Welsh fragments of legends' (*LGB*, p. 196). Some of the sketches in *Rest and Unrest*, written that year and published in 1910, mention Welsh folk material. 'Mothers and Sons', which is set in a Welsh-speaking family, has a moment when 'the eldest boy sang "Morfa Rhuddlan" and "Hob y deri dando"', which the narrator describes as 'the most mournful and the merriest of the old Welsh songs'.[7] The former commemorates the Battle of Rhuddlan Marsh in 796, when Caradog, King of Gwynedd, was killed by Offa, King of Mercia. The latter, a traditional song, is 'one of the most popular tunes for choruses at the "noson lawen"' (*NCLW*, p. 320).

In another sketch in this collection, 'The Fountain', the narrator imagines 'the way of life' of a woman he meets by chance out walking: he likens her to the 'fairy-bride . . . who consented in the old days to live with a mortal husband until he should have struck her three times', at which point she returns 'to her father's palace below the lake in the hills'.[8] This is an allusion to two Welsh myths: firstly, the legend of Llyn y Fan Fach, discussed earlier, and secondly, a legend associated with two lakes in the Brecon Beacons, Llyn Cwm Llwch and Llyn Syfaddan, below which, every May Day, a secret door opens into a drowned palace of the Tylwyth Teg. The penultimate sketch, 'Snow and Sand', manipulates the myth of Cantre'r Gwaelod, discussed above.

The same pattern is evident in a 1911 collection of short stories, *Light and Twilight*. In one of the sketches, 'Olwen', a Welsh girl is described in ways that allude to the legend 'Culhwch and Olwen', which is 'the most primitive and probably the oldest of the *Mabinogion* tales' (*NCLW*, p. 126), and one that Thomas retells in full in his 1911 *Celtic Stories*. In the *Mabinogion* tale, Olwen, a giant's daughter, cannot get married because there is no suitor who can complete all the tasks demanded of him. Thomas adapts the story to the present day, and retells it with comic realism: Olwen, 'strong as a man', is about to get married, but her fiancé falls pathetically short of her hopes for him.[9] The sketch 'Winter Music' develops a story in *The Red Book of Hergest* in which a red and a white dragon, symbolising the Welsh and the Saxons, battle over a Snowdonia lake for the island of Britain. Another sketch, 'The Castle of Lostormellyn', is a retelling of a quest myth set in fictional medieval Welsh castles, while 'Home' is an adaptation of 'The Patriot', a short story previously published, as we have seen, in *Nationalist*. Here, the folk tradition epitomises the way in which the Welsh are different from the modern British. The dying soldier remembers his father 'singing the songs of his country' (*LT*, p. 27), an experience which is associated with his memory of the London train station where people 'were talking in the tongue in which his father used to sing' (*LT*, p. 29). The train carries a 'proud freight of living men looking ahead towards their country', a line that points to not only the end of their journey, but also a future time when their country becomes a nation (*LT*, p. 33). The final lines, in which the speaker recalls 'the land of his father and of his father's fathers, and of those who sang the same songs', refer to the Welsh national anthem *Hen Wlad Fy Nhadau* (Land of My Fathers), while the last clause seems to allude to the exiled Welsh – of whom 265,000 then lived in England – who nonetheless 'sang the same songs' (*LT*, p. 36). This suggests that Welsh identity can continue to be sustained by folk songs played beyond its geographic borders. One notebook entry of 1899 suggests that Thomas shared his speaker's love of such traditional materials:

> What yearning thoughts filled my brain as Janet played the tune of 'Y Ferch o Landebie' and 'Moli merched Cymru lan!' and when I hummed the 'Gwlad Gwlad' of the national anthem, my heart broke with thoughts of what I might be and am not, of what I may be – ah! The future in some bookish cottage in the pastoral Towy with Helen![10]

R. George Thomas records Thomas's 'Welsh folk-song evenings' with friends in London in 1904 (*ETAP*, p. 115). Thomas's interest in Welsh folk material continues into his only novel, *The Happy-Go-Lucky Morgans*, a depiction of a middle-class London Welsh household at the turn of the century. Aside from the references to Iolo Morganwg, already discussed, there are several retellings in this text of Welsh folk material, as well as stories from the literary tradition. Chapter Three, for example, contains the tale of 'the Wild Swans' (*HGLM*, pp. 17–21), which originates in the *Mabinogion*, and in which four children, changed by a sorceress into four swans, have their sorrow allayed when they are enabled to speak Welsh. Chapter Eighteen depicts one of the characters 'singing mightily':

> Foul fall the hand which bends the steel
> Around the courser's thundering heel,
> That e'er shall dint a sable wound
> On fair Glamorgan's velvet ground! (*HGLM*, p. 142)

The title of the song is not mentioned, and the narrative moves quickly on, but it is 'The War-Song of the Men of Glamorgan', and this second verse celebrates a medieval Welsh cavalry victory over the English at Caerphilly. *The Happy-Go-Lucky Morgans* is full of references such as this to Welsh culture which, being unexplained, are easy for the reader unfamiliar with Welsh culture to miss.

On another occasion, the narrator visits the now-deserted home of the Welsh-speaking Morgan family in Wiltshire, and listens to a neighbour as she tells a story once told by Ann, a Welsh-speaking servant, about a man returning from a country fair who sees people 'dancing and musick-ing' in a 'grand, gorgeous house close by the road'. After joining them, he fell asleep 'in a soft warm bed, but in the morning he woke up under a hedge' (*HGLM*, p. 154). The story is perhaps adapted from the romance of 'Geraint and Enid' in which a hedge of mist guards a field where enchanted games are played. When Thomas incorporates Welsh folk songs and stories into the text in this way, without explicitly drawing attention to the fact that he is doing so, the reader is aware of a 'difference', but one that is not translated in terms that present it fully to the English reader. The title of Chapter Four, 'Hob-y-deri-dando', referring to a song popular at 'noson lawen' (boisterous evening entertainment), also fulfils this function. In using a Welsh-language word that remains untranslated, the text, as Kirsti Bohata argues, 'asserts the cultural difference of "English"-language Welsh writing' (*PR*, p. 122). Thomas also uses this device in *Beautiful Wales* when he incorporates into the text the Welsh for cataract: 'jutting out of every hedge-bank a little *pistyll* of fair water, curving and shining in the heat, over a slice of stone or through a pipe, into the road' (*BW*, p. 164).

In Thomas's critical study, *George Borrow: the Man and His Books*, finished in Laugharne in December 1911, he does more than demonstrate his knowledge of Welsh folk and literary material. Unlike his subject, the English Borrow (who claimed to be intimately familiar with the literary and folk history of a nation to which he did not belong), Thomas explicitly asserts possession of that material. Borrow, he reports, 'kissed the silver cup at Llanddewi Brefi and the tombstone of Huw Morus at Llan Silin' (the former is a relic connected to St David and the latter the seventeenth-century Welsh poet.[11] Thomas here calls Morus by his folk name of 'the Nightingale of Ceiriog', a description repeated from *Beautiful Wales* (*GB*, p. 267). There are further references to Borrow's translation of 'an ode of Lewis Glyn Cothi', the fifteenth-century Welsh bard (*GB*, p. 305), and a repetition of the myth (found in *Beautiful Wales* and *The Happy-Go-Lucky Morgans*) that Arthur sleeps at Craig-y-Ddinas (*GB*, p. 318). More significantly, Thomas indicates his own, greater, familiarity with Welsh folk and literary material:

There is no evidence that [Borrow] knew the great nineteenth-century collections of Welsh manuscripts and translations. He says nothing of the

Mabinogion. He had apparently never heard of the pedestrian Iolo Morganwg. He perhaps never saw Stephens' *Literature of the Kymry*. His knowledge was picked up anyhow and anywhere from Welsh texts and Lhuyd's *Archaeologia*, without system and with very little friendly discussion or comparison. Wales, therefore, was as wonderful as Spain, and equally uncharted. (*GB*, p. 276)

As Eiluned Rees and Philip Henry Jones suggest, it was only with the publication of the *Journal of the Welsh Bibliographical Society* in Swansea from 1910, and monographs published by the University of Wales Press from the 1920s, that more systematic analysis of Welsh manuscript material was even attempted, so Thomas's awareness of some of the extant material, as early as 1911, was impressive.[12] As well as pointedly demonstrating his own knowledge of the material, Thomas identifies more with the people described than with the visiting author. Instead of accepting Borrow's claims that Wales is 'uncharted' and 'wild', he puts them down to his subject's ignorance of the literary and manuscript materials that already existed. This leads to a telling insight that anticipates postcolonial criticism: 'The chief fault of his Welsh portraits', argues Thomas, 'is [Borrow's] almost invariable, and almost always unnecessary, exhibition of his own superiority. He is nearly always the big clever gentleman catechizing certain quaint little rustic foreigners' (*GB*, p. 287).

   Thomas's interest in the Welsh literary tradition slips into books that are about ostensibly different, even English, subject matter. His 1909 book *The South Country*, the record of a walk across the south of England, mentions Taliesin and 'the chess-playing in *The Dream of Rhonabwy*' from the *Mabinogion*.[13] It features a woman who had lived in England for fifty years but nonetheless 'hums a Welsh tune' (*SC*, p. 232). There are passing references to Welsh folk traditions: the bardic motto on 'the chair of the bards of Beisgawen' (*SC*, p. 160), and a description by Gerald of Wales (*SC*, p. 151). Thomas's biography, *Richard Jefferies*, published in 1909, compares his subject's appreciation of women's beauty to his love of nature by invoking the character of Blodeuwedd, the beautiful woman created out of flowers in the fourth branch of the *Mabinogion*: 'as if, indeed, they were made, as Blodeuwedd was made by Gwydion, of the blossoms of the oak and the blossoms of the broom and the blossoms of the meadowsweet'.[14] Even in his 1912 volume, *Lafcadio Hearn*, dedicated to Gwili, a biography of the journalist, literary translator and travel writer who emigrated from Britain to Japan via the United States, he refers to his subject's upbringing 'in Wales and Ireland', in order to emphasise that 'he was weary of the whole Anglo-Saxon system of life and civilization'.[15]

Thomas's book *The Country*, published in 1913, is concerned with England but has as its epigraph an extract from a W. H. Davies poem about Wales:

> Can I forget the sweet days that have been,
> The villages so green I have been in;
> Llantarnam, Magor, Malpas, and Llanwern,
> Liswerry, old Caerleon, & Alteryn?[16]

This recalls the list of Welsh place names in Thomas's book on Borrow: 'Llangarmon, Sycharth, Bala, Machynlleth, Devil's Bridge, Plinlimmon, Pont Rhyd Fendigaid, Strata Florida, Tregaron, Lampeter, Pumpsaint, Llandovery, Llangadog, Gwynfe, Gutter Fawr (Brynamman), Swansea, Neath, Merthyr, Caerphilly, Newport and Chepstow', names associated with 'the places mentioned by the Welsh bards' (*GB*, p. 265). Thomas includes a similar catalogue in *Beautiful Wales*:

> Llangollen, Aberglaslyn, Betws-y-Coed, the Fairy Glen, Capel Curig, Colwyn, Tintern, Bethesda, Llanfairfechan, Llanrhaiadr, Llanynys, Tenby (a beautiful flower with a beetle in it), Mostyn, Glyder Fach and Glyder Fawr, Penmaenmawr, Pen-y-Gader, Pen-y-Gwryd, Prestatyn, Tremadoc, the Swallow Falls, the Devil's Bridge, the Mumbles, Harlech, Portmadoc, Towyn and Aberdovey (with its song and still a poet there). I have read many lyrics worse than that inventory. (*BW*, p. 9)

The 'song' associated with Aberdyfi is the Welsh folk song 'Clychau Aberdyfi' ('The Bells of Aberdyfi'), linked to the legend of Cantre'r Gwaelod because it imitates the chiming of the lost city's underwater bells. The idea that an 'inventory' of place names is a set of 'lyrics' in itself is echoed in Thomas's praise for folk ballads: 'their observation of life so fresh, so fond of particular detail – its very lists of names being at times real poetry' (*SC*, p. 242). Later in *The Country* the narrator refers to 'the valley of the river Uther', also in Wales, and comments: 'That is my world in spite of everything. Those fifteen or twenty square miles make the one real thing that I know and cannot forget, in spite of a hundred English scenes wantonly visited and forgotten and unintelligible'.[17] Here, as in his book on Borrow, the narrator explicitly identifies with Wales in a way that Borrow, for example, an Englishman writing about the country, does not.

In Pursuit of Spring is a 1914 travel narrative in which Thomas and an unnamed 'other man' walk from London in a south-westerly direction in March. It ends with the men 'finding' spring in Wales, even though they never leave England:

> Down the slopes I looked across the flat valley to the Mendips and Brent Knoll, and to the Steep and Flat Holms, resting like clouds on a pale, cloudy sea; what is more, through a low-arched rainbow I saw the blueness of the hills of South Wales.[18]

At this point they discover 'the first bluebells and cowslips' by the side of the road, and the connection to Wales is reaffirmed. Epiphany here, like the end of the quest in *The Heart of England*, is associated with Wales:

> Even to have seen them on a railway station seat in the rain, brought from afar off on an Easter Monday, would have been something; here, in the sun, they were as if they had been fragments fallen out of that rainbow over against Wales. I had found Winter's grave; I had found Spring.[19]

The Icknield Way, published in 1916, is another England-based travel narrative that includes much about Wales. Here, Thomas's interest is slightly different: it is an interest in the Welshness of England. 'You will find Welsh ways all over England', he writes, listing the street names associated with the drover practice of driving flocks of Welsh sheep to markets in London.[20] He identifies different features of the English land-scape as landmarks for these itinerant Welsh drovers, the recurrence of which in his poetry will be discussed in Chapter Six (*IW*, p. 27). In this book, its dedication written at the 'Dolau Cothi Arms, Pumpsaint, Carmarthen-shire', Thomas argues that 'it is a dream in the *Mabinogion* which gives one of the most majestic scenes of travel' (*IW*, p. 7). He then relates the 'dream of the Emperor Maxen', one of the stories that appeared in Lady Charlotte Guest's 1849 translation of the *Mabinogion*; this, he suggests, is the source for the street name 'Sarn Helen', one of 'the great ancient roads leading North and South across Wales' (*IW*, p. 7), and he discusses alternative etymological interpretations by Sir John Rhŷs (*IW*, p. 7), and Geoffrey of Monmouth (*IW*, p. 37).[21]

The text most obviously concerned with material from the *Mabinogion* is *Celtic Stories*, published in 1911, in which Thomas retells four Welsh and seven Irish tales. While this chapter has shown how Thomas's interest in Welsh culture, both literary and folkloric, informs his work in a range of genres, and ostensibly about a range of subjects, *Celtic Stories* is a text in which he tackles the subject head-on. It links Irish and Welsh concerns in a colonial context, a matter that will be explored in more depth in Chapter Five as part of a sustained investigation of Thomas's interest in Irish literature. The collection presents traditional Welsh material that would be recycled again in the poetry, an aspect of Thomas's work considered later in Chapter Four.

Acknowledging his 'debt' to Guest's seminal translation of the *Mabinogion*, Thomas introduces *Celtic Stories* by suggesting that his version would have a readership among people who had not yet encountered Guest's work, an evident concern to widen the popularity of Welsh traditional materials.[22] There is an indicator of his success in the 1914 purchase by the Australian government of several thousand copies for schools (*ETAP*, p. 215). While this must have helped at a financially difficult time for Thomas, it also fulfilled his aim of widening the availability of Welsh and Irish folk stories among English-speaking emigrants. This is a significant development as it illuminates Thomas's sense of his own cultural positioning, working on the edges of an emerging tradition of 'other' Anglophone literatures.

The four Welsh tales in *Celtic Stories* are 'Bran and Bronwen', 'Kilhugh and Olwen', 'The Dream of Rhonabwy' and 'The Dream of Maxen'. The first story, from the second branch of the *Mabinogion*, narrates the life of the giant Bran, who waded across the Irish Sea to avenge the Irish king's treatment of Bran's sister Branwen. When the Irish use the 'cauldron of rebirth' to bring their dead soldiers back to life, Bran is killed and the Welsh are defeated. Bran's head is eventually taken by the seven survivors of the battle to Tower Hill, London, where it is buried, facing in the direction of France, to ward off invaders. 'Kilhugh and Olwen' retells the oldest of the *Mabinogion* tales, found in *The Red Book of Hergest*, in which the hero Culhwch, along with Arthur, undertakes a series of tasks in order to win Olwen as his bride. 'The Dream of Rhonabwy', also found in *The Red Book of Hergest*, is another Arthurian tale, and the first example in Welsh literature of the dream motif used as a framework for a story in which several unconnected scenes are related. In 'The Dream of Maxen', one of the few tales in the *Mabinogion* with an identifiable historical basis, the narrator relates the story of the marriage of the fourth-century Roman Emperor, Macsen Wledig, to Helen of Wales, or Elen Luyddog, which resulted in the building of roads across the country.

In this chapter so far, we have seen how Thomas's interest in Welsh cultural materials is evident in his prose publications from 1902, towards the beginning of his career, to 1914, when he turned to poetry. It informs genres including his review work, and the travel narratives *Beautiful Wales*, *The Heart of England*, *The South Country*, *In Pursuit of Spring* and *The Icknield Way*, as well as biographical-critical work such as *Richard Jefferies*. It also features in collections of sketches including *Horae Solitariae, Rest and Unrest, Light and Twilight*, and his only novel, *The Happy-Go-Lucky Morgans*. In *George Borrow: the Man and His Books*, Thomas seems to want to emphasise his own familiarity, in contrast with his subject, with manuscript and secondary material, while in *Celtic Stories* he offers his own versions of classic Welsh folk tales.

Naturally, these powerful cultural preoccupations surface, too, in Thomas's poetry, all written – as already noted – between November 1914 and January 1917. Thomas's adaptation of Welsh-language forms and metres into his English-language poetry is the aspect of his work to which this chapter will next pay attention, before considering how, in terms of its subject matter, his poetry contains both explicit references and buried allusions to the Welsh-language folk and classic literary traditions.

Cynghanedd, an intricate system of sound-chiming peculiar to Welsh verse, contains four basic types, to illustrate which I borrow examples in English provided by *The New Companion to the Literature of Wales* (p. 139). The first two, *cynghanedd groes* and *cynghanedd draws*, divide the poetic line into two feet. In *cynghanedd groes*, the consonant sounds of the first foot are repeated in the second ('A ro*s*e *bl*oomed / whe*r*e I*s*o*b*el walked'); in *cynghanedd draws*, also based on a repetition of consonant sounds across two halves of the line, some consonant sounds may be unmatched ('*L*o*ll*ing / beneath the *l*i*l*ac'). A third type, *cynghanedd sain*, divides the line into three feet. Here, there is internal rhyme between the first two feet, and repetition of consonants between the second and third ('By the br*eeze* / the *tr*ees / en*tr*anced'). The fourth type, *cynghanedd lusg*, occurs when the penultimate syllable is accented and when it rhymes with a word earlier in the line ('The flowers wel**come su**mmer'). The *cynghanedd* system is entirely based on repetition of consonant sounds, and internal rhyme. While critics have focused on Thomas's adaptation of blank verse to speech rhythms, and on the influence on his work of Frost's 'sound of sense', the sound and stanza experiments, as well as the internal rhymes, that occur in his poetry have been commented on less frequently. Matthew Hollis is one of the few critics to identify in Thomas's verse 'musical phrasings' that distinguish his poetry from that of Frost.[23] A logical place to look for the source of these metrical and rhythmic innovations is the classic Welsh-language tradition of *barddas* that has continued to evolve from the sixth century to the present time.

One of Thomas's poetic innovations involves the creation of intricate sound systems, based on internal rhyme and the repetition of consonant sounds. In 'The Bridge', for example, the rhyme and sound pattern of the stanzas is without precedent in the English language:

> I have come a long way today:
> On a strange bridge alone,
> Remembering friends, old friends,
> I rest, without smile or moan,
> As they remember me without smile or moan. (*ACP*, p. 66)

The internal rhyme within the first and third lines, as well as the refrain to end lines four and five, establish a pattern that is repeated across the poem's three stanzas. The internal rhyme in lines one and three approximate to Welsh metres in its adaptation of *cynghanedd lusg*, albeit for a stressed line end, while the refrain to end the stanza is adapted from folk songs in both Welsh and English traditions.

'The Green Roads' is another experimental poem: a series of non-rhyming couplets in which the end-word of each first line is 'forest'. In addition, the end-rhyme of the second line is anticipated at some point in the second line, usually by the word before the caesura in the second line:

> The green roads that end in the forest
> Are strewn with white goose feathers this June,
>
> Like marks left behind by someone gone to the forest
> To show his track. But he has never come back. (*ACP*, p. 128)

The internal rhyme in the second line of each pair recalls the similar technique in the third and fourth types of *cynghanedd*. Although the use of the metre is not exact, a more relaxed interpretation of its rules is in keeping with the view of Thomas's friends, O. M. Edwards and Gwili, both of whom called for the easing of the strict rules of *cynghanedd*. Thomas's distinctive use of internal rhyme and consonant sounds suggests a poet with an imprecise knowledge of how these devices work in Welsh prosody, but with the vision to experiment with their adaptation into English.

In 'Gone, gone again', the four-syllable lines of the opening stanza manipulate consonant sounds and internal rhyme:

> Gone, gone, again,
> May, June, July,
> And August gone,
> Again gone by. (*ACP*, p. 131)

Here, 'gone' recurs four times in a four-line stanza of four syllables per line, and its consonants are echoed twice in the word 'again'. Even the 'n' sound in 'June' and 'and', as well as the 'g' in 'August', recall the stanza's dominant word. The effect is to disrupt the traditional English ballad stanza of *abcb* to the point at which internal rhyme and repetition of consonants impose a stronger sound pattern onto the verse. While Thomas does not employ a strict *cynghanedd* metre, the techniques central to it – internal rhyme and consonant repetition – effectively revolutionise the traditional form, which is pared down to the extent that it becomes something else.

A similar technique is evident in the bleak opening lines of 'Rain', which allow the internal rhyme of 'rain' and the consonant patterns of 'r' and 'n' to dominate the expected iambic pentameter of the blank verse lines:

> Rain, midnight rain, nothing but the wild rain
> On this bleak hut, and solitude, and me
> Remembering again that I shall die
> And neither hear the rain nor give it thanks
> For washing me cleaner than I have been
> Since I was born into this solitude.
> Blessed are the dead that the rain rains upon. (*ACP*, p. 105)

Here, the repetition of 'rain' three times in the opening line establishes a beat that supersedes the expected iambic rhythm of the blank verse. As a result, it is impossible not to hear 'rain' in the phrase 'remembering again', in the 'rain' of line four, as well as echoes of it in the 'n' of 'been' and 'born', before the spondee of 'rain rains' hammers home the point. This demonstrates how even lines written in the English tradition of blank verse can be utterly altered by techniques of internal rhyme and consonant repetition that have their origins in *cynghanedd*.

Another metre commonly used in Welsh verse is the *triban*, a four-line stanza, usually seven or eight syllables per line, in an *aaba* rhyming pattern, in which the end word in the third line rhymes with a word in the fourth line. Three of Thomas's poems adopt an *aaba* rhyme pattern which, although they do not keep to its strict syllable count, may be an echo of the Welsh *triban* metre. One of them, 'The Ash Grove', mentions a Welsh folk song of the same name, its final stanza reading:

> The song of the Ash Grove soft as love uncrossed
> And then in a crowd or in distance it were lost,
> But that moment unveiled something unwilling to die
> And I had what most I desired, without search or desert or cost.
>
> (*ACP*, p. 108)

The end word in the third line, 'die', is echoed in both 'I' and 'desired' before the caesura of the fourth line. The 'song of the Ash Grove' refers to 'Llwyn Onn', a Welsh harp tune, the most popular version of which was John Jones's interpretation, published in 1862, as 'Gogoniant i Gymru' ('All hail to you, Wales').[24] The first lines of it read:

> Gogoniant i Gymru,
> Anwyl wlad fy nhadau,
> Pe medrwn mawrygwn
> Dy fawredd a'th fri;[25]
>
> (All hail to you, Wales,
> The land of my fathers,
> I would I could make you
> Immortal in song).

While Thomas's version lacks the patriotic lyrics, the *aaba* rhyme pattern (broadly speaking) of Jones's version may have encouraged a similar pattern in Thomas's poem, while the mountains – as in the closing lines of 'The Patriot' – suggest a Welsh setting.

Two more poems adopt a similar *aaba* form. In 'March the Third', the pattern is employed, this time to a stricter pattern of eight-syllable lines, and feature, in three of the five stanzas, a half-rhyme between the end word in the third line and a word in the middle of the fourth.[26] In 'An Old Song I', Thomas adapts the English folksong 'The Lincolnshire Poacher' from an *abab* rhyming pattern to an *aaba* one that echoes the *triban*:

> I was not apprenticed not ever dwelt in famous Lincolnshire;
> I've served one master ill and well much more than seven year;
> And never took up to poaching as you shall quickly find;
> But 'tis my delight of a shiny night in the season of the year.
>
> (*ACP*, p. 46)

Another formal innovation found in Thomas's poetry is the mixing of long and short rhyming couplets, in patterns that involve strict syllable counts. There is a Welsh precedent for this in the metrical form of the *cywydd*. While there are four types of *cywydd*, the most popular, *cywydd deuair hirion*, is a rhyming couplet of seven syllables, written in *cynghanedd*, with each couplet consisting of one stressed and one unstressed final syllable. A second type, *cywydd deuair fyrion*, is a rhyming couplet, also written in *cynghanedd*, in which the first line has seven syllables, and the second line has four. A third type, *cywydd llosgyrnog*, has a more intricate rhyme pattern, one which also involves internal rhyme, and in which there are lines of two, three or four syllables, together with one of seven. Finally, *toddaid byr* is another rhyming couplet in which there are ten syllables in the first line and six in the second.

There is an echo of *toddaid byr* in the opening lines of 'After Rain', which sets up a pattern of rhyming couplets where the first line has nine to eleven syllables, and the second has between four and six:

> The rain of a night and a day and a night
> Stops at the light
> Of this pale choked day. The peering sun (*ACP*, p. 38)

The internal rhyme and sound echoes do not follow a strict pattern, but they occur through most of the poem. In this instance, the first 'night' anticipates the end word of the first line, while the first 'day' anticipates the word before the caesura in line three. Words like 'border', 'trees' and 'leaves' drip through the internal rhyme scheme like the raindrops the poem describes.

Many of Thomas's poems display formal characteristics – in terms of syllable count and rhyme pattern – which have something in common with the Welsh metres described above. For example, the four-syllable line coupled with a rhyming seven- or eight-syllable line that Thomas employs in 'Song' echoes *cywydd deuair fyrion*. A similar syllable pattern is employed in unrhymed lines in the stanzas of 'The New House' and 'Digging'. In 'The Mill-Water', two four-syllable lines are sandwiched between six- and ten-syllable lines. While this clearly adapts the English 'In Memoriam' stanza, it also pays homage to the varied line lengths of the Welsh metre *cywydd*. The formal development that Thomas achieved in 'Words' and 'After you Speak' involves delayed rhyming couplets in which the partner line is distributed at a seemingly random point in the poem. The lines, between two and six syllables in length (or five in the case of 'After you Speak'), also display internal rhyme. Although he departs from the strict syllable counts associated with the traditional use of the Welsh metres, Thomas's experiment here echoes the use of two, three and four syllable lines, together with internal rhyme and couplets in the Welsh metre *cywydd llosgyrnog*.

Thomas is also responsible for another innovation in his use of the single-stanza poem. 'Thaw', 'Cherry Trees', 'In Memoriam' and 'When he should laugh' are discussed by Edna Longley in terms of their relation to Imagism.[27] However, while acknowledging their originality, Longley does not consider a Welsh source for Thomas's innovation in this area: the Welsh *englyn*, the oldest recorded Welsh form, which most commonly occurs as a short single-stanza poem, comparable to the haiku. Although there are rhyme and syllable patterns associated with particular types of *englyn*, it is an adaptable form that can be lyrical or proverbial, epigrammatic, elegiac, or occasional. Thomas's most economical poems, these four-line stanzas, can be read as adaptations of the *englyn* into English-language verse. The *englyn* lends itself to memorials (*NCLW*, p. 219), and Thomas's four-line stanza 'In Memoriam (Easter 1915)' is one such elegiac poem:

> The flowers left thick at nightfall in the wood
> This Eastertide call into mind the men,
> Now far from home, who, with their sweethearts, should
> Have gathered them and will do never again. (*ACP*, p. 80)

The dead soldiers, evoked by describing place – in particular, the presence of the 'flowers left thick' in the wood – recalls the medieval *englynion y beddau* ('the stanzas of the graves') found in *The Black Book of Carmarthen*; they are lyrical and elegiac poems that contrast the activity of a warrior's life with the desolation of his burial place. Here in Thomas's poem, abundance is used to imply absence and desolation. Another one of Thomas's single-stanza quatrain poems is the little-commented-on 'When he should laugh', which has an epigrammatic, proverbial quality and a humorous tone that is reminiscent of the *englyn*.

One of the characteristics of *englyn unodl union*, a popular form of *englyn*, is an initial rhyming couplet in which the first line consists of ten syllables and the second, six. The end-rhyme of the first line is anticipated in the seventh syllable of the same line, while the remaining syllables, or the *cyrch*, form *cynghanedd* with the syllables of the second line (in other words, they repeat the consonant pattern). The opening line of 'Head and

Bottle', another short, single-stanza poem, is an almost perfect adaptation of the form into English: 'The downs will lose the *sun*, white a**lyssum** / **Lo**se the bee**s**' hu**m**' (*ACP*, p. 81). Here, a ten-syllable line is followed by a four, a pattern that is broadly repeated through the poem. The sixth syllable of the first line, 'sun', half-rhymes with the end-rhyme 'sum', while the pattern of consonants in the *cyrch* of 'white alyssum' ('l', 's', 'm') forms near-*cynghanedd* with the consonants at the end of the first foot ('l', 'z', 'n' in 'lose the sun'), and forms near-*cynghanedd* with the syllables in the second line ('l', 'z', 'm' in 'lose the bees' hum').

In its metrical and formal innovations, Thomas's poetry, as we have seen, shows the influence of the classic, ancient Welsh-language poetic tradition. And, as if complementing this, the concerns of the Welsh folk and literary traditions also pervade the subject matter of Thomas's poetry. As we shall see, specific references occur in such poems as 'The Ash Grove', 'The Child on the Cliffs', 'Roads', 'Words', 'Man and Dog', 'The Wind's Song' and the 'cuckoo poems'. In addition to these, there are buried allusions to these sources in many of the concerns that feature most strongly in Thomas's poetry, including the idea of a shared language with the birds, and the hope for 'a language not to be betrayed'. Other allusions include Thomas's adaptation of the Welsh vaticinatory – or prophetic – tradition, and his adaptation of Candlemas poetry. The rest of this chapter sets out these connections in more detail.

'The Ash Grove', as we have seen, imagines a girl singing the Welsh folk song of the same name, but specific references to Welsh folk stories do not stop there. 'The Child on the Cliffs' alludes to the folk story of Cantre'r Gwaelod, its speaker, sitting on a cliff, hearing bells from the submerged city off the Welsh coast:

> Fishes and gulls ring no bells. There cannot be
> A chapel or church between here and Devon,
> With fishes or gulls ringing its bell, – hark! – (*ACP*, p. 65)

Thomas mentions this myth in *Beautiful Wales* and in *Rest and Unrest*. The poem 'Roads' mentions Helen, from 'The Dream of Macsen' in the *Mabinogion*, a character previously mentioned in *The Icknield Way*, and whose story is retold at greater length in *Celtic Stories*:

> Helen of the roads,
> The mountain ways of Wales
> And the *Mabinogion* tales,
> Is one of the true gods

. . .
And it is her laughter
At morn and night I hear (*ACP*, p. 106)

There is another specific reference to Welsh literary material, this time to popular seventeenth-century poetry, in 'Words', one line of which reads: 'Wales / Whose nightingales / Have no wings' (*ACP*, p. 92). These wingless Welsh nightingales are the Welsh poets given the pseudonym 'Eos' or 'nightingale', one of whom is the poet Huw Morus, referred to in *Beautiful Wales* as 'Eos Ceiriog' or 'the Nightingale of Ceiriog' (*BW*, p. 5). The central lines of 'Words' describe a culture whose words are 'old / worn new / again and again'. This echoes Thomas's translation of the Welsh folk song 'Eluned' (again in *Beautiful Wales*), in which Eluned's singing 'made the new [songs] / Seem old, and the old / As if they were just born' (*BW*, p. 82). This context suggests that the line in 'Words', 'Choose me, you English words', may be read as that of a poet from outside the English nation, but one who nonetheless writes in the English language, as indeed is implied by the main inversion here: that the words choose the poet rather than vice versa (*ACP*, p. 92).

Another reference to literary material concerns the ninth-century *englyn* sequence, 'Llywarch Hen', a cycle of monologues and dialogues about an old man and his sons who have gone off to war. In one of these, 'Cân yr Henwr' ('The Song of the Old Man'), Llywarch, now lame, muses on old age, reflecting on what he achieved in his youth and on his sons who have gone off to their deaths in battle. The poem ends when he laments his impending death, suggested in the image of a leaf blown by the wind. Thomas refers in *Beautiful Wales* to 'the poem of the old princely warrior Llywarch Hên' (*BW*, p. 39), and his poem, 'Man and Dog' is surely a modern-day retelling of 'The Song of the Old Man'. It is a dialogue poem that describes a chance meeting with an 'old man... straight but lame', who reflects on what he has done 'since he left Christchurch in the New Forest, one / Spring in the seventies' (*ACP*, p. 57). Like Llywarch, who hints at his impending death, the old man tells the poem's speaker that he will soon 'fall' 'to another world' (*ACP*, p. 57). His sons, like those of Llywarch, are soldiers ('His sons, three sons, were fighting'), and again like the character in the *englyn*, he is compared to a wind-blown leaf in a way that suggests death:

Stiffly, he plodded;
And at his heels the crisp leaves scurried fast,

> And the leaf-coloured robin watched. They passed,
> The robin till next day, the man for good. (*ACP*, p. 57)

There is a clue to the Welsh origins of the old man in the description of his dog: 'the small brown bitch / With spots of blue / [whose] foxy Welsh grandfather must have paired / Beneath him. He kept sheep in Wales and scared / Off strangers, I will warrant' (*ACP*, p. 57).

In Welsh tradition, the cuckoo is associated with death, a connection that has its origins in 'Cyntefin Ceinaf Amser', a series of stanzas in *The Black Book of Carmarthen*, in which positive descriptions of spring always end in a cuckoo's call evoking memories of the dead. The noted scholar, Ifor Williams, suggested that the constant repetition of 'cw', which in Old Welsh means 'where?', reminds the poet of kinsmen who had died, as if the cuckoo is asking 'where are they? where have they gone?' (*NCLW*, p. 141). R. S. Thomas rather intuitively suggests that his namesake's interest in cuckoos stems from 'lines such as Llywarch Hen's "Yn Aber Cuawc yt gagnant gogeu" – "At Abercuawg the cuckoos sing" [which] seems to have fascinated Thomas'.[28] Three of Thomas's poems refer to the cuckoo, 'The Cuckoo', 'Melancholy' and 'She dotes', and all of them make the association between the cuckoo and death. The first of these depicts an old man, now deaf, who says that 'even if I could lose my deafness / The cuckoo's note would be drowned by the voice of my dead' (*ACP*, p. 54). 'She dotes', which describes a woman who does not understand her lover's death, perhaps in war, ends with the seemingly inexplicable line 'And she has slept, trying to translate / The word the cuckoo cries to his mate / Over and over' (*ACP*, p. 84). Finally, 'Melancholy' ends with:

> All day long I heard a distant cuckoo calling
> And, soft as dulcimers, sounds of near water falling,
> And, softer, and remote as if in history,
> Rumours of what had touched my friends, my foes, or me
> (*ACP*, p. 85)

While 'dulcimers' clearly allude to Coleridge's 'Kubla Khan', the way that the cuckoo evokes memory of the dead suggests that Thomas is here updating this Welsh tradition into the present day, as well as establishing an English-language Welsh tradition. This is not as far-fetched as it might seem: as early as 1898, Thomas had written, in a letter to Helen Noble, of his love for Welsh poetry, concluding that his work 'would have given me a sort of name if written in Welsh; even in English I might do something by writing of Wales'.[29] This suggests his regret at not being proficient in Welsh, and offers, incidentally, an interpretation of the 1899 diary entry mentioned in the last chapter in which, on singing the 'Gwlad Gwlad' of the national anthem, Thomas wrote that his 'heart broke with thoughts of what I might be and am not'. It implies, too, that, well before his turn to poetry, Thomas was aware of the possibility of writing at a point where the two linguistic traditions meet.

The title of Thomas's poem 'The Wind's Song' echoes 'Canu y Gwynt' ('The Song of the Wind'), found in *The Book of Taliesin*. It is the inspiration for Dafydd ap Gwilym's fourteenth-century *cywydd* 'Y Gwynt' ('The Wind'). As we have seen, Thomas was familiar with the sixth-century work of Taliesin (including one of his poems in his 1907 *Pocket Book of Poems and Songs for the Open Air*) and with the poetry of Dafydd ap Gwilym (translations of whose work he reviewed). In Thomas's similarly titled poem, the speaker muses that 'there could be no old song so sad / As the wind's song; but later none so glad / Could I remember as that same wind's song' (*ACP*, p. 118). While these lines obviously refer to the wind itself, the poem also seems to suggest the existence of more than one 'song' of the wind, an oblique nod, perhaps, to the poems of Taliesin and ap Gwilym. Again, the implication is that Thomas is extending this native Welsh-language tradition into English.

Aside from the specific references to Welsh cultural material, the thematic concerns of its lore, legends and poetic tradition often feature in Thomas's poetry. The idea of a shared language with the birds is a frequently recurring motif. In 'March', the speaker describes the communication between him and the thrushes: 'Something they knew – I also, while they sang / And after' (*ACP*, p. 35). In 'The Unknown Bird', the speaker remarks that 'I alone could hear him / Though many listened' (*ACP*, p. 55). In 'The Owl', 'the bird's voice' is 'telling me plain what I escaped'. It is 'speaking for all who lay under the stars, / Soldiers and poor, unable to rejoice' (*ACP*, p. 65). 'Home' links speaker and migrating birds: 'one nationality / We had, I and the birds that sang, / One memory' (*ACP*, p. 81). In 'She dotes', the female speaker 'dotes on what the wild birds say / Or hint or mock at'. Here, the 'hawk, heron, owl, and woodpecker . . . / Never say a word to her / About her lover'; she is instead 'trying to translate / The word the cuckoo cries to his mate' (*ACP*, p. 84). 'Sedge-Warblers' refers to 'the small brown birds / Wisely reiterating endlessly / What no man learnt yet, in or out of school' (*ACP*, p. 91). Finally, 'The Word' describes how the speaker cannot forget 'a pure thrush word' that 'some thrushes learn to say' (*ACP*, p. 93). While these references to understanding the language of birds are part of a common European medieval inheritance, including Geoffrey Chaucer's *Parlement of Fowles*, they also have their origin in the *Mabinogion* tale of 'Culhwch and Olwen', retold by Thomas in *Celtic Stories*. In this story, Thomas writes about 'Gwyhyr' (Gwrhyr), 'who knew all tongues of men and birds and beasts', and who helps Culhwch fulfil his quests and marry Olwen (*CS*, p. 95). These involve talking to 'the Blackbird of Cilgwri' (*CS*, p. 103), 'the Owl of Cwm Cawlwyd' (*CS*, p. 104), and the Eagle of Gwernabwy (*CS*, p. 105), to which Thomas also refers in *Beautiful Wales*.

In the story of 'Lludd and Llefelys', which appears in the *Mabinogion* as well as in a thirteenth-century Welsh translation of Geoffrey of Monmouth's *History of the Kings of Britain*, the Coraniaid invade Britain. According to Sioned Davies, this is a misreading of 'Cesariaid', the Romans.[30] One of their legendary attributes, which enables them to conquer part of the island, is remarkable hearing. The wind betrays the native Welsh, carrying their conversation to the ears of the invaders, forewarning them of any plans to repel them. This suggests a reading of Thomas's 'I never saw that land before', the third stanza of which refers to 'the breeze / That hinted all and nothing spoke' (*ACP*, p. 120). In the final two stanzas, the speaker declares:

> if I could sing
> What would not even whisper my soul
> As I went on my journeying,
>
> I should use, as the trees and birds did,
> A language not to be betrayed;
> And what was hid should still be hid
> Excepting from those like me made
> Who answer when such whispers bid. (*ACP*, p. 120)

The idea of a language that is 'not to be betrayed' alludes, within the Welsh tradition, to hopes of resisting invaders, and possibly to the contemporary suppression of the Welsh language. The notion that the 'birds', unlike humans, speak a language which is 'not to be betrayed' recalls Gwrhyr, who, as we have seen, 'knew all tongues of men and birds and beasts' (*CS*, p. 95). This language puts Thomas's speaker in the privileged position, like Gwrhyr, of being the only one, 'excepting from those like me made', to understand it.

Another of the traditions of Welsh literature is vaticination, or prophetic poetry, which had its origins in poetry that anticipated, among
other things, 'that the Welsh will regain sovereignty over the Isle of
Britain . . . and the English will be defeated for all time' (*NCLW*, p. 753).
Gwyn A. Williams describes prophetic poetry as 'an underground verse,
anti-English, . . . expressly political and couched in the terms of redemption
by a political saviour' (*WWWH*, p. 103). An example occurs in the folk
tale 'Hanes Taliesin' ('The Story of Taliesin'). The story goes that
Ceridwen's son, Afagddu, is to be given the power of foreknowledge in
order to compensate him for his ugliness. This power comes from a potion
that must be stirred for a year in the 'Cauldron of Foreknowledge'.
Ceridwen appoints her little servant boy Gwion to this task, while she adds
the necessary ingredients. At the end of the year, three drops intended for
Afagddu spill onto Gwion's finger, which he puts in his mouth, acquiring
knowledge of the future. He flees from a wrathful Ceridwen, shape-
changing into various animals. The final metamorphosis sees him become
a grain of wheat and she a hen that promptly consumes him. But after a
nine-month gestation period, she gives birth to a beautiful boy (Tal-iesin
means 'beautiful brow') who grows up to become the magician Taliesin.
In popular memory, over time, this magus became conflated with the
sixth-century poet Taliesin, who, thanks to this association, comes to be
seen as a poet-prophet.

Thomas's poetry is often conversely concerned with the speaker's
inability to predict what the future holds. This has rightly been attributed
to the immediate historical situation in 1915, in particular his decision
whether to go to America or enlist, and the likelihood of death at the front,
but it is also part of the longer, Welsh tradition of vaticinatory verse. For
example, in 'This is no case of petty right or wrong', the speaker, 'dinned /
with war and argument', turns to the vaticinatory tradition:

> Two witches' cauldrons roar.
> From one the weather shall rise clear and gay;
> Out of the other an England beautiful
> And like her mother that died yesterday.
> Little I know or care if, being dull,
> I shall miss something that historians
> Can rake out of the ashes when perchance
> The phoenix broods serene above their ken. (*ACP*, p. 104)

The 'two witches' cauldrons' are certainly connected with the idea of
predicting the future outcome of the war, and have an obvious literary

precedent in Shakespeare's *Macbeth*. However, given Thomas's knowledge of the Welsh literary tradition, it is plausible that one of the cauldrons is the 'Cauldron of Foreknowledge' from 'Hanes Taliesin'. The poem suggests the impossibility of knowing what 'historians' will say about the present moment in time and, thereby, about the future. In a sense, therefore, the poem is a meeting between 'witches' and 'historians', between the vaticinatory tradition of a divined future, and the modern view of an indifferent, historical time. The second cauldron in the poem may allude to one from another tale in the Welsh tradition, also connected with war: the so-called 'Cauldron of Rebirth' in the story of Bran, retold by Thomas in *Celtic Stories*. As any dead person who is placed in the cauldron will rise from it reborn, it is taken by the Welsh to Ireland as a means of guaranteeing victory in war. It is, however, used instead by the Irish, with the result that the Welsh are defeated. In Thomas's poem, the image of 'the phoenix' risen 'perchance' from the 'ashes' alludes to this second cauldron. It undermines the speaker's confidence that, after the war, 'an England' shall 'rise', while the use of 'an' questions what sort of nation it will be. In spite of the poem's rather forced ending in which the speaker pledges his allegiance to England, it succeeds in undermining the country's moral case, subverting its anti-German propaganda, distancing its speaker from the media's jingoistic patriotism, and implying that the outcome of the war is far from clear.

Other poems which seem to conduct a conversation with this prophetic tradition include 'No one cares less than I', 'As the team's head-brass', 'It was upon' and 'How at Once'. The last is another poem in which vaticinatory verse meets historical cataclysm. The opening image of 'the swift's black bow' 'stretched in the harvest blue' captures the present moment in a reassuring way. The speaker knows that one day, some time in August, the swift will migrate, suddenly and without warning, but that it will return 'next May'. The second stanza develops this meditation on the present and the future by alluding to the war and the changes it brings: 'With other things I but fear / That they will be over and done / Suddenly / And I only see / Them to know them gone' (*ACP*, p. 130). Time here has become historical. There is no prospect of return next year, only the possibility that what he sees will suddenly disappear.

'It was upon' recalls a July evening twenty years previously, when a passing 'stranger', 'a wandering man', predicts that 'the lattermath / Will be a fine one' (*ACP*, p. 126). The lattermath is a late harvesting of the grass for winter hay. The speaker recalls how, at this 'prophecy', he was 'flushed with desire'. Like Gwion in 'Hanes Taliesin', he had acquired knowledge of what was to happen: 'the earth outspread, / Like meadows of the future, I possessed' (*ACP*, p. 126). The poem then fast-forwards twenty years to the same speaker who can now only ask the 'question, wondering, / What of the lattermath to *this* hoar Spring?' (my italics). In the 'interval' of 'twenty years', the speaker seems to have entered history, and become swept up in events for which there is no certain future.

Similar themes are explored in 'As the team's head-brass'. Thomas employs reported speech stretched over blank verse, which captures in its enjambment and mid-line caesuras the rhythm of the dialogue between Thomas and a ploughman, a conversation characterised by long periods of silence and snippets of talk as the plough team turns. The war, the dominant subject of their conversation, has irrevocably changed the world in which they live: the fallen tree on which Thomas sits would have been cleared were it not for the war, and one of the farm workers has been killed. Only two teams work on the farm this year, the rest having gone to France. The subtext is the men's attempts to come to terms with the changes brought by war: Thomas tells the ploughman that were it not for war, 'I should not have sat here. Everything / Would have been different. For it would have been / Another world', to which the ploughman replies, 'If we could see all all might seem good' (*ACP*, p. 123). The implication is that, in this brave new world, foreknowledge is impossible. History affects participants and onlookers alike. An individual's fate is in the hands of an indifferent history. The thwarted vaticinatory poet, who now knows he belongs only to the world of 'the ploughshare and the stumbling team', turns lines as the ploughman his furrow, 'for the last time'.

Another facet of literature that depicts a future where enemies are vanquished, is the tradition of poems and stories in which the pain of past defeat is forgotten. In the story of 'Bran and Bronwen', adapted from the *Mabinogion* in Thomas's *Celtic Stories*, the Welsh leaders who survive defeat in Ireland return to Harlech, where, 'as they sat eating and drinking, the three birds of Rhiannon flitted up into the darkness of the rafters and began singing' (*CS*, p. 90). The birdsong induces memory loss: 'they were seven years sitting at this repast and listening to the birds of Rhiannon, and the seven years were no longer than a summer's day' (*CS*, p. 90). This is followed by a journey to the island of Gwales on which 'they remembered nothing of the past' until, opening a door they had been told not to open, 'they remembered all things, their misery and losses, just as they had happened and as freshly as if those eighty years had never been' (*CS*, p. 90). It is significant that this loss of memory with its loss of the past, is associated in the Welsh tradition with national defeat. It suggests a context in which those many poems by Thomas that are concerned with feeling unmoored in time may be read. For example, Thomas's second poem 'Home' begins:

> Often I had gone this way before:
> But now it seemed I never could be
> And never had been anywhere else
> 'Twas home; one nationality
> We had, I, and the birds that sang,
> One memory.
>
> They welcomed me. I had come back
> That eve somehow from somewhere far:
> The April mist, the chill, the calm,
> Meant the same thing, familiar
> And pleasant to us, and strange too,
> Yet with no bar. (*ACP*, p. 81)

Thomas's use of the word 'home' will be further discussed in Chapter Six. In this instance, its association with a 'nationality' that seems to have an ethereal or 'out of time' quality to it suggests parallels with the Welsh situation. The poem is not a retelling of the 'Bran and Branwen' story: it seems to be set in the Hampshire village in which Thomas lived. None-theless, the connection between 'the birds that sang' and loss of memory, and the poem's defamiliarisation of the speaker's experience of return, all suggest parallels to the story that Thomas had retold four years before in *Celtic Stories*.

Another Welsh folk tradition involves poets wishing success to crops at Gŵyl Fair (Candlemas): the seeds are blessed, there is usually a refer-ence to the cold weather, and this is contrasted to the hearth and the hoped-for kisses from the women inside. In 'Sowing', Thomas alludes to this tradition. Written at the right time of year, on 23 March 1915, the poem looks back on 'a perfect day / For sowing'. The speaker works at dusk, 'between the far / Owl's chuckling first soft cry / And the first star', until, 'the early seeds / All safely sown', he returns inside, from where he listens to 'the rain / Windless and light / Half a kiss, half a tear, / Saying good-night' (*ACP*, p. 69). The key elements of the Welsh tradition are all present in the poem, even if the hoped-for kisses have been transmuted into the rain's 'half a kiss'.

Finally, 'I built myself a house of glass', a two-quatrain poem, refers twice to a building made of glass: 'a house of glass' and a 'palace of glass'. Edna Longley rightly suggests the presence in this poem of the proverb 'people in glasshouses should not throw stones' (*ELN*, p. 242), as well as the connection to a story Thomas tells in his 1915 book *Four-and-Twenty Blackbirds*. However, the 'palace of glass' is also associated with the underworld in the pre-Norman poem 'Preiddiau Annwfn' ('The Spoils of Annwfn'), a poem in *The Book of Taliesin*; the underworld is here depicted as a four-cornered glass fortress. The poem's reference to a 'palace of glass' in which neighbours live 'alone' may, exploiting this Welsh tradition, allude to the presence, in the midst of those left behind, of the dead. This would then involve an oblique reference, through the Welsh tradition, to the slaughter at the front (*ACP*, p. 91).

As I hope the foregoing discussion has demonstrated, it has proved fruitful to approach Thomas's work through stage one of Casanova's 'Irish paradigm'. It has enabled the unearthing of a weight of evidence that suggests the centrality of many aspects of the Welsh cultural tradition to his work (folklore and popular poetry, as well as ancient Welsh historiography, the *barddas* tradition, the *Mabinogion* and classic medieval poetry), evidence that has, for almost a century, been overlooked by critics on both sides of the border. To recover it is to begin to reposition Thomas as a Welsh writer, one of the first in the English-language Welsh tradition to import such a wide range of Welsh cultural references into his work. The next two chapters will continue this process by viewing his work through subsequent 'potentialities' offered by a revised version of Casanova's developmental model. Building on the Welsh foundation established in this chapter, it will be argued that Thomas should be read, not as the 'quintessentially English' figure so often described by English critics, nor as the traitorous Welshman depicted by Tony Conran, but, through a more transnational prism, as a subversive figure operating within British literary space.

5

Edward Thomas and English 'as a foreign tongue'

The previous chapter, which built on the modifications to Casanova's theory proposed in Chapter One, looked at Thomas through the prism of stage one of Casanova's 'Irish paradigm', showing the extent of his use of material from the Welsh cultural tradition. Another modification to Casanova's model, also suggested in Chapter One, amended her 'Irish paradigm' so as make it less deterministic in its use of history. That allowed her model to be more loosely applied by dispensing with the need to confine a writer to one of its stages alone, and indeed replacing the presupposition of a chronology inherent in Casanova's stages with the notion of potentialities. This chapter therefore considers Thomas from the perspective of the fourth stage or potentiality in Casanova's 'Irish paradigm'. This concentrates on the 'marginal' writer's ostensible assimilation to a dominant cultural centre that he or she then proceeds to subvert. For Casanova its best exemplar is the career of George Bernard Shaw. I shall argue that Thomas likewise uses his chosen position as a Welsh writer to subvert Anglocentric British literary space in specific ways. The first part of my argument suggests that his literary journalism demonstrates an interest in writing in the English language by non-English writers, especially those from Ireland and the United States. Here I also argue that his work is less ideologically opposed to the modernist ideas of Ezra Pound than subsequent critics have suggested. The second part of this chapter contends that Thomas challenges the provincialism of British literary space by importing into it the lessons of French symbolism, especially the work of Paul Verlaine and Maurice Maeterlinck. The final part of my argument, again mainly based on his literary journalism, reveals his positive reviews of gay writers and critics at a time when, in the aftermath of the Oscar Wilde trial, it was dangerous to do so.

The fourth stage in Casanova's 'Irish paradigm' rescues Shaw and other exiles like him from their excommunication from national literary history. She argues that in spite of his exile in London and his ostensible rejection of Irish nationalist values, Shaw nonetheless subverted British norms from within. By rejecting the way nationalist Ireland appropriated literature for political purposes, and by moving to London in order to write as an Irishman without political interference, Shaw, argues Casanova, performed a vital function in the eventual establishment of a national literary space within Ireland. As I proposed in Chapter One, Casanova's argument that a writer in a literary centre is able to operate without political interference is flawed, as is her idea that by writing in London he necessarily contributes to what she calls the 'autonomy' of Irish writers. Nonetheless, I want to retain her useful idea that Shaw subverts British space and that, in this, there is a structural similarity between him and Thomas. In this argument, of course, Casanova follows in the wake of the Irish critic Declan Kiberd who, in 1995, made the case for Shaw's importance to Irish literary history by including him in his groundbreaking study *Inventing Ireland*. Shaw, he argues, 'used England as a laboratory in which he could define what it meant to be Irish'.[1]

Casanova makes some of her argument through the case of Norway. She argues that by the end of the nineteenth century, Norway, partly through its writers, had gained autonomy from Danish occupation, and thereby become an example to other dominated small nations (*WRL*, p. 248). She traces how Joyce in particular uses the Paris-based, Norwegian playwright, Henrik Ibsen, the 'self-exiled playwright', as a means of attacking the icon of English literary space, Shakespeare (ibid.). In this, she argues, Joyce developed the subversive work of Shaw whose life in England 'made him highly sensitive to the problems faced by an author from a country on the periphery of the European literary world' (*WRL*, p. 161). Following the 1889 premiere of *Peer Gynt*, Shaw promoted Ibsen, an act which was one of 'the first signs of international recognition of Norwegian culture' and which simultaneously drew attention to 'the hegemonic instincts of the English' (ibid.). Welsh interest in Ibsen at this time would bear sustained examination, but in the present context it is more important to note that Thomas too promoted Ibsen's work in London. He reviewed *Selections from Peer Gynt* in the *Morning Post* on 24 May 1909, while a letter dated 12 December 1904 reveals his early interest in Grieg, who wrote the music for the play (*LGB*, p. 171). Nevertheless, during the first and second decades of the twentieth century, the main inspiration for writers from a small country like Wales, dominated by an Anglocentric Britain, was Ireland, a country which, through its literary revival, had reasserted its cultural independence from Britain, and reignited its aspirations for political independence.

Thomas's interest in the dissemination of traditional Welsh materials leads him both to its Irish equivalent, and to the writers most associated with its *littérisation* in Ireland. This is evident in Thomas's correspondence, review work, published prose and his poetry. As we have seen, Edna Longley argues that 'Thomas's "England"' contains 'trace elements of Yeats's Ireland, Frost's New England, and bardic Wales' but her notion of 'trace elements' effectively romanticises these places and subsumes them into a Greater England.[2] Elsewhere, by stating that his 'main allegiance' was to the 'English literary tradition', which is then contrasted with 'American and Irish rebellion', Longley suggests Thomas's minimal interest in both these nations' literary scenes, as well as that of the Welsh (*PW*, p. 32). Contrary to her assertion, Irish writers are a major interest and an inspiring example to Thomas. In making this case, I hope to complicate further his critical reputation as a 'quintessentially English' poet, and to suggest that, as a writer whose main allegiance is to Wales, he found common cause with writers of the Irish Revival at the very time when the Irish example was a compelling one for many associated with the Cymru Fydd movement.

The main form through which Thomas promoted Irish writing was his literary journalism. Casanova identifies eight Irish writers who were responsible for the nascent Irish folk tradition at the turn of the twentieth century: W. B. Yeats, Lady Gregory, Edward Martyn, George Moore, George Russell, Pádraic Colum, J. M. Synge and James Stephens (*WRL*, p. 305). Collectively, according to Casanova, these writers 'undertook to manufacture a national literature out of oral practices, collecting, transcribing, translating, and rewriting Celtic tales and legends' (ibid.). Thomas consistently used his position as an influential London reviewer to promote writers associated with the Irish Revival (including authors not mentioned by Casanova). Incredibly, with the exception of Martyn, Thomas reviewed all the Irish writers she mentions here, as well as others. He finds in emerging Irish literature a parallel in which Welsh writers and scholars are found lacking, and he exploits the difference to urge on the Welsh.

Thomas views Yeats as a leader of 'the modern Irish movement in English', which he describes in the *Morning Post* on 13 April 1908 as a movement with the 'driving power [of] sincerity illumined by vision'

(*R*, vol. 4, p. 59). Between 1902 and 1909, Yeats was reviewed by Thomas on at least eleven occasions. In his review of *Celtic Twilight* in the *Week's Survey* on 13 September 1902, Thomas argues that the work emerges out of 'notes from the talk of Irish peasants about fairies and ghosts' (*R*, vol. 3, p. 2). The comment suggests an awareness of the potency of Yeats's *littérisation* of folk material, and the status that such efforts had achieved for his national literature: there is good reason, Thomas argues, 'for comparing the Irish with the Greek mythology' (*R*, vol. 1, p. 99). Thomas's interest in Yeats's work extends not only to the practice of turning folk material into a national literature centred on an idealised peasantry, but also to Yeats's attempts to build readerships and audiences for this kind of work. Yeats, he argues, 'is gazing as much forward as backward', and he hints at Yeats's political project when he notes how revisions to *The Shadowy Waters* 'bring his scenes a little nearer to life as the majority know it by touches of common speech or thought' (*R*, vol. 4, p. 100). Thomas's interest in Yeats's drama can be seen in the same light. In 1903, he read the *United Irishman* in which Yeats had published his play, *Where There is Nothing* (*LGB*, p. 46). In a 1907 letter he writes that *Deirdre* (which was reviewed by Thomas in the *Daily Chronicle* on 28 September 1907, and in the *Bookman* in October 1907) 'is perhaps the most perfect thing Yeats has done' (*LGB*, p. 151). Horatio Sheafe Krans's *William Butler Yeats and the Irish Literary Revival* was negatively reviewed by Thomas in the *Daily Chronicle* on 22 April 1905:

> [Krans] begins with a mistake, and goes on with a mistake, and ends with a mistake. For he is not content to deal with Mr Yeats alone; nor, on the other hand, has he space or desire to examine the domestic or literary history of his time . . . He leaves history alone. (*R*, vol. 2, p. 66)

Thomas's comments suggest not only an interest in how Yeats's work might be read in its 'domestic' or immediate historical context, but also a firm belief that it should.

There are other references to Yeats in Thomas's prose: the epigraph at the beginning of his book *The South Country* is a long quotation from Yeats's play *Where There Is Nothing*, the title of which is also suggested in lines in Thomas's poem 'The Mountain Chapel': 'Till there is nothing I shall be' (*ACP*, p. 43). Other poems in which Yeats's work is alluded to include 'The Lofty Sky'; here the line 'I / Would arise and go far / To where the lilies are' echoes 'The Lake Isle of Inisfree' (*ACP*, p. 53). Finally, *The Heart of England* ends with a Yeats poem, 'The Song of the Happy Shepherd' from *Crossways* (1889), which is quoted in full.

In his review of Yeats's *Collected Works* in the *Morning Post* on 17 December 1908, Thomas argues that Celtic literature cannot simply be seen in Arnoldian terms as a corrective for the philistine English middle classes: 'many must have suspected that Arnold was too definite and simple on this difficult matter'. Instead, he endorses Yeats's point that 'the Celtic alone has been for centuries close to the main river of European literature' (*R*, vol. 5, p. 32). While the focus on a Celtic tradition in the European mainstream marginalises the English tradition, it is, as Daniel Williams has pointed out, 'difficult to see how [Yeats's] analysis modifies Arnold's argument in any way'.[3] Thomas, importantly, goes further. In this review, he describes Yeats as a leader of the 'modern Irish movement in English', a phrase that stresses his Irishness (not simply his 'pan-Celtic' qualities), and hints at the usefulness of 'Celtic' as a basis for further classifications along national lines ('Irish' is used in this review and 'Welsh', as we shall see, is employed elsewhere).[4]

In *Beautiful Wales*, Thomas distinguishes between a romanticised, 'English' use of the word 'Celt', and a different use that suggests, in more hard-headed terms, the difference of the Welsh and Irish from the English. He describes authors who are 'lovers of the Celt' as writers who 'go about the world in a state of self-satisfied dejection, interrupted, and perhaps sustained, by days when they consume strange mixed liquors to the tune of all the fine old Celtic songs which are fashionable' (*BW*, p. 10). He accuses such writers of being 'a class of "decadents" . . . preferring *crème de menthe* and *opal hush* to metheglin or stout', and angrily parodies them for their self-fulfilling mentality of self-defeatism: 'that *once we were*, is all we have left to boast of; that *once we were*, we have record upon record' (*BW*, p. 11). This is a charge repeated elsewhere in *Beautiful Wales* where Thomas describes Owen the innkeeper as 'a perfect Celt according to the English superstition. For there never was such a failure who was also such a swaggerer as he' (*BW*, p. 59). These critiques of Celtic defeatism are significant. Daniel Williams refers to Yeats's failure to challenge such associations, pointing out, indeed, that Yeats 'repeats Arnold's view that it is the Celts' "conquered" status that gives them their insights into "charms", "dreams" and "visions"' (*ECA*, p. 128). Williams's reading here offers a challenge to the widely held view that Yeats 'appropriate[s] the stereotypes ascribed to his people by an imperial power and turns them into positive attributes', views most influentially put forward by Robert Welch and Edward Said (*ECA*, p. 131). Thomas's dismissal of the association of the Celtic nations with defeat as an 'English superstition' is therefore significant. It anticipates postcolonial insights into the ways in which a colonising power maintains the myth of its own supremacy, as well as providing an example of how a writer from a dominated nation begins the process of 'decolonising the mind' (not to mention proving a clearer example than Yeats for so doing).

Thomas goes on to write that he prefers 'the kind of Celt whom I met in Wales one August night' (*BW*, p. 13), a man who, 'finding that I could pronounce Bwlch-y-Rhiw, was willing to talk and share the beer in my satchel' (*BW*, p. 14). The distinction between the two types of Celt is significant: Thomas's 'kind of Celt' is also identified with a nation, in this case Wales. The speaker meets him halfway (literally in 'the shelter of a bridge'), makes the effort to learn his language, and shares his (non-decadent) drink (*BW*, p. 13). Thomas goes on to describe this man as one who 'played many parts – he was always playing . . . he had been a booking-office clerk, a soldier, a policeman, a gamekeeper, and put down what he called his variability to "the feminine gender"' (*BW*, p. 14). Thomas's description, in the way it connects Wales, the feminine, and the role-playing necessary to the different jobs undertaken in a colonised society, anticipates (without fully articulating) postcolonial insights into the hybridity and gendering of those in colonial situations.

Thomas reviewed J. M. Synge at least four times: *The Shadow of the Glen* and *Riders to the Sea* were reviewed by him in the *Daily Chronicle* on 19 July 1905, while *The Playboy of the Western World* (a play that Thomas saw when it came to London), was covered in the same paper on 13 September 1907 and in the August 1907 *Bookman*. In this latter review, Thomas argues that the effect of 'Irishmen, like Messrs Yeats and Synge' is comparable to that of Coleridge and Wordsworth in *Lyrical Ballads* (*R*, vol. 3, p. 81). In his *Daily Chronicle* review of the same play, Thomas demonstrates an awareness of its controversial Irish reception: 'This play caused a disturbance at the Abbey Theatre in Dublin, one paper saying it was a "gross and wanton insult to the Irish people"; and it turns out to be a very good play' (*R*, vol. 4, p. 36). The same positive response to Synge's work is evident in Thomas's correspondence: 'but *The Playboy*. Have you read and seen it? I daresay it is the greatest play of modern times . . ., utterly new and altogether fine' (*LGB*, p. 189). Synge's *Poems and Translations*, reviewed in the *Daily Chronicle* on 26 July 1909, was also privately praised: 'Have you seen Synge's poems? They are raw poetry and something more – wonderfully lean and bare and yet compelling us to clothe them in the warm and radiant life which they disdain' (*LGB*, p. 190).

Thomas's interest in Irish writers extends beyond Yeats and Synge. In January 1908, he reviewed Lady Gregory's *Saints and Wonders* for the *Bookman*, while his book *The South Country* refers to her 'Irish tale of the poor old blind woman who recovered her sight at St Brigit's well' (*SC*, p. 26). In the *Daily Chronicle* of 1 July 1911, he reviewed George Moore's *The Apostle*. He also reviewed George Russell's *The Divine Vision and Other Poems* in the *Week's Survey* on 7 May 1904, while Russell's *Collected Poems* was covered in the *Daily Chronicle* in September 1913. James Stephens was reviewed twice by Thomas: his *Hill of Vision* in the *Daily Chronicle* on 19 April 1912, and *Insurrections* in the *Morning Post* on 19 June 1908. Thomas also reviewed at least four works by Pádraic Colum.[5] He remarks too that he corresponded with Colum and indicates his intention to read Colum's *New Songs: a Lyric Selection* (1904), observing that Colum is 'quite important in Dublin, I hear' (*LGB*, p. 123). Other writers of the Irish Literary Revival whom Thomas reviewed include Katherine Tynan, Joseph Campbell, Alfred Percival Graves, Seosamh Mac Cathmhaoil and Thomas MacDonagh. The latter was one of the subsequently executed leaders of the Easter Rising, immortalised in Yeats's poem 'Easter 1916'; Thomas wrote in the *Bookman* in April 1913 that MacDonagh's work contains 'much promise' (*R*, vol. 6, p. 129).

Some of Thomas's reviews contrast the effectiveness of translations from Irish- and Welsh-language literature. A review of Evelyn Lewes's *Life and Poems of Dafydd ap Gwilym*, published in the *Daily News* on 24 April 1914, leads Thomas into making the comparison:

> That there is not a volume of translations from Dafydd [ap Gwilym] and the other half dozen Welsh poets which is worth mentioning in the same breath with Kuno Meyer's *Ancient Irish Poetry* is a reproach either to the devotion or ability of Welsh scholars. Some years ago, a more or less complete translation was whispered about. It was by a Professor in North Wales, but it was said to have been withheld in dread of criticism from a younger generation. It is time the younger generation repaired the loss, if there was anything to lose. (*R*, vol. 6, p. 122)

The point that Welsh scholars had failed where their Irish counterparts had not is suggested elsewhere in Thomas's journalism. A review of Magnus Maclean's *The Literature of the Celts*, published in the *Daily Chronicle* on 21 October 1903, argues that 'the most important work to be done is to present Celtic Literature to the world'. This work is urgently required in the case of the Welsh-language literary tradition, Thomas continues, because 'we may say of Welsh lyrics that they are worse than untranslated because they are abominably translated' (*R*, vol. 1, p. 114).

Thomas's review of Evelyn Lewes criticised her poetic translations and advised her to read 'the prose versions published by Mr Idris Bell in the Welsh *Nationalist*', a journal that often featured translations of Welsh poetry, and one to which, as we have seen, Thomas himself contributed (*R*, vol. 6, p. 122).

As a reviewer, Thomas is supportive of Irish writers in English and translators from Gaelic. The review of Colum's *Broad Sheet Ballads* points out that 'much of the flavour of these songs seems to have come through the process of transmuting Gaelic into English'. Their 'peculiar rhythms and rhymes are traceable to Gaelic' (*R*, vol. 6, p. 146). Elsewhere he praises the work of Douglas Hyde, 'an Irishman and a scholar . . . in touch with the modern development of his country and her literature' and 'deeply versed in Irish matters' (*R*, vol. 5, p. 132). Thomas reviewed other Gaelic texts in translation, including *Fis Adamnáin: an Irish Precursor of Dante* and *The Poem Book of the Gael* by Eleanor Hull. Of the latter, Thomas writes in the *Bookman* in January 1913 that 'there is no anthology half as welcome as this is, and none so necessary' (*R*, vol. 6, p. 134). Kuno Meyer's *Selections from Ancient Irish History* is given the accolade in the *Daily Chronicle* of 4 August 1911 of being 'the best volume of poetry published in 1911' (*R*, vol. 6, p. 45). *Táin: an Irish Epic*, translated by Mary A. Hutton, is described by Thomas in the *Morning Post* of 30 January 1908 as a 'national literary fortune' (*R*, vol. 5, p. 3).

The book in which Thomas most vividly suggests the parallels between the Welsh and Irish cultures is his *Celtic Stories*, the 'Notes' to which tell us that the tales are 'the work of Welshmen and Irishmen when Wales and Ireland were entirely independent of England' (*CS*, p. 126). His comment suggests that he sees parallels in the colonial experiences of Ireland and Wales, and a value in their literature's separation from that of England. There is also a sense in which Thomas is here recovering these stories in order that they gain relevance in the present. He is at pains to stress the present (and possible future) reality of these figures: 'Probably Finn did exist, or some one of the same name; he is as real as Agamemnon; and as for Arthur, is it not told that he did not die, but passed away?' (*CS*, p. 127). The allusion to the myth that Arthur will again return to rescue the Welsh from the Saxons echoes the same point made in Thomas's review of O. M. Edwards's *Wales* a decade before.

While the seven Irish tales in *Celtic Stories* are Thomas's own interpretation, his 'Notes' acknowledge his source material: *Cuchulain of Muirthemne* by Augusta Gregory, *The Tain* by Mary Hutton, *Old Celtic Romances* by P. W. Joyce and *Manners and Customs of the Ancient Irish* by Eugene O'Curry. Thomas also mentions 'Professor O'Looney's rendering of a poem on *Uisin in Tir-nan-oge* ("Transactions of the Ossianic Society")' and 'Dr Kuno Meyer's *Ancient Irish Poetry*' (*CS*, p. 6). Most of the Irish tales centre on the character of Cuchulain: his 'Boyhood', his relation with his son in 'Father and Son', 'The Battle of the Companions' and his 'Death'. Also included are stories entitled 'Deidre and Naisi', 'The Palace of the Mountain Ash Trees' and 'The Land of Youth'.

There are several connections between the Irish tales in *Celtic Stories* and Thomas's poetry, written between three and five years later. Part of the first story, about the boyhood of Cuchulain, is set in a 'smithy' at a 'crossways', anticipating the setting for the poem 'Aspens', which is likewise set at a 'cross-roads' where there is a 'blacksmith's cavern' (*ACP*, p. 97). In the same story, there is a 'ford' setting, where someone is always 'keeping watch', and which is linked to a sense of impending battle (*CS*, p. 12). The ford is similarly depicted in 'Father and Son'. Both Irish stories anticipate Thomas's two-quatrain poem 'The Watchers':

> By the ford at the town's edge
> Horse and carter rest:
> The carter smokes on the bridge
> Watching the water press in swathes about his horse's chest.
>
> From the inn one watches, too,
> In the room for visitors
> That has no fire, but a view
> And many cases of stuffed fish, vermin, and kingfishers. (*ACP*, p. 119)

The poem is set at a 'ford', overlooked by an inn from where the speaker 'watches' the carter and his horse in the river, and where the speaker in turn is watched by the stuffed animals that line the room. The act of watching is an activity in contrast to the impending battle at the front. Critics have tentatively suggested a Welsh location for the ford, but *Celtic Stories* implies that something else is also going on here. Cuchulain's ford is being relocated from the Ulster border to Wales; it is being moved in temporal terms too, transferred from a mythical time, pre-history, to the First World War. This subtle registering of different modes of time will be explored at greater length later in this chapter.

To recap, Thomas's interest in Irish writing forms a significant part of his work as a literary journalist. The comparisons to Welsh writers and scholars (who are often found wanting), and to Welsh folk and literary stories (put alongside their Irish equivalents, and valued for their independence from English culture) suggest that Thomas sees a structural affinity between the Irish and Welsh literatures. One of the pioneering aspects of Irish writing, in this respect, is its use of the English language. In a review of *The Dublin Book of Irish Verse*, published in the *Morning Post* on 6 January 1910, Thomas describes Irish writing in English as 'in a real sense foreign, though written in English', and announces his interest in poetry in which 'English is used as a foreign tongue by writers who were born to it' (*R*, vol. 5, p. 75). This notion seems at first to be paradoxical. The idea that English can be both a writer's first language, yet also remain 'foreign' to her or him, suggests Thomas's awareness of how a writer's background affects her or his relation to the language, an idea that is implied by his mention of those who are not able to write in 'a medium perfectly and by long traditional use adapted to their modes of feeling and thought' (ibid.). Thomas's sensitivity to the position of these writers stems from his own situation as a writer one generation removed from the Welsh language, and anticipates later, postcolonial insights into their work. For example, Kirsti Bohata argues that Welsh writing in English is a new literature in that it displays 'the defining characteristic of postcolonial writing in a European language', namely that the 'writer approaches the language from the outside, often as a second language, or even as a first language which does not quite reflect the history and culture of the speaker' (*PR*, p. 105).

Judy Kendall has traced a similar interest in English approached from the perspective of an outsider in Thomas's interest in the Japanese writer Yone Noguchi, whom Thomas reviewed three times. Thomas draws attention to Noguchi's 'intimate foreign English', asking his readers how Noguchi could 'learn English and yet be so little tinged by our use of the language'.[6] A similar concern for the ways that English might be 'used as a foreign tongue' even by 'writers who were born to it' lies behind Thomas's interest in writers from the US. The comment is echoed in his description of Frost's use of 'English with just that shade of foreignness'.[7] This suggests that his interest in American writers, like his interest in the Irish, stems from the parallel he saw with his own position as an English-language writer from a non-English nation. He portrays Frost as a descendent of Wordsworth and Whitman, a poetic ancestry that brings to mind the well-known Wordsworthian use of rural speech patterns in *Lyrical Ballads*. But Frost, as Matthew Hollis points out, and as Thomas's review implies, also 'shared [Whitman's] manifest interest in the destiny of a new people'.[8] Many British writers of the early twentieth century shared Frost's interest. As discussed earlier, Huw Walters has shown how, in the 1910s, Thomas's friend Gwili introduced Welsh writers in the Ammanford area to the work of Whitman and Edward Carpenter, an area that M. Wynn Thomas has gone on to explore in more depth. Discussing the phenomenon of Whitman's 'internationalism', M. Wynn Thomas draws attention to the American poet's power 'to appeal to societies that also speak English, but an English very different from his own' (*TC*, p. 259).[9] Welsh culture from both sides of the linguistic divide found in Whitman 'significant points of self-recognition' (*TC*, p. 239). One such writer was Ernest Rhys, London-based Welsh author and editor, acquaintance of Thomas and, along with Yeats, among others, a founding member of the Rhymers Club in the fin-de-siècle (*TC*, p. 230). Rhys's work was reviewed on three occasions by Thomas.[10] As editor of the *Everyman* series, Rhys commissioned Thomas to write an introduction to an edition of George Borrow's *The Bible in Spain* (1906). Rhys's interest in Whitman is 'related exclusively to his Welshness', notably to Rhys's own attempts to 'reconnect . . . to his Welsh Celtic background' (*TC*, p. 233). Rhys made 'common cause' with Yeats, the latter finding in Whitman 'hope for the de-Anglicising of our people' in the model his work provides for how to build 'a national literature which shall be nonetheless Irish in spirit from being English in language' (*TC*, p. 235). Yeats's phrase recalls O. M. Edwards's hopes for a literature 'English in language but Welsh in spirit'.[11] These references to Whitman – in the context of Thomas's connections to Gwili, Rhys, Edwards and Yeats – indicate a transnational pattern to Thomas's interest in the writer, echoed in the hope, expressed in a review of Leon Bazalgette's *Whitman: L'Homme et son Oeuvre*, that 'the active sympathies of France, which long ago accepted Poe, may accept Whitman as heartily' (*R*, vol. 4, p. 74). Whitman, of course, is another source for Thomas's interest in the relation between written forms infused with oral speech rhythms and nascent national literary traditions.

Examining Whitman's work within this wider international context enables us to consider Thomas's own emigration plans in a new light. Writing to Frost on 13 November 1913, four months after his decision to enlist, he repeated his desire to leave England: 'I realize – I think no more about it – that England will be no place for me when all is over'.[12] This echoes an earlier letter in which Thomas suggests that emigration to the US would 'set me free from English journalism' and would enable him to 'find a market out there for what I really want to do. What that is I am not perfectly sure yet. But I have begun to write in verse and am impatient of anything else' (*LGB*, p. 244). This desire to emigrate is not a momentary consequence of his new-found relation with Frost. Rather, hopes of escaping from 'English journalism' and of establishing himself as a writer on the other side of the Atlantic are at one with his interest in other English-language literary traditions. One letter, written over a year before he met Frost, asks the opinion of Cazenove, his literary agent, on the likelihood of finding 'literary work' in the US.[13] With this aim in mind, he cultivated American contacts among journalists: one letter refers to a Llewellyn of the *Chicago Evening Post* (probably the Welsh-sounding Llewellyn Jones, the paper's then literary editor), for whom Thomas hoped to write, while another refers to dinner with the 'English advisor to the Minneapolis *Bellman*, a pretty good weekly that may be persuaded to print me' (*EF*, p. 53). Correspondence with Frost repeatedly displays similar hopes in which Thomas imagines what he would do if he got to New York or Boston (*EF*, p. 62), and in which he writes of his hope of making 'connections that would make it worthwhile staying for good' (*EF*, p. 69).

Not only did Thomas hope to find a market for his poetry in the United States; his success in getting poems placed in Harriet Monroe's *Poetry*, in the February 1917 issue (which also contained work by Pound and Emile Verhaeren), suggests an openness to the American modernism which that journal did so much to promote.[14] Indeed, a reconsideration of Thomas's journalistic work on Pound reveals that Thomas is far from the anti-modernist critic that is usually depicted. Between 1908 and 1914, Thomas reviewed Pound at least five times, and his journalism displays a respect for the innovations that Pound brought to poetry. Comments in the earlier reviews and some of his correspondence are sometimes glowing: Pound 'has very great things in him', he wrote in 1909; 'Nearly all [his poems] are extraordinary achievements' (*LGB*, p. 185). Thomas's 1909 *Daily Chronicle* review of *Personae* displays an interest in what lies behind Pound's 'disdain' for 'conventional form' (*R*, vol. 4, p. 13), while in a 1909 review of the same collection, which appeared in the June 1909 issue of *English Review*, Thomas recognises that the American's work is distinct from both the 'superficial good qualities of modern versifiers' with 'their wavering uncertain languor', and also from the Tennysonian tradition's 'smooth regularity'.[15] Thomas is open to Pound's 'lack of obvious grace' as well as to his 'carelessness of ordinary effects'.[16] While it is certainly true that Thomas can be more trenchant in his criticism of Pound, the tone of the reviews reveals Thomas's interest in Imagism. One 1914 review by him referred to it as a movement that will 'interest readers as theorists, and touch them as men'. The same review displays a respect for Imagists' 'sincere and sensitive attempt to write poetry without admitting any commonplaces of verse, in form, language or sentiment', hardly the work of a writer for whom modernism constitutes a foreign 'aberration' (*R*, vol. 6, p. 126). Clive Wilmer, a critic sympathetic to modernism, describes the brilliance of Thomas's reviews, wondering 'if anyone, even critics of Pound's circle, ever caught the feel of his work as precisely as Thomas does here'.[17]

That Thomas positively reviewed Pound, and that such reviews were controversial, is corroborated in the memoirs of Edgar Jepson, member of a literary club that Thomas had also joined, who recalls the reaction to Thomas's favourable view of *Personae of Ezra Pound*:

> You could not be a poet in those days unless they discovered and made you. They would not allow it . . . Then E.T. fairly tore it: in a review he praised the verse of Ezra Pound! I shall never forget the meeting of the Square Club a few days after that monstrous action: the pale, shocked, contorted faces of the poet-makers . . . Poor Edward Thomas! He did look so hot and bothered. His protest that he had acted in good faith, that at the time of the writing of the review he had really fancied that he liked the verse of Ezra Pound, drew from his colleagues only horrid rumblings. How could he have liked the verse of a man whom none of them had discovered, much less made? Why, none of them even knew him! The thoughtlessness! The betrayal! The shattering blow to English Literature![18]

The subversion implied by some of Thomas's reviews of Pound is echoed in Thomas's interest in continental modernists, including the Italian Futurists. On 20 August 1912, after a day in the company of poets Walter de la Mare and Ralph Hodgson, Thomas wrote, 'we talked comfortably about Futurists . . . till near midnight'.[19] F. T. Marinetti's London launch of the Futurist manifesto had taken place in August 1910, while the Futurist art exhibition opened in the Sackville Gallery, London in March 1912. Lawrence Rainey has shown that Marinetti's 1912 performance was 'fully reported in the *Daily Chronicle*', a paper for which Thomas wrote regular reviews at the time.[20] Thomas's familiarity with the modernist scene is also confirmed in his correspondence with Frost, a 1915 letter to whom recording the publication of the second and final issue of the avant-garde journal *BLAST* (*EF*, p. 88). Nonetheless, Thomas's interest is especially drawn to the French and Belgian modernists, in particular to the writers Paul Verlaine and Maurice Maeterlinck. The former's use of 'nuance' influenced the incorporation of speech rhythms into Thomas's own verse, while the Belgian, Maeterlinck, was reviewed by Thomas more often than any other writer (with the possible exception of Yeats). By bringing their work into British literary space, Thomas challenged its provinciality.

Thomas is widely acknowledged as a poet who successfully incorporates oral rhythms into traditional stanza forms and blank verse. An unacknowledged source of Thomas's innovation in this area is the work of Verlaine. Critics familiar with Frost often assume that Thomas developed his poetics from the American writer, who had, by the time he met Thomas in October 1913, already developed his 'sound of sense' poetic theory. Jay Parini, for example, argues that what the two poets share in terms of their poetics derives from 'Frostian influence on Thomas'.[21] Andrew Motion, seeing Thomas within a native 'English' line, contends, on the contrary, that Thomas's 'insistence on speech owes nothing to Frost's example'. He argues that Thomas, working alone, 'clarified the means by which blank verse might be made to imply the vocal inflections, accents and gestures of its author' (*PET*, p. 62). Both critics fail to realise the significance of French symbolism to Thomas's development as a poet.

According to Peter Nicholls, French symbolism was a shaping force in the development of proto-modernism. Characterised in particular by an interest in Verlaine and Mallarmé, proto-modernism as a literary movement was brought from the continent to Britain by three principal texts: *Confessions of a Young Man* by George Moore, *The Symbolist Movement in Literature* by Arthur Symons and *Egoists: A Book of Supermen* by James Gibbons Huneker.[22] Thomas reviewed all three writers. He was too young (in 1888) to review Moore's *Confessions*, although he did review later work by the same author. He did, however, review Huneker's *Egoists* when it came out in 1909. Symons's book was reviewed too, and also mentioned in positive terms in Thomas's 1911 critical biography of Maurice Maeterlinck.

The Symbolist Movement in Literature is a series of eight essays on French symbolist writers: Villiers de l'Isle Adam, Joris-Karl Huysmans, Jules Laforgue, Maeterlinck, Stéphane Mallarmé, Gérard de Nerval, Arthur Rimbaud and Paul Verlaine. Thomas's diaries demonstrate that he had read many of these authors, an aspect of his work that has received scant critical attention. In December 1903, and in January 1909, he was reading Huysmans; in March and April 1909, he was reading Verlaine (and Nietzsche); in July 1909, he read unspecified 'French Poetry', following Huneker's *Egoists* the month before.[23] He read, in addition, Mallarmé in July 1904, while Baudelaire, already reviewed twice, was read for pleasure in May 1912.[24] *Poems in Prose* demonstrates 'Baudelaire's exquisite gift in the fantastic use of prose' (*R*, vol. 2, p. 113), while *Century of French Poets*, edited by Francis Yvon Eccles, was described as 'an excellent book' in a 1909 *Daily Chronicle* review (*R*, vol. 4, p. 124). Maeterlinck's works were reviewed on twelve occasions between 1901 and 1911, journalism that provided the basis for Thomas's critical study, *Maeterlinck*.

French symbolism was not only a concern for Thomas as a literary journalist; it also influenced his poetry. While it is difficult to ascertain the exact source for Thomas's use of speech rhythms in verse forms, there is certainly explicit reference to the French symbolist tradition in the first line of Thomas's first poem, 'Up in the Wind', written in November 1914. Its opening line, which reads 'I could wring the old thing's neck that put it there!', directly alludes to Verlaine (*ACP*, p. 31). The sixth stanza of Verlaine's 1884 poem, 'L'Art Poétique', begins 'Prends l'éloquence et tords-lui son cou!' ('Take rhetoric and wring its neck!'), a line that, according to Nicholls, 'assumed a sort of programmatic significance' in its emphasis on 'suggestiveness, nuance, [and] an "uneven", partly accentual rhythm' (*M*, p. 44). 'Verlaine's poem', Nicholls continues, 'presented these as the antithesis of metrical conformity and rhetoric' (ibid.). The idea of taking rhetoric and wringing its neck also recalls an often-quoted May 1914 letter to Frost in which Thomas describes his intention to pursue Frost's aim of writing a literature informed by oral rhythms: 'I do so daily and want to begin all over again with them and wring all the necks of my rhetoric' (*EF*, p. 9). While the line is certainly evidence of Frost's influence on Thomas's turn to poetry, it also indicates Thomas's indebtedness to Verlaine, a writer with whom he was familiar long before his October 1913 meeting with Frost. As we have seen, Thomas's diary records that he read Verlaine in March 1909, while the very poem alluded to here, 'L'Art Poétique', is described by Thomas as a neat summary of 'Verlaine's doctrine of poetry' in his 1911 critical study of the Belgian symbolist.[25] This shows that his journalistic work – his interest in drawing attention within Britain to French symbolism – also informs the poetry. If anything, the depth of Thomas's interest in the French scene also serves to downplay the importance of the relation with Frost in Thomas's turn to poetry.

Casanova argues that, at the beginning of the twentieth century, there is a structural affinity between Belgium and Ireland whose writers' 'shared literary destitution leads them to take each other as models and historical points of reference, to compare their literary situations and to apply common strategies based on the logic of prior experience' (*WRL*, p. 247). She describes Belgium at the beginning of the twentieth century as 'a sort

of model for small countries in Europe', and points out the similarities
with Ireland:

> Linguistically, politically, and religiously divided, and under the cultural
> domination of France, Belgium furnished a model for each of the two
> contending factions: the Anglo-Irish could identify with the poets [Maurice]
> Maeterlinck and [Emile] Verhaeren . . . and the Gaelicizing Irish looked to
> the example of Hendrik Conscience, who had undertaken to revive the use
> of Flemish. (*WRL*, p. 248)

Nicholls also draws attention to Verhaeren, citing a 1913 critic who
describes the Belgian as 'indisputably the most modern and the most
massive force in the whole of European poetry'.[26] Although Thomas never
reviewed Verhaeren, their literary paths crossed. Thomas's literary journalism appeared in the journal, *Poetry and Drama*, alongside Verhaeren's
poetry, while Thomas's own poetry appeared in the same issue of the
American journal *Poetry* as Verhaeren's verse. Thomas's general interest
in Belgian literature is implied by his *Daily Chronicle* review, on 15 June
1911, of Jethro Bithell's *Contemporary Belgian Poetry*. Moreover, while
Yeats famously met Maeterlinck in Paris, Thomas corresponded with
Maeterlinck during the research for his 1911 study of the author. He
reviewed the author many times.[27] Patrick McGuinness, who has done
more than any other critic to capture the significance to contemporary
readers of 'one of modern theatre's quietest, but most radical, innovators',
points out that Maeterlinck held a 'lifelong attachment to the language
and culture of his native Flanders, even at the height of his fame as a
"French" writer'.[28] Thomas's interest in Maeterlinck, like that of Yeats,
reveals a felt relation to his own position as a writer from a nation dominated by a neighbouring nation in whose language he writes. Thomas
thereby anticipates the affinity between Wales and Belgium that intensified
during 1914, partly fuelled of course by Lloyd George's fateful paralleling
of 'poor [over-run] Belgium' with Wales, a comparison correctly calculated
to act as a potent recruiting weapon for the front. Belgian artists, led by
Verhaeren, featured heavily in the journal *The Welsh Outlook* during 1914
and 1915 in particular, but the wartime relation should not blind us to
the pre-war Welsh interest in Belgium as a nation that had successfully
emancipated itself from a culturally dominating neighbour.[29] As the
anonymous reviewer of Verhaeren wrote in the October 1914 issue, the
Belgian 'literary renascence', led by Maeterlinck and Verhaeren, 'should
be of special interest to us in Wales' because it 'has been compared with

the recent Irish revival . . . which is also analogous to the present movement in our own country'.[30] In yet another connection, P. Mansell Jones, Welsh scholar and translator of Verhaeren's poetry, published in the journal *Aberystwyth Studies* a pioneering defence of the free-verse form employed by the Belgian poet, in which he invoked the example of Whitman, another of Thomas's interests, as we have seen.[31] These networks and affinities between writers identified with nascent national literary spaces in Wales, Ireland, the US, Belgium and Norway in the first two decades of the twentieth century have yet to be fully explored, although Thomas is clearly aware of, and actively building, these connections.

Casanova also makes the connection between Ibsen and Maeterlinck. In Paris, both playwrights were interpreted for the stage by Lugné Poë, who, in 1895, brought both men's work to London (*WRL*, p. 163). According to Casanova,

> [the] passionate interest in the work of the Belgian playwright shown by the decadent young poets of the capital, admirers of Oscar Wilde, excited the disapproval of Victorian public opinion and, on the start, a few days later, of Wilde's first trial, encouraged bitter attacks from opponents of innovation in the theatre. (*WRL*, p. 163)

Maeterlinck, who invented Symbolist theatre, was acclaimed in 1890 by Octave Mirabeau as the 'Belgian Shakespeare', a label that was contested when his plays were brought to England five years later (*WRL*, p. 163). By encouraging an interest in Maeterlinck, Thomas is supporting a playwright who, like Ibsen, threatened to challenge the dominant position of Shakespeare in British theatrical space.

Another aspect of Thomas's journalism hitherto neglected by the critics is his interest in gay writers. In many ways, Oscar Wilde is a writer Casanova could have chosen to represent the fourth stage of her paradigm: an Irish writer, Wilde, like Shaw, used his position in London to challenge the British norms. His imprisonment for homosexuality in 1895 threw down the glove to avant-garde writers tempted to use their position to address society's taboos in this area. He became an iconic figure, yet one whose influence went underground. Ann L. Ardis goes so far as to argue that Wilde is the unacknowledged father of Anglo-American modernism, and traces how key figures in the field are conspicuously silent in their criticism of him. The first two volumes of Virginia Woolf's letters 'include no reference to Wilde'.[32] Pound, with one exception, 'never mentions Wilde in his letters', while Eliot refers to Wilde 'only once'; these are silences that Ardis attributes to the writers' conservative politics and hostility to 'perceived effeminacy' (*MCC*, p. 46). Incidentally, the only record of Pound's view of Thomas (aside from a review of Thomas's posthumously published poetry), is as 'a mild fellow with no vinegar in his veins', which suggestively feminises the Welshman.[33]

Thomas, in contrast to these writers, reviewed Wilde positively four times.[34] He also reviewed Leonard Cresswell Ingleby's reminiscences of Wilde and W. W. Kenilworth's study, both in the *Daily Chronicle* on 11 September 1912. In his review of Wilde's *The Works*, Thomas declares that, 'No writer of such reputation has in recent times equalled Wilde's versatility'. He describes *Salomé* as a 'tribute to Flaubert and M. Maeterlinck' and argues that *The Critic as Artist* 'is equal to almost anything that has been written about criticism by anyone since Coleridge' (*R*, vol. 4, p. 60). Private correspondence connects his own project as a reviewer to that of Wilde:

> I have just finished the 'Critic as Artist' again and am astonished to think how much I owe to him, & in fact am not sure if there is ever anything but him in my criticism – anything worth having. (*LGB*, p. 132)

Thomas's public and private defence of Wilde, indeed his wider critical interest in, and support for, gay writers, in the context of the first decade of the twentieth century, is an important intervention in the field, and one that has received absolutely no recognition.

As Mark Lilly argues in *Gay Men's Literature in the Twentieth Century*, Walter Pater was a key figure among homosexual writers at the end of the nineteenth century.[35] Thomas published a full-length book on Pater in 1913. In 1912, moreover, he had published a critical study of Algernon Charles Swinburne, another gay writer and, in the same year, he proposed to his agent, Cazenove, a full-length work on the homosexual poet and critic Arthur Symons.[36] He reviewed Swinburne six times, and Symons on ten occasions.[37]

Thomas also reviewed the openly gay Edward Carpenter.[38] In *Lads: Love Poetry of the Trenches*, Martin Taylor singles out Edward Carpenter's *Iolaus*, 'known in the book trade as "the Bugger's Bible"', as an example of the tradition of depicting homosexual relationships 'in terms of the Greek ideal of male love'.[39] Thomas's review of this book refers in a discreet, even coded, way to homosexuality: 'probably two diabolic Greeks were just as perfect friends as two Whitechapel "blokes"' (*R*, vol. 1, p. 43). His correspondence too reveals a familiarity with Carpenter's *From Adam's*

Peak to Elephants, published in 1892 (*LGB*, p. 153), while he also mentions Carpenter in *Richard Jefferies*.[40] Thomas, moreover, reviewed books about Carpenter, including one by Mrs Havelock Ellis, whose husband, along with J. A. Symonds, wrote *Sexual Inversion*, an early investigation of homosexuality. Her book, *Three Modern Seers: James Hinton, Nietzsche, Edward Carpenter*, was reviewed by Thomas in the September 1910 issue of *Bookman*. Taylor argues:

> Carpenter helped to evolve a language of male love that, although discreet, distinguished it from the conventions of heterosexual love, and his poetic influence can be observed in Harold Monro's volumes *Before Dawn* (1911), *Children of Love* (1914) and *Strange Meetings* (1917). (*LLP*, p. 45)

Monro was another personal correspondent of Thomas's. He received informal advice about his poetry from Thomas, who visited him for the weekend in November 1912, and who once received an invitation to Monro's holiday home on the Italian island of Capri (*LGB*, p. 225). Monro ran the Poetry Bookshop, and edited *Poetry and Drama*, where Thomas was a regular reviewer. Thomas reviewed Monro's work on several occasions.[41]

Walt Whitman's 'philosophy of "the institution of the dear love of comrades"' is also mentioned in Taylor's analysis of World War I love poetry (*LLP*, p. 46). It was 'admired by such soldier-poets as . . . Edward Thomas' (ibid.). Taylor does not provide any evidence of Thomas's interest in Whitman, but he might have referred readers to Thomas's reviews of Symons, in one of which Thomas writes that his subject 'has all the sympathy which Mr Whitman desired to have' (*R*, vol. 5, p. 16). Thomas also reviewed James Thomson's *Walt Whitman* in the *Morning Post* on 12 September 1910 and Leon Bazalgette's biography of Whitman in the *Daily Chronicle* on 11 July 1908. Frost is described as one of Whitman's literary descendants in Thomas's review of *North of Boston*, published in *New Weekly* on 8 August 1914. Whitman is also mentioned in various of the books of prose by Thomas.[42] Works by Michael Field, a pseudonym for the female collaboration between K. H. Bradley and E. E. Cooper, whom later critics have identified as possible lesbian writers, were reviewed by Thomas on six occasions.[43] Thomas noted in his *Bookman* review of Field's *Mystic Trees* that it 'seems to need a key', a comment that hints at the partly-formed codes employed by female homosexual writers at the turn of the century (*R*, vol. 6, p. 118). There is also a 1913 review of *Songs of Three Counties*, an early publication by Radclyffe Hall, later author of the influential 1928 lesbian novel *The Well of Loneliness* (*R*, vol. 6, p. 115).

There is little homosexuality in Thomas's poetry, but this is hardly surprising given the legal context at the time. Nonetheless, his poem 'Tonight' comes close:

> Harry, you know at night
> The larks in Castle Alley
> Sing from the attic's height
> As if the electric light
> Were the true sun above a summer valley:
> Whistle, don't knock, tonight. (*ACP*, p. 86)

This first stanza's celebration of the 'electric light' rather than the 'true sun' implies a relation that is supposedly 'unnatural'. According to Edna Longley, the poem 'appears to dramatise forbidden love, whether hetero-sexual or homosexual'.[44] But, however tempting, it would be no more than speculation to link this 'Harry' to Thomas's friend, the gay writer, Harold Monro.

In Thomas's correspondence, there are further coded references to homosexuality. He shared rooms in Chelsea from September to December 1904 with Arthur Ransome, and there are suggestions in Thomas's corres-pondence that their relation was briefly sexual. Looking back from 1908 on his relation with Ransome, Thomas writes in a letter to Bottomley, 'I cherished him because he was the nearest approach to a blithe youth I happened to know, and it is natural that I should be angry with him for a rather speedy disillusionment'.[45] The following year, Thomas privately fought to ensure that incriminating material did not appear in Ransome's autobiography. A later letter suggests that he was successful: 'He is sparing of his autobiography to me now, though he threatened to return to these parts' (*LGB*, p. 205). Just how close Thomas came to a potentially ruinous situation is clear from events in 1913 when Lord Alfred Douglas sued Ransome, whom Thomas elsewhere describes as 'rash',[46] for what he had written in his recently published biography of Wilde. Ardis, incidentally, describes Ransome's biography of Wilde as one of a number of 'isolated attempts to grant Wilde centrality in a genealogy of modern writing' (*MCC*, p. 47). Ransome's assertion that Wilde's 'attitude in writing gave literature new standards of valuation' echoes Thomas's correspondence on the importance of Wilde's criticism (*MCC*, p. 46). In a 1913 letter, Thomas argues that 'Douglas must be ¾ mad and ought not to have been allowed to victimize Ransome' (*LGB*, p. 229). Eighteen years on, the forces behind the 1895 Wilde trial were still powerful, and revelations of homosexuality could still lead to a prosecution.

One of Thomas's poems in which these elements are presented is 'The Other', an eleven-stanza work, the first stanza of which introduces a first-person narrator who emerges from the 'forest' only to be stopped by unknown interrogators:

> 'twas here
> They asked me if I did not pass
> Yesterday this way. 'Not you? Queer.
> Who then? And slept here?' I felt fear. (*ACP*, p. 40)

The interrogatory tone conjured by the single-stress words, the question about where the speaker 'slept' and the end-rhyme of 'queer' and 'fear' suggest criminalised homosexuality as a subtext here. In subsequent stanzas, the speaker doubts his own identity, resolving to pursue his quarry 'until myself I knew'. This 'goal' is described as 'a new desire, to kiss / Desire's self beyond control, / Desire of desire', a passion focused on a male 'other' whom the speaker pursues doggedly from pub to pub, but about whom to a 'landlady' and 'children' he remains guarded, lest from 'an answer indiscreet' his 'purpose' is revealed. His consummation eventually arrives one 'night' in which 'still / The roads lay as the ploughland rude, / Dark and naked, on the hill'. Up to this point, the poem reads as a coded reference to the difficulties of pursuing a homosexual relationship in early twentieth-century Britain. Indeed, the man pursued is described as one who lived 'under a ban'. Nonetheless, while the poem alludes to such matters, it also presents them as a drama of the speaker's self. His brief and temporary moment of consummation occurs when he is alone and involves:

> Happiness and powers
> Coming like exiles home again,
> And weaknesses quitting their bowers (*ACP*, p. 40)

Here, the 'other' seems to have momentarily disappeared, revealed as a projection of half of the speaker's polarised self (the other half being the narrator). The terms 'exiles' and 'powers' are telling, implying a national dimension and recalling Thomas's self-description as an exiled Welshman.

Kiberd's analysis of Wilde's use of the double is instructive here. Citing the psychologist Otto Rank, Kiberd argues that for Wilde, the double (a device used in *The Importance of Being Earnest*) 'may epitomise one's noble soul or one's base guilts, or indeed both'.[47] Matthew Hollis pursues a similar line with Thomas's 'the other man', reading him as a 'projection of his alter ego', and tracing him to a character that the narrator pursues in the earlier prose text, *In Pursuit of Spring*.[48] But in a comment that is also relevant to Thomas's poem, Kiberd goes on to suggest that for Wilde 'the Double is a close relation of the Englishman's Celtic Other'.[49] When the imperialist English culture externalises its repressed aspects in a Celtic other, those characteristics come back to haunt their begetters. As Arnold's Celticism shows, the creative, non-utilitarian aspects that are exiled and used as a justification for colonial rule become the very qualities required for the salvation of the imperial culture. One way of reading Thomas's 'other' is to see him as an externalised amalgamation of those parts of the self which have been suppressed – be they his Welshness or feelings of homosexuality – and which return to haunt the speaker who exiled them, to become what the speaker's remaining self seeks above all else, indeed upon which his own existence mysteriously depends. This might begin to explain the final lines of the poem in which the fate of the two characters, by now separated again, is shown to be inextricably interlinked:

> He goes: I follow: no release
> Until he ceases. Then I also shall cease. (*ACP*, p. 41)

Moreover, as we have seen, the prose text in which Thomas's 'other man' makes his first appearance presents a 'pursuit' – the discovery of spring – which is only ended when the narrator finds spring and Wales together. What the use of queer metaphors implicitly recognises is the relation between nationality and sexuality, as if, through the poem, Thomas is searching for a space where the binaries on which these kinds of identity are currently based might be dissolved, revealing new possibilities both of nationhood and sexuality.

In his writing about himself, even in correspondence to trusted friends, Thomas is understandably careful not to implicate himself. Even so, there is a candid, confessional quality to one 1906 letter to Bottomley, in which he writes of his need for the kind of 'salvation' that 'depends on a person & that person cannot be Helen [his wife]' (*LGB*, p. 129). The letter continues:

> It is unlikely to be a woman because a woman is but a human being with
> the additional barricades of (1) sex and (2) antipathy to me – as a rule. And
> as to men – here [at Steep, in Hampshire, not far from Bedales School] I
> am surrounded by schoolmasters, while in town I can but pretend to pick
> up the threads of ancient intercourse, a task as endless as the counting of
> poppy seeds or plovers in the air. (*LGB*, p. 129)

Here, the reference to poppy seeds is linked to the slim chance of establishing an exclusively male bond, and 'threads of ancient intercourse' picked
up on his frequent trips to London. Perhaps this is an allusion to the
poppies in Virgil's *Second Eclogue*, one of the flowers with which Corydon
courts Alexis, and, according to Taylor, one of the classical texts that, by
the second decade of the twentieth century, had become a coded means
of expressing homoeroticism (*LLP*, p. 31).

In Thomas's correspondence, a recurring prospect of a male bond was
the chance to live with Frost in America. As early as 19 May 1914, seven
months after their first meeting, he looks forward to it:

> Today I was out from 12 till sunset bicycling to the pine country by Ascot
> and back. But it all fleets & one cannot lock up at evening the cake one ate
> during the day. There must be a world where that is done. I hope you & I
> will meet in it. I hardly expect it of New Hampshire more than of old. (*EF*,
> p. 9)

'New Hampshire' is a reference to their shared dream of making a living
from farming, writing poetry and setting up a summer camp together. It
exists in another 'world' from the one in which Thomas then found himself.
He was then living in Steep, 'old' Hampshire, while the Frosts were in
Beaconsfield, Buckinghamshire, where they would remain until returning
to New Hampshire in February 1915.

Other correspondence between the two develops this closeness
by making coded reference to homosexuality. For example, when, in
December 1914, Thomas produced his first poems, he wrote to Frost,
famously calling him their 'only begetter' (*EF*, p. 38). The phrase suggests
that Thomas saw Frost, metaphorically speaking, as the father of Thomas's
poetry; it also, of course, alludes to the epigraph of the 1609 publication
of Shakespeare's sonnets in which the author calls 'Mr W. H.' their 'onlie
begetter'. There has been critical debate about the mysterious 'Mr W. H.'
ever since, particularly over the ambiguity of his relationship to Shakespeare. To some he is patron, to others, male muse. Certainly, Thomas's

use of the phrase implies creative possibilities in two men conceiving a text together. Another intriguing aspect of their correspondence during 1914 is Thomas's repeated allusion to Verlaine's phrase 'wring the necks of rhetoric' which, as we have seen, occurs in the letter to Frost of 19 May 1914, and in the first line of the first poem he ever wrote in December of that year: 'I could wring the old thing's neck that put it there'. While this implies the two men's discussion of Verlaine, any allusion to the French symbolist in correspondence between two male poets must also bring to mind his notoriety: certainly the allusion to a homosexual poet who scandalised Paris by having an affair with Rimbaud would not have been lost on either Thomas or Frost. Indeed, in his 12 April 1909 *Morning Post* review of E. Lepelletier's *Paul Verlaine: his Life and Work,* Thomas directly refers to Verlaine's life with Rimbaud (*R*, vol. 5, p. 43). Almost a year later, the Verlaine reference is echoed in a letter to Frost (now back in New Hampshire) dated 3 May 1915:

> I tell you – I should like another April week in Gloucestershire with you like that one last year. You are the only person I can be idle with. That's natural history, not eloquence. If you were there, I might even break away from the *Duke* [*of Marlborough*, his latest book] for 3 days, but it would be hard. (*EF*, p. 51)

While this letter shows the closeness of their friendship, the mention of 'natural history, not eloquence' is another allusion to Verlaine's 'Prends l'éloquence et tords-lui son cou!'

The allusion to Verlaine, associated in Thomas's mind with the memory of their time in Gloucestershire, works in the same way as the allusion to 'Mr W. H.': it knowingly employs a coded homosexual reference in order to suggest the closeness of his literary relationship with Frost. Michael Hofmann, in his 'Foreword' to the collected correspondence between the two poets, is at pains to point out that there was no 'homosexual component' to the relationship.[50] Instead, he argues that 'something of what one thinks of as merely or exclusively sexual – the gallantry or flirtatiousness of seduction – inheres in many, if not most, great friendships'.[51] However, read in the context of Thomas's interest in gay writers, the above allusions suggest that there is indeed a 'homoerotic component' to Thomas's descriptions of their literary relations. This continues into the correspondence of July 1915 in which Thomas informs Frost of his fateful decision to enlist. Joining Frost in New Hampshire would have to wait until after the war:

I would plough & hoe & reap & sow & be a farmer's boy . . . But try & forgive me everything by thinking what an asset I shall be in summer camp if I have been in the trenches as well as at Oxford. I believe you know that to find myself living near you & not working for editors would be better than anything I ever did & better than I dare expect. There is no one to keep me here except my mother. She might come too. But I couldn't in this present mess pack up again and be born again in New Hampshire. (*EF*, p. 82)

In this letter, dated 22 July 1915, the prospect of being 'born again' in New Hampshire recalls the earlier letter to Bottomley, suggesting that Frost was held aloft as the man in whom Thomas would find his 'salvation', while the notion of what he 'dare expect' recalls the May 1914 letter to Frost in which he discusses his idealistic hopes for their joint venture. In another letter to Frost, dated 27 July 1915, Thomas describes his decision to enlist as 'punish[ing] myself with (other people's idea of) virtue & what a married man ought to do &c &c' (*EF*, p. 84). Both letters imply that the attachment to Frost was deeper than that to his wife and children. In this sense, the friendship with Frost challenged conventional ideas of 'what a married man ought to do'. While there is no evidence of any homosexual relationship between the two men, Thomas certainly employs homoerotic allusion to describe the intensity of their literary relations. This, along with Thomas's positive reviews of gay writers, subverts society's expectations, and constitutes an act of defiance.

What this study has been suggesting is that this subversion and act of defiance needs partly to be understood as being aligned to the sense of being an 'outsider-insider'; a significant aspect of that self-identification was that Thomas was more 'Welsh' than 'English'. Accordingly, the next chapter will explore this positioning further – still from the perspective of stage four of Casanova's Irish paradigm, but considering in more depth its applicability to Thomas's ambivalent relation to Englishness.

6

Edward Thomas and England's Failed Locales

It is Walter de la Mare who describes Thomas's work as 'a mirror of England', and Andrew Motion who writes of the 'specifically English' context of his poetry, impressions that the last two chapters have complicated. Nonetheless, there is a sense in which Thomas is not simply Welsh but chooses an English identity. Kirsti Bohata suggests that 'an obvious way to avoid the inferiority attached to Welshness was to become English – a solution denied to most subjects of the British Empire' (*PR*, p. 132), yet one available to Thomas as an English-speaking Welshman brought up in London, and educated at Oxford. In this chapter, I consider this significant self-division, again through the prism of stage four of Casanova's 'Irish paradigm': his strategy of assimilation to, and yet subversion of, British literary space. Shifting attention to Thomas's poetry, I employ Ian Baucom's theory of Englishness in the British Empire in order to suggest a way of reconciling my 'Welsh' reading of Thomas's work to the Englishness with which his poetry is often exclusively associated.

Thomas's writings and actions in the last three years of his life suggest an internal conflict about his national affiliation. On the one hand, his prose and poetry, as we have seen, are informed by Welsh cultural traditions. Moreover, there are statements of his intention to leave 'English journalism' and England: 'I realize – I think no more about it – that England will be no place for me when all is over' (*EF*, p. 106). On the other hand, some of his correspondence suggests that Thomas went through a conversion to English patriotism at the outset of the First World War. In an August 1914 letter to de la Mare, he writes, 'If the war goes on I believe I shall find myself a sort of Englishman'.[1] Another, written in autumn 1914, declares 'I am slowly growing into a conscious Englishman'.[2] These comments suggest that Thomas did not see himself as an Englishman before, a view that is supported by an earlier letter in which, as we have seen, he declares 'I am Welsh'.[3] The statements admit to surprise, even reluctance, on becoming 'a sort of' or 'conscious' Englishman, and show the extent to which Englishness is an identity that could be adopted, at least by an Oxford-educated Welsh person. On one level, we should, of course, take this conversion at face value. Thomas's transformation into an Englishman registers a growth in English patriotic feeling brought about by the war. Some of the poems – all written after the outbreak of hostilities – record Thomas's affinity to a rural or folkloric England where way of life was fast disappearing. 'The Manor Farm', 'The Combe', 'Tears', 'Lob', 'Words', 'This is no case' and 'The Child in the Orchard' all explicitly mention 'England'. As we shall see, however, the Englishness depicted is both uncannily haunted by a Welsh presence, and at odds with the British nation state at a time when its war effort is destroying this England.[4]

Another aspect of Thomas's English patriotism is pragmatic: the wartime shrinking of the literary marketplace. Ian Norrie reports that the number of titles published in Britain slumped from 12,379 in 1913 to 7,716 in 1918.[5] Cazenove, Thomas's literary agent, suggests the desperate straits of those who made a living from writing: 'publishers are simply not paying', while 'shortage of paper' and demand for news from the front squeezed out any room for literary matters.[6] Cazenove concludes that 'the author who has not been able to accumulate a good deal of money and the smaller professional man will suffer as badly as anyone'. This is reflected in a letter Thomas wrote to a friend at the time: 'I have of course no prospect of earning any sort of living while the war lasts.'[7] While Cazenove – who, like Thomas, depended on writing to make a living – made a decision to join up (and subsequently died at the front), Thomas initially looked for financial security elsewhere. He asked the influential editor, Edward Garnett, to lobby on his behalf for a Civil List pension, suggesting that 'others might speak to Lloyd George'.[8] His 1915 plea to Garnett, 'Anything rather than a continuation of the insecurity of the last three years', indicates his desperation.[9] The decision to enlist, which guaranteed an income and a pension, must be seen, at least in part, in this context. There is also some evidence that Thomas foresaw a greater market for his poetry once he had joined up. One letter to his parents dated 9 July 1915, the month he enlisted, remarks that 'the *English Review* rejects my poem. Perhaps if I am in khaki they will be more genial'.[10]

One kind of writing that still commanded reasonable commissions was patriotic journalism. Austin Harrison, editor of *English Review*, agreed to pay £25 for 5,000 words on the effect of war on the English provinces. 'Tipperary' (October 1914), 'It's a Long, Long Way' (December 1914) and 'England' (April 1915) were each written with this commission in mind. These articles led to another commission, 'This England', an article published in *The Nation* in November 1914. Unsurprisingly, perhaps, some of Thomas's most English-patriotic and often-quoted lines occur in these texts and the correspondence that surrounds them. According to R. George Thomas, these articles in turn 'led directly' to Thomas's final commissioned prose: the anthology, also called *This England*, and his biography of the wartime leader, *The Life of the Duke of Marlborough* (*ETAP*, p. 239).

A letter from Cazenove to Thomas on 26 August 1914 shows how informal mechanisms of censorship operated at the time. Cazenove relays Austin Harrison's editorial decree at the *English Review* that 'nothing must be said which will stop recruiting', a 'consideration, he says [which lies] at the bottom of everything the press is publishing at the present moment'.[11] Cazenove tells Thomas that he 'will have to handle it very carefully and make it quite clear to him that he is going to get the sort of stuff he wants'. The focus here on 'the sort of stuff' demanded by Harrison, along with knowledge of Thomas's financial predicament in a shrinking literary marketplace, suggests that his decision to write patriotic wartime articles, biographies and anthologies is as much pragmatic as it is heartfelt.

There is, nonetheless, a deeper engagement with Englishness than this analysis allows for. In order to examine how a 'sort of' Englishness informs Thomas's aesthetic, this chapter now turns to the theory of Ian Baucom, whose work considers English identity within the wider context of the British Empire. In *Out of Place: Englishness, Empire and the Locations of Identity*, Baucom argues that over the past 150 years, 'Englishness has been generally understood to reside within some type of imaginary, abstract or actual locale, and to mark itself upon that locale's familiars'.[12] He describes how a number of 'simultaneously literal and metaphorical spaces have each been understood as a synecdoche of the nation's space (even when they are physically present in imperial territory)' and how 'the struggles to define, defend, or reform Englishness' during this period are 'struggles to control, possess, order, and dis-order' these local spaces (*OOP*, p. 4). Baucom suggests that these spatial struggles 'have also been apprehended as temporal contests, primarily as struggles to determine the meaning and authority of the "English" past, and to define the function of collective memory in a discourse of collective identity' (ibid.). These local spaces, he continues, are central to 'the ideologies of English nationalism, the cult of English memory, the discourses of Englishness and Britishness, and, above all, the imperial and post-imperial reformations of English identity' (*OOP*, p. 6).

Baucom argues that, at the beginning of the nineteenth century, the English Romantics, led by William Wordsworth,

> awarded the resonant English locale the power to preserve Englishness against Enlightenment modernity, England – with only the slightest hyperbole – against France, and, in time, Englishness against the British Empire. (*OOP*, p. 30)

Baucom further argues that Wordsworth's famous return to England – his election of Englishness over 'Frenchness' – is dramatised and enabled by his discovery of 'spots of time', redemptive locales which are also Burkean 'spots of tradition' that 'bind together those who are living, those who are dead, and those who are to be born' (*OOP*, p. 31). This redemptive localism and an understanding of Englishness as a species of mnemonic localism are, according to Baucom, evident in the emphasis on tradition and custom in the 'Preface' to *Lyrical Ballads*, and in 'The Ruined Cottage' and 'Michael'. In each of these poems, the reader is taught 'the discipline of reading – and in reading, being bettered by – the locale' (*OOP*, p. 33). Baucom argues that, as the nineteenth century unfolded, this ideology of localism became useful to the empire's administrators 'as they attempted to preserve the Englishness of all those men and women whom the Crown dispatched "beyond the seas"' (*OOP*, p. 34).

Baucom traces the influence of Wordsworth on John Ruskin, who wrote that he 'used Wordsworth as a daily text-book from youth to age, and have lived, moreover, in all essential points according to the tenor of his teaching' (ibid.). He shows how, for Ruskin, like Wordsworth and Burke before him, the

> need to define English culture entailed a struggle to define the national past, to secure the obedience of the present and the future to that past, and to defend that privileged past from the depredations of a metropolitan and imperial modernity. It also meant that these struggles would hinge on the nation's ability to preserve, inhabit, and read those public spaces which physically located England's past – and with that past its true identity. (*OOP*, p. 35)

Ruskin's particular innovation in this sphere is his development of the notion of anticipatory nostalgia: 'the anticipated pleasure of looking back on the present from afar, from a distance at which the present becomes an absent past that may be nostalgically recuperated' (*OOP*, p. 51). It occurs, for example, in an essay, 'The Lamp of Memory', in *The Seven Lamps of Architecture*, in which Ruskin writes how a building 'connects forgotten and following ages with each other, and half constitutes the identity, as it concentrates the sympathy, of nations' (*OOP*, p. 52). Baucom argues that, in constructing national identity in this way, 'Ruskin codes memory as a form of saving nostalgia that resolves the identity of the nation by connecting forgotten and following ages and erasing the present' (*OOP*, p. 55). Ruskin's concept of memory, suggests Baucom, can be read as an allegory of redemption 'in which the past redeems the nation's present, and in which the present will be redeemed as some future's past' (ibid.).

Baucom extends his thesis by focusing on the existence of these 'identity-securing sites . . . not only in England, but in the colonies', where they perform the function of securing 'the cultural identity of the colonists' and Anglicising, reforming and civilising 'the colonised' (*OOP*, p. 17). In other words, they answered the stipulation by nineteenth-century theorists of imperial rule that 'the empire should create a body of colonial subjects who were in the words of Thomas Babington Macaulay's *Minute on Indian Education*, "English in taste, in opinions, in morals, and in intellect"' (*OOP*, p. 20).

In a brilliant turn of argument, Baucom then shows that this policy had unintended consequences. He argues that:

> by creating for English localist rhetoric a global theater of address, the British Empire ensured that England would lose sovereign command of its 'own' spaces of identity. . . . As [colonised] subjects took their places within the locations of Englishness, they also took partial possession of those places, estranging them, and, in the process, transforming the narratives of English identity that these spaces promised to locate. (*OOP*, p. 38)

Baucom devotes the majority of his study to showing how 'the shadow of a localist ideology' has fallen over Rudyard Kipling, E. M. Forster, C. L. R. James, Jean Rhys, V. S. Naipaul and Salman Rushdie (in sites in the British empire), and how that ideology is open to reinterpretation by the very people it is intended to Anglicise (*OOP*, p. 39). For example, with regard to C. L. R. James, Baucom shows how, by laying cricket fields across the British Empire, the English 'invoked an absent England and expressed their belief that, in re-presenting that England, both they and their subjects would be re-made in the image of the re-located past'. James's texts show, however, that 'in laying those pitches, the landscapers of empire also made the English past available to a colonial act of re-invention, a disobedient labor of remembrance'. Not only do such sites of Englishness 'alter the identities of the persons inhabiting, viewing, or passing through them', Englishness itself is subject to change as a result of the reinterpretation of these sites by subjects of empire (*OOP*, p. 39).

Baucom's thesis offers a useful way of considering Thomas's poetry. It is my contention that Thomas approaches sites of Englishness as a Welshman, and that his poetry shows how the ideology of localism – through which an English identity situated itself within a British imperial project – no longer worked in the historical circumstances in which Thomas wrote. Even though it is often set in rural England, supposedly the place where the idea of a continuing England is most easily supported, his poetry, I argue, actually demonstrates the failure to find a locale in which Englishness can be secured. In particular, it records the failure of memory to redeem the nation's present, as well as the inability to imagine a future that looks back on the present with nostalgia. In this, it unwittingly registers the failure, at the onset of World War I, of this aspect of the English localist ideology as it had developed through Burke, Wordsworth and Ruskin. My argument augments that of Baucom, in that it suggests that Thomas's poetry demonstrates the failure of those identity-securing locales even within England's geographic borders. This failure is only possible because of the peculiar circumstances of Wales's relation to England.

In terms of Baucom's argument, it is important to point out that while the policy of Anglicisation in one British colony has much in common with the same policy in another, the ways in which a writer subverts a particular 'identity-securing locale' are always refracted through the particular circumstances of the colonised nation. In the case of Thomas, the particular characteristics of Wales's colonial status determine the way that he undermines the ideology of the locale upon which Englishness is based. One aspect of Wales's colonial status is unique to Wales: much of England (and parts of Scotland) now sit on land that was once considered Welsh, and there is a traditional association of Welsh culture to lands that now form part of England. A great deal of the earliest Welsh literature – that of Taliesin, for example – comes from Welsh cultures in what is now north-west England. Wallbrook, in the City of London, has its origins in the name 'wealh' or Welsh. In this sense, the relatively new Welsh-speaking communities in London and Swindon, with which Thomas was familiar, are part of a longer (if disrupted) tradition. Thomas calls Swindon 'a little Wales' (*ETAP*, p. 80). Baucom's '[English] identity-securing locales', even though they may exist in England, are formed in lands that were once Welsh. This is a cultural 'memory' (among nations colonised by England) unique to the Welsh, and one which – to a Welsh person – immediately undermines their supposedly incontestable power as pristine aboriginal sites of Englishness.

While critics acknowledge that some of Thomas's poems are set in, or inspired by, Wales (for example, 'March', 'The Mountain Chapel', 'Over the Hills', 'A Dream', 'Old Song II', 'Child on the Cliffs', 'The Watchers' and 'I never saw that land before'), no critic has attached any importance to Thomas's association of certain features of the *English* landscape with Wales. In *Icknield Way*, as we have seen in Chapter Four, he identifies 'Welsh ways all over England' (*IW*, p. 22). He goes on to list the street names associated with the practice of driving flocks of Welsh sheep and cattle to markets in London (*IW*, p. 22), as well as different features of the English landscape – including chalk pits, hawthorns, fir clumps, church towers and combes – used as landmarks for these itinerant Welsh drovers (*IW*, p. 27). These features recur frequently in Thomas's poetry. Clumps occur in several poems ostensibly set in England, including 'Up in the Wind':

> And it's the trees you see, and not the house,
> Both near and far, when the clump's the highest thing
> And homely, too, upon a far horizon (*ACP*, p. 31)

'The Wind's Song' is inspired by a 'lone pine clump' on the downs (*ACP*, p. 118), and in 'Roads', just before the mention of 'Helen' and 'the *Mabinogion* tales', the speaker sees 'upon the crest / The close pine clump' (*ACP*, p. 107). Another poem is titled and set in 'The Chalk Pit' (*ACP*, p. 88), and another is titled and set in 'The Combe' (*ACP*, p. 48), while 'A Private' is about a ploughman who used to sleep 'At Mrs Greenland's Hawthorn Bush', on the Wiltshire downs 'beyond "The Drover" [inn]' (*ACP*, p. 50). Although these poems are set in England, they are set in places that Thomas associates with Wales. The existence of such 'sites of Welshness' within England suggests how Thomas's poetry subverts Baucom's '[English] identity-securing locales'.

In 'The Glory', the speaker opens in Wordsworthian fashion by declaring, and then describing, 'the glory of the beauty of the morning'. Midway through, however, the poem is unable to sustain its Romantic tone: the speaker confesses how 'the glory invites me, yet it leaves me scorning / All I can ever do, all I can ever be'. The Romantic past, for this speaker, cannot redeem either his present alienation or his imagined future. The poem's despairing conclusion addresses Ruskin's concept of memory as an allegory of redemption:

> And shall I ask at the day's end once more
> What beauty is, and what I can have meant
> By happiness? And shall I let it all go,
> Glad, weary, or both? Or shall I perhaps know
> That I was happy oft and oft before,
> Awhile forgetting how I am fast pent,
> How dreary-swift, with naught to travel to,
> Is Time? I cannot bite the day to the core. (*ACP*, p. 87)

The speaker's anticipation of the question he will again ask himself 'at the day's end' amounts to the failure of what Baucom describes as Ruskin's proleptic nostalgia: the future will not redeem the present. Indeed, its supposed capacity to do so is exposed as a sham, dependent on 'forgetting how I am fast pent'. When Ruskin's anticipatory nostalgia fails (premised as it is on the concept of a present occupied only in a future memory), the bonds that connect the past, through the present, to the future have been broken. The speaker has only the experience of a present that disappears before he can grasp it: the sense that he 'cannot bite the day to the core'.

My argument is that this poem exemplifies how Thomas's poetry records the failure of English localist ideology as inherited from Burke, Wordsworth and Ruskin. He was certainly familiar with all three writers, and there is an intriguing entry in his diary for 27 April 1901 that connects the poem (yet to be written) with his reading of two of them: in a discussion on the nature of beauty, ostensibly the main theme of 'The Glory', he writes 'but what is beauty. I don't find answer in Burke or Ruskin'.[13] In *The Isle of Wight* (1911), there is an even more telling passage in which Thomas makes the connection between 'Ruskin', 'England' and 'locality': during a dialogue between three voices on the subject of 'a solitary yew', one speaker remarks on finding a 'landscape' that is 'changed' in order to become 'the legitimate setting for some poem or romance'.[14] The speaker points out that:

> Ruskin, you may remember, regarded it as something curious and precious
> . . . that his wandering over England took him to places where 'his romance

was always ratified to him by the seal of locality – and every charm of
locality spiritualised by the glow and the passion of romance'. We have to
be fortunate to have any such experience.[15]

As far as Thomas's speaker is concerned, therefore, Ruskin's 'seal of
locality', which is 'ratified' through his experience of the English landscape, is less easily attained.

One of many poems to deal directly with the failure of memory to
redeem the present is 'Over the Hills':

> Often and often it came back again
> To mind, the day I passed the horizon ridge
> To a new country, the path I had to find
> By half-gaps that were stiles once in the hedge,
> The pack of scarlet clouds running across
> The harvest evening that seemed endless then
> And after, and the inn where all were kind,
> All were strangers. I did not know my loss
> Till one day twelve months later suddenly
> I leaned upon my spade and saw it all,
> Though far beyond the sky-line. It became
> Almost a habit through the year for me
> To lean and see it and think to do the same
> Again for two days and a night. Recall
> Was vain: no more could the restless brook
> Ever turn back and climb the waterfall
> To the lake that rests and stirs not in its nook,
> As in the hollow of the collar-bone
> Under the mountain's head of rush and stone. (*ACP*, p. 52)

The poem initially presents a positive memory, that of an occasion which
'often and often . . . came back again'. This is a picture which, in the way
the moment is imagined extending into an 'endless . . . after', echoes
Ruskin's vision of a proleptic nostalgia. The act of leaning and seeing it
and thinking 'to do the same / Again' serves to allow the memory to
redeem the present.

Nonetheless, within this idealised scenario, there are the seeds of its
own demise: in retrospect, there is something ominous in 'the pack of
scarlet clouds', while the 'half-gaps that were stiles once' suggests decay,
alluding to rural depopulation and a less-maintained countryside, caused
by the agricultural depression of the last quarter of the nineteenth century.

The central line in this poem, 'Recall / Was vain', challenges the notion that memory can redeem the present. The act of recollection does not lead to any action beyond the act of recollection. If anything, it leads to inaction: merely 'to lean and see it and think to do the same'. The poem closes with a different mode of time: not one in which the present is occupied by an imagined future; nor one in which the Romanticised past redeems the present. Instead of any binding together of past, present and future, the future becomes unpredictable, contingent on factors beyond the power of memory to shape. The poem's closing image, which best captures this broken temporal relation, is, perhaps, a Welsh one: a 'restless brook' which cannot 'ever turn back and climb the waterfall' to the lake under the mountain – a description that echoes that of the mountain stream in *Beautiful Wales* (*BW*, p. 176). This locale, the poem suggests, is the source of a different, historical, mode of time that does not conform to the speaker's attempts to bind together memory, an imagined future and the present in Englishness.

This poem depicts its speaker's inability to project a future in which the present moment will be viewed nostalgically. Another poem, which more clearly expresses this loss of faith in the future, is 'No one cares less than I':

> 'No one cares less than I,
> Nobody knows but God,
> Whether I am destined to lie
> Under a foreign clod,'
> Were the words I made to the bugle call in the morning.
>
> But laughing, storming, scorning,
> Only the bugles know
> What the bugles say in the morning,
> And they do not care, when they blow
> The call that I heard and made words to early this morning.
>
> (*ACP*, p. 123)

Written in late May 1916, almost a year after Thomas's enlistment, the poem makes clear the reasons for its speaker's loss of faith in the future: war. Thomas here parodies Rupert Brooke's 1914 sonnet 'The Soldier' ('there's some corner of a foreign field / That is forever England') in which the soldier-speaker looks forward to his own death. Brooke's confident use of an imagined future to redeem present action is rejected. Instead, Thomas's poem presents a bleak view of time: the future is unknowable, and therefore cannot redeem his current actions. His words are ineffectual. Time is indifferent to the speaker, and he responds by professing indifference to what it has in store for him. This should not be confused with resignation to his fate: the act of writing the poem, and of professing that indifference, is itself a rebellion against the powers that have put him in this predicament. Crucially, too, the poem focuses on the early morning call-to-parade, the ritualised moment when the individual men are brought together and have their group identity as British soldiers reasserted. The poem explodes that particular myth, and in doing so, explicitly connects the failure of the future to a British identity.

This idea that British identity conflicts with, even caused the death of, an English identity based on localist ideology, is not so far-fetched: Baucom's thesis concerns itself centrally with the conflicts and difficulties of positioning Englishness within the context of the British Empire (*OOP*, p. 38). A poem that explicitly addresses these problems is 'Tears', written in January 1915 (*ACP*, p. 52). Although one of the poems cited by de la Mare in support of his claim that Thomas's poetry constitutes a 'mirror of England', it is more complex than he allows. Written seven months before Thomas himself enlisted, 'Tears' may be read as a veiled anti-war poem, and a demonstration of how the promotion of British identity at a particular point in history rendered obsolete English localist ideology:

> It seems I have no tears left. They should have fallen –
> Their ghosts, if tears have ghosts, did fall – that day
> When twenty hounds streamed past me, not yet combed out
> But still all equals in their rage of gladness
> Upon the scent, made one, like a great dragon
> In Blooming Meadow that bends towards the sun
> And once bore hops: and on that other day
> When I stepped out from the double-shadowed Tower
> Into an April morning, stirring and sweet
> And warm. Strange solitude was there and silence.
> A mightier charm than any in the Tower
> Possessed the courtyard. They were changing guard,
> Soldiers in line, young English countrymen,
> Fair-haired and ruddy, in white tunics. Drums
> And fifes were playing 'The British Grenadiers'.
> The men, the music piercing that solitude
> And silence, told me truths I had not dreamed,
> And have forgotten since their beauty passed. (*ACP*, p. 52)

Edna Longley suggests that the poem's 'Tower' refers to the Tower of London, a location that is, on the one hand, an iconic seat of English imperial power, built by William I before he extended Norman power over the rest of England, as well as the other British and Irish nations. On the other hand, it is the place, according to Welsh legend, where the head of the warrior Bran was buried in order to protect Britain from invasion, a story retold by Thomas in *Celtic Stories*. Here, Bran, 'at the point of death' commands his soldiers: 'cut off my head, and take it and bear it to the White Mount in London, and bury it there with the face towards France' (*CS*, p. 89). This dual English-Welsh significance reflects the double readings that I suggest emerge from the poem.

The poem recalls two memories: an English hunting scene, as well as the ceremonial changing of the guard. The idea of a broken temporal relation helps to explain the strangeness of the opening and closing lines. The fact that the speaker has 'no tears left' implies that they have all been shed, leaving him unable to redeem the present. Instead, the memories are recounted, and the 'truths' they tell are left open for the reader's interpretation, the speaker claiming that he has 'forgotten' them. One of these implied 'truths', I would suggest, is that imperial British identity is leading to the death of England.

The poem may be read as a Romantic portrayal of English countrymen turned by their patriotism into 'British Grenadiers'. Stan Smith rightly disagrees, pointing out 'the gulf' between the English countrymen and the British Grenadiers: the former, he suggests, 'are innocent in their pastoral pathos' while the latter 'carries the burden of an imperial ideology and the exultant violence which sustains it'.[16] However, rather than simply depict a 'gulf' between the two, the poem implies that one is now destroying the other. The soldiers, described as 'equals in their rage of gladness' metamorphose into 'a great dragon', the very enemy that England's St George was supposed to defeat. The poem, at this point, implies that a newly militarised Britain is the beast that England is failing to defeat, a reading supported by the line, 'A mightier charm than any in the Tower / Possessed the courtyard'. While this can be interpreted as a Romantic portrayal of soldiers wearing 'white tunics' for the changing of the guard, the word 'possessed' implies a pejorative reading of the patriotism that convinces men to enlist in the first place. Here, the word 'charm' connotes a spell that has onlookers and guards alike in its power. British patriotism, in the modern day, has the power to cast a spell over 'English countrymen' which turns them into 'British Grenadiers'. In this sense, it possesses a 'mightier charm' than anything 'in the Tower' upon which more traditionally rooted national identities were founded. Given the 'estranging' implications of these 'British Grenadiers', it is hard to resist the temptation to see the ancient 'dragon' first of Roman banners and subsequently of the Welsh flag in this image. It is as if a quintessentially English scene suddenly turned 'uncanny', ghosted by 'foreign' anterior presences. The poem recalls the opening paragraphs of Polish immigrant Joseph Conrad's *Heart of Darkness*, in which the mouth of the Thames, gateway to the imperial capital of London, is suddenly, and uncannily, seen as a place subject to colonisation by the Romans. Given this study's reading of Thomas, we might see both him and Conrad as writers who approach the English language from outside, from a perspective that is not, in a national sense, English.[17]

This sense of an uncannily haunted English patriotism is present even in poems that are usually considered as expressions of Englishness. Even 'Lob', undoubtedly one of the most patriotic of Thomas's 'English' poems, contains the line 'As English as this gate, these flowers, this mire'. These are images that work in more than one direction. Here, the 'gate', linked to nationality, is a liminal place, a point of entry or exclusion, just like the English identity that Thomas, as a London-born, Oxford-educated Welsh-man, could see from both sides. 'Flowers' are not, of course 'English' in any 'natural' way (rather it is their vernacular names that may be described as 'English'). In 1915, 'mire' cannot but allude to the environment at the front (there is another allusion in the poem's mention of 'no man's land'), darkly suggestive of the end to which a sense of English patriotism had led many young men.

Thomas's 'The Combe', written on 30 December 1914, develops the idea of contradictions between British, English and Welsh suggested in 'Tears' (*ACP*, p. 48). By taking an epoch-long perspective on a half-forgotten English rural locale, Thomas is able to unsettle the Englishness of the location:

> The Combe was ever dark, ancient and dark.
> Its mouth is stopped with bramble, thorn, and briar;
> And no one scrambles over the sliding chalk
> By beech and yew and perishing juniper
> Down the half precipices of its sides, with roots
> And rabbit holes for steps. The sun of Winter,
> The moon of Summer, and all the singing birds
> Except the missel-thrush that loves juniper,
> Are quite shut out. But far more ancient and dark
> The Combe looks since they killed the badger there,

> Dug him out and gave him to the hounds,
> That most ancient Briton of English beasts. (*ACP*, p. 48)

Although one of Thomas's most anthologised poems, it is also one of his most difficult to interpret. Those critics who have ventured to tackle the poem echo wider reaction to Thomas's work: most see its focus as England, while some interpret it as a reference to Wales. Michael Kirkham takes the former line. He argues that as far as 'national' levels of meaning are relevant to the poem, it can be read 'as an emblem of divided England'.[18] Smith seems less certain about the specifically English locus of the poem. In his interpretation of the poem, he refers to

> a Britain of obscure and hidden corners before [the Roman] Empire had brought it under the semblance of rule, surviving now only in the swarthy, taciturn peoples of Wales and the West. It is just such a dark backward that the combe seems to represent. (*ET*, p. 22)

Smith in his criticism, like Thomas in his poem, moves from pre-Roman times to 'now', and in doing so, implies that the poem has something to say about contemporary Wales. He goes on to describe the 'tension between "Briton" and "English"', noting how the term 'England' was used almost as early for this island as 'Britain'. However, having made these distinctions, he concludes that the poem is concerned, above all, with England. In Smith's view, the badger 'becomes the figure of an aboriginal heart of England endangered by the new, shallow and unfounded discourses of Empire to which the concepts of "Briton" and "English" have been recruited' (*ET*, p. 22). Smith suggests that the aggressor within the poem is both an imperialist England and an imperialist Britain, yet for him the victim of this imperialism is 'an aboriginal heart of England'; the brief reference to contemporary Wales is marginalised in the thrust of an argument about England. Indeed, Smith does what he accuses others of doing: conflating the terms 'England' and 'Britain'. Somewhere in his phrase 'the aboriginal heart of England' – a phrase that implies an indigenous people, subject to colonisation – Wales has disappeared. In his eagerness to show how Thomas's poem uncovers an imperialist ideology in language and landscape, Smith misses something that the poem has to say about the history and multiple identities of Britain.

The combe, critics suggest, is in England. Edna Longley places it in Hampshire (where Thomas lived), but it might equally have been in Wiltshire (perhaps the Downs above Swindon), both areas that Thomas knew well, and both areas in which 'juniper' could be found at the time Thomas was writing. The word 'combe,' one of the few English words with Celtic origins, is similar to the Welsh word for valley, 'cwm'. The 'stopping' of 'its mouth' implies a physical denial of speech, alluding perhaps to the suppression of the Welsh language. Certainly, 'bramble, thorn and briar', three words for the same plant, have etymological roots in Old Norse and Anglo-Saxon, languages and cultures which, at various points in their histories, contributed to the marginalisation of old and modern forms of Welsh.

There is a powerful, historically influential tradition in Welsh letters that sees *Lloegr* (England) as land that was Welsh long before the waves of Anglo-Saxons, Vikings and Normans forced the British inhabitants to retreat to the territory that would become Wales. Thomas refers in *Icknield Way* to 'the so-called laws of *Dynwal Moel Mud*', an account of the laws and institutes of Wales 'before the crown of London and the supremacy of this island were seized by the Saxons' (*IW*, p. 37). The Welsh-speaking community in Swindon, Wiltshire – Thomas's 'Little Wales' – not to mention the more substantial Welsh communities in London in which Thomas grew up, might be read as part of a tradition of Welsh habitation of land now considered as part of England. By setting 'The Combe' in a typical English locale, and subverting its Englishness, Thomas alludes to this tradition of Welsh thought.

This 'etymological' reading enables the poem to subvert the assumed supremacy of English over Britain's Celtic languages. Casanova suggests that even dominant languages like English try to legitimise their perceived supremacy by extending it back into history (*WRL*, p. 240). W. W. Skeat, for example, author in 1873 of *Questions for Examination in English Literature*, insists that schoolboys should be taught that 'the language which we speak now is absolutely one in its essence with the language that was spoken in the days when the English first invaded this island and defeated and overwhelmed its British inhabitants'.[19] Thomas's 'The Combe', by emphasising an English word with 'roots' in the language of the 'ancient' British, subverts the perceived 'supremacy' to which Skeat contributed. By invoking the cultural memory of a time before England existed, the poem's use of the past serves to undermine the notion that memory redeems the national present, thereby creating a sense of continuity between the two. If anything, the past here unsettles the present, suggesting that fracture and violence were used to secure the present English hegemony.

The notion of a failed locale and, by extension, of a failure of the localist ideology upon which Englishness was based, pervades Thomas's poetry.

It is there in 'Man and Dog', in which the speaker encounters a landless
worker in the woods walking from Chilgrove, 'where he had pulled up
docks', to Alton, where he hoped to find work:

> His mind was running on the work he had done
> Since he left Christchurch in the New Forest, one
> Spring in the seventies, – navvying on dock and line
> From Southampton to Newcastle-on-Tyne, –
> In seventy-four a year of soldiering
> With the Berkshires, – hoeing and harvesting
> In half the shires where corn and couch will grow.
> His sons, three sons, were fighting, but the hoe
> And reap-hook he liked, or anything to do with trees. (*ACP*, p. 56)

In *The Country and the City* (1973), Raymond Williams presents Thomas
as a typical Georgian poet, arguing that his poetry represents 'a dream of
England, in which rural labour and rural revolt, foreign wars and internal
dynastic wars, history, legend and literature, are indiscriminately enfolded
into a single emotional gesture'.[20] He places Thomas firmly on the side
of 'the high English imperialist' (*TCC*, p. 257). He goes on to argue, in
a line of criticism that would be famously developed by Edward Said,
that Britain's nineteenth-century development into an urban, industrial
society, would have been impossible without colonial development. As
a result, rural–urban relations changed. In particular, 'distant lands became
the rural areas of industrial Britain, with heavy consequent effects on its
own surviving rural areas' (*TCC*, p. 280). Williams identifies a 'larger
context' in which 'every idea and every image was consciously and un-
consciously affected' by the existence of empire (*TCC*, p. 281).

By using Thomas as an example of high English imperialism, Williams
sets his argument on shaky foundations. He misses the ways in which
Thomas's poetry represents a challenge to that imperialism. The main
character in 'Man and Dog' reflects the late nineteenth-century economic
and social change that Williams describes: displaced from his home, he
becomes an itinerant worker, and joins the Berkshires – presumably
because of poverty – before returning to itinerant work. This regiment
fought battles in India throughout the 1870s. The poem's movement from
actual locales ('Christchurch' and 'New Forest') to place names that have
become army regiments ('the Berkshires') suggests the cultural move
from a nation of local places to an imperialist nation. The old man's
aimlessness (over forty years), and the fact that his three sons, like him,
have also enlisted, implies criticism of this imperialism. The mention of

his itinerant work harvesting 'corn and couch' alludes to the displacement caused by the agricultural depression from the 1870s to the 1890s, the effects of which, 'more marked in grain', were the result, according to Williams, of an imperialist economic model in which 'manufactured goods were exported against imports of cheap foreign food' (*TCC*, p. 187). More importantly, 'Man and Dog' registers the failure of the localist ideology behind Englishness, and begins to trace the effect of the British Empire on England itself. If, as I argue in Chapter Four, 'Man and Dog', on one level, is a reworking of the Llywarch Hen story from the native Welsh literary tradition, then it is significant that (as in 'Over the Hills') there is an implied Welsh source to this poem's depiction of the failure of an ideology of Englishness.

Williams goes on to argue that 'to protect such an [imperialist] order, young officers from the country-houses led other Englishmen, and the expropriated Irish and Scots and Welsh, to the colonial battles in which so many died', and remarks on the irony that 'the superfluous landless worker, the dispossessed peasant: each of these found employment in killing and disciplining the rural poor of the subordinated countries' (*TCC*, p. 283). While Williams accepts that the whole of British society, 'even at the lower ends of the scale', benefited materially from imperialism, and he does not ignore the crimes against humanity carried out in the name of 'Empire', he also makes the point that 'for many of these advantages British workers had to pay: with blood in repeated wars which had little or nothing to do with their immediate interests; and in deeper ways, in confusion, loss of direction, deformation of the spirit' (ibid.).

Thomas's poetry records the effect of this imperialism on one of those groups identified by Williams: the rural poor. While 'Man and Dog' focuses on a superfluous landless worker, 'A Private' depicts the consequences for one rural worker of fighting in a war remote from his interests:

> This ploughman dead in battle slept out of doors
> Many a frosty night, and merrily
> Answered staid drinkers, good bedmen, and all bores:
> 'At Mrs Greenland's Hawthorn Bush,' said he,
> 'I slept.' None knew which bush. Above the town,
> Beyond 'The Drover', a hundred spot the down
> In Wiltshire. And where now at last he sleeps
> More sound in France – that, too, he secret keeps. (*ACP*, p. 50)

This poem is clearly influenced by Thomas Hardy's 'Drummer Hodge' and, like Hardy's poem on the Boer War, it subtly criticises the war in

France by pitching the speech, humour and vitality of a locality – in this case, 'Wiltshire' – against the silence and anonymity of his unknown grave. If Drummer Hodge's grave is unmarked, the whereabouts of the grave of Thomas's unnamed private is simply unknown. More importantly, on many nights, 'None knew' where the ploughman slept; it is a 'secret'. There is more to this than an oblique reference to the hardship endured by the late nineteenth-century rural workforce. The ploughman's home, like his final resting place, is unknowable to anyone but the ploughman. This indicates one of the differences between Hardy and Thomas: for the former, the local home was more clearly identified; for the latter, home was elusive. It is significant, once again, that the subversion of the patriotic idea of dying for King and Country has a faint Welsh association, not only in terms of the Welsh community in Wiltshire, but also the reference to 'the drover', associated in Thomas's work with the Welsh. The poem echoes Thomas's sketch 'The Patriot' in which, as we have seen, a young Welsh soldier, 'dying in a foreign land', realises that 'his country [is] not the country he had fought for' (*P*, p. 43). The sketch, which Williams had not read, counters his suggestion that Thomas is on the side of the high imperialist English.

In the second half of the nineteenth century, the localist ideology of Englishness paid special attention to the place of home. Williams argues that from the 1880s onwards, the existence of empire, in particular the number of English people abroad, had produced 'a marked development of the idea of England as "home", in that special sense in which "home" is a memory and an ideal' (*TCC*, p. 281). A particular focus of this notion of home is rural England: 'its green peace contrasted with the tropical or arid places of actual work; its sense of belonging, of community, idealised by contrast with the tensions of colonial rule and isolated alien settlement' (ibid.). Far from suggesting the notion of England as a settled 'home', each of Thomas's three poems titled 'Home' demonstrate, by contrast, the impossibility of finding it.

'Home ("Not the end")' operates as a riddle. It describes a homeland from which its speaker has come, and yet one to which he has never been:

> I would go back again home
> Now. Yet how should I go?
>
> This is my grief. That land,
> My home, I have never seen;
> No traveller tells of it,
> However far he has been. (*ACP*, p. 64)

The poem alludes to Hamlet's 'To be or not to be' soliloquy, the most famous literary example of a moment in which an imagined future fails to redeem a possible action in the present: Hamlet's inability to know what lies in the future, on the other side of death, leaves him at an impasse. He is a literary precursor to Thomas's demonstration of the failure of Ruskin's anticipatory nostalgia. Moreover, by presenting his predicament or 'grief' as a search for home, Thomas himself is making the connection between spatial and temporal metaphors, as Baucom would later theorise them. The poem concludes with a defiant admission that he is living in a new mode of time. Neither memory nor an imagined future can any longer redeem the present, leaving the speaker to face whatever time has in store for him:

> No: I cannot go back,
> And would not if I could.
> Until blindness come, I must wait
> And blink at what is not good. (*ACP*, p. 64)

'Home ("Often I had gone")' also explores the idea in temporal terms. In this second poem, moreover, the speaker confidently declares in the opening stanza that he has arrived 'home':

> Often I had gone this way before:
> But now it seemed I never could be
> And never had been anywhere else;
> 'Twas home; one nationality
> We had, I, and the birds that sang,
> One memory.
>
> They welcomed me. I had come back
> That eve somehow from somewhere far:
> The April mist, the chill, the calm,
> Meant the same thing familiar
> And pleasant to us, and strange too,
> Yet with no bar. (*ACP*, p. 81)

Again, however, the speaker's understanding of 'home' seems to pose more questions than it resolves. The poem tackles positively the idea that memory no longer redeems the present. Any memory of elsewhere, as well as any desire to be elsewhere, has disappeared. Only then can the speaker declare ''Twas home'. At this point, the use of 'nationality' raises more questions. For one, birds do not have a nationality if, by nationality, we mean a shared identity based on social, cultural and political affiliations. The emphasis on '*one* nationality' and '*one* memory' suggests that the visionary moment of identification with nature presents a solution to Thomas's sense of having more than one nationality, and it suggests that the issue of memory at some level concerns national identity. However, the 'one memory' that the speaker shares with 'the birds that sang' is in fact a total absence of memory. The speaker does not know how he arrived, or where he came from. He has escaped from history, from the complex sense of nationality and memory that it necessarily gives him, and from the 'bar' that a historical consciousness erects between him and his place in nature. Like the birds, he has 'no bar' – no memory, no language, no need to interpret, no consciousness – between him and his place in nature. The ecstatic vision of home achieved by Thomas in this poem might perhaps be explained in material terms as a reaction to the loss of faith in memory and an imagined future as means of redeeming the present. In a sense, Thomas turns the problem on its head: he begins from the premise of a loss of memory and loss of future, and occupies the present, not in the way that Ruskin would have done (as a form of proleptic nostalgia), but as an ecstatic experience in which the lack of a before and after enables him to occupy the moment in and of itself.

> The thrush on the oak top in the lane
> Sang his last song, or last but one;
> And as he ended, on the elm
> Another had but just begun
> His last; they knew no more than I
> The day was done.
>
> Then past his dark white cottage front
> A labourer went along, his tread
> Slow, half with weariness half with ease;
> And, through the silence, from his shed
> The sound of sawing rounded all
> That silence said. (*ACP*, p. 81)

The fact that the speaker links himself to the birds who 'knew no more than I / The day was done' emphasises his loss of faith in the future as a means of redeeming the present. While this might apply to the birds, it certainly does not apply to the speaker, who even if he did not know then, would have known later, and certainly, with the benefit of a restored memory, at the time of writing, that 'the day was done'. This is a description of the speaker's consciousness at his moment of vision. It is a description that is achieved by the conceit of isolating this one moment, and suppressing what happens next – as memory returns.

This notion of home is premised on the poem's unacknowledged conceit: one moment is isolated from its 'before' and 'after' in order for the speaker to arrive at 'home'. The problem of memory which so plagued the speaker in the earlier poem, 'Home ("Not the end")', has been circumvented by denying all memory; the speaker has lost his historical consciousness; the labourer's speech and consciousness have been suppressed. While the conceit works insofar as it describes a moment of ecstatic vision without a 'before' or 'after', it fails to acknowledge that there clearly must have been an 'after' in order for the poem to be written at all. Poetry, used in this instance as a means of escaping from historical consciousness and thus finding its speaker a 'home', offers the prospect of a way out, but also, simultaneously, betrays its speaker's entrapment within the nightmare of history, his inability to find 'one nationality', and his lost 'home'. In this sense, the poem obliquely demonstrates my argument that Thomas's poetry reveals the failure of a cult of memory in which past memory and an imagined future redeem the present, and provide the continuity across time required for a viable national identity. The mention of 'nationality' suggests that on some level Thomas connects this failure with the difficulty of now locating Englishness, while the framing of these issues within the context of a search for 'home' further implies some criticism of an imperialist project that made easy use of an English rural home. Moreover, as I argued in Chapter Four, this reaction has its origins in the Welsh folk tale of 'Bran and Branwen', retold by Thomas in *Celtic Stories*, in which the defeated Welsh spend seven years on an island beyond the reach of memory and historical time. The implication is that, once again, Wales is the source of Thomas's subversion of Englishness.

'Home ("Fair was the morning")' presents a more political angle on the notion of home. The speaker describes the moment when one of a group of British soldiers on a day's walk away from their army camp mentions the word 'home':

> The word 'home' raised a smile in us all three,
> And one repeated it, smiling just so
> That all knew what he meant and none would say.
> Between three counties far apart that lay
> We were divided and looked strangely each

> At the other, and we knew we were not friends
> But fellows in a union that ends
> With the necessity for it, as it ought. (*ACP*, p. 113)

There is clearly a political overtone to this part of the poem. It subverts any illusion of a sense of 'home' shared by three soldiers. It seems to reject the wartime propaganda that attempted to unite the three of them in the imperial British cause, insisting instead that each soldier's understanding of 'home' comes from each of the 'three counties' they came from. 'Union' is a politically charged word to use, as Edna Longley suggests.[21] It is especially charged given Thomas's interest in Home Rule, and the historical context of the poem, written around Easter 1916, time of the Easter Rising in Dublin, and just after lesser known major anti-war protests in Glasgow. Prior to the outbreak of war in Serbia in 1914, war in Ulster had seemed a likely prospect. The break-up of the union must have seemed even more likely in the aftermath of the battles in Dublin and Glasgow. These events certainly drew attention to the diverse range of identities within the Union. To Thomas, who was then an army map-reading instructor who taught hundreds of soldiers before they went to the front, they must have brought home the range of sometimes conflicting allegiances within Britain and Ireland. Matthew Hollis remarks that 'events in Dublin seemed curiously not to register with Thomas who had been schooled in Irish Home Rule', but an awareness of the potential disunity of the United Kingdom, which after all long predated the events in Dublin 1916, is certainly present in this poem.[22] The lines 'a union that ends / With the necessity for it' recognises the end of the temporary 'union' between those brought together as soldiers in wartime, while implying a possible end to the four-nation political 'union' (something that of course transpired after the end of the First World War).

A national reading of the poem is supported by Thomas's critically neglected *The Happy-Go-Lucky Morgans*. Chapter Fifteen of the novel begins with 'someone with a precocious sneer ask[ing] if England was now anything more than a geographical expression' (*HGLM*, p. 122). In response, there is a patriotic speech by Mr Stodham – to a predominantly Welsh audience – which descends into a confused explanation of the relation between England and Wales: 'Do you love Wales? If you do, you love what I understand by "England". The more you love and know England, the more deeply you can love the Wilderness and Wales. I am sure of it' (*HGLM*, p. 124). However, the speech descends into farce: Mr Stodham, who cannot articulate his patriotic Englishness, 'ran away', while Higgs, who 'came nearest to laughing . . . struck up "Rule Britannia" with evident pride'. The narrator describes how 'this raised my gorge; I could not help shouting "Home Rule for Ireland", whereupon Higgs swore abominably, and I do not know what would have happened if Ann had not said: "Jessie, my love, sing *Land of my Fathers*"'. This song, the Welsh national anthem, is rightly described in the novel as 'exulting without self-glorification or any other form of brutality'. In contrast to the British national anthem and 'Rule Britannia', it is 'the national anthem of any nation that knows, and would not rashly destroy, the bonds distinguishing it from the rest of the world without isolating it'. The performance of the anthem partly resolves the earlier conflict: 'everyone but Higgs joined in the chorus and felt that it breathed the spirit of patriotism which Mr Stodham had been trying to express' (*HGLM*, p. 124). Higgs's exclusion from this chorus suggests that his British patriotism is not at one with Irish or Welsh Home Rule, or even with the version of English patriotism unsuccessfully expressed by Stodham.

The scene ends with another character declaring that he 'really did not know before that England was not a shocking fiction of the journalists and politicians' (*HGLM*, p. 125). The implied answer to the earlier question is that England is now indeed nothing more than a 'geographical expression', and 'a shocking fiction of the journalists and politicians'. The phrase 'geographical expression' has an immediate political significance. On one level, Thomas is here turning the tables on England, using the same phrase, 'merely a geographic expression', with which William James, Anglican Bishop of St David's, infamously described Wales in the 1880s (*WWWH*, p. 229). On another level, according to the line of argument developed through this chapter, it is as if England's places once gave it a meaning it no longer possesses. It is the loss of this England, founded on geographical locales, that is depicted in Thomas's poetry, which was written between two and four years after the novel.

This book has been conceived of as a revisionist contribution to three areas of study: the life and work of Edward Thomas, British literatures, and world literary studies. As far as the first of these is concerned, the book challenges the prevailing critical consensus on Thomas in several ways. It puts him back into the context of turn-of-the-century debates about the position of literature within Welsh political and economic society. It provides evidence that Welsh cultural traditions are central to his project as a journalist, prose writer and poet, and is one of the first books to draw attention to his writing across these genres. It also insists on a transnational reading of Thomas's output, showing for the first time that his reputation as a quintessentially English poet is complicated not only by these Welsh concerns, but also by his interest in Irish and American writers, by his use of French and Belgian literature, by his openness to modernist innovation (relative to his reputation as an anti-modernist), and by his poetry's critique of Englishness. The book also reveals, again for the first time, Thomas's daring, socially subversive post-Wilde defence of gay writers. And by such means as these, it takes issue with Edna Longley, the critic who has most shaped the field of Thomas studies for the last forty years, by complicating her Larkin-inspired presentation of him as the 'missing link' in a native English tradition.

This study has also opened up the question of Thomas's appropriation by different national traditions within British literatures. In particular, it has exposed the national-ideological agendas behind his depiction, after the First World War, and either side of the Second, as a quintessentially English soldier-poet. This has also raised awareness of the way that writers with a Northern Irish allegiance have, since the 1970s, linked Thomas to one of the foundation myths of British Ulster identity: its blood sacrifice for the 'union' in the First World War. The book challenges these appropriations by suggesting ways that Thomas may alternatively be recovered for a Welsh literary tradition in which his position was formerly uncertain. It contributes to a more confident English-language Welsh culture, one that moves away from what M. Wynn Thomas describes as 'the old anglo-centric ideology of Britishness' and towards his 'cultural equivalent of a council of the islands' (*I*, p. iii). At the same time, it suggests that there is a long way to go before M. Wynn Thomas's vision can be realised. That a writer considered so 'quintessentially English' can be radically repositioned in this way has consequences for English nationhood. It raises the question of whether the same might be argued of other writers from Wales and other dominated nations within Britain. If writers with non-English national allegiances can no longer be Anglicised in the way that they once were, where does this leave English identity? Is it possible to read English writers through a prism in which England is seen as a dominated nation within Britain? What kind of relations is a post-imperialist England likely to have with its British neighbours? In this sense, this study aims to bring us, 'intellectually and imaginatively', a little closer to 'a decentred world where England now takes its place in an intricate constellation of island cultures' (*I*, p. iii).

The third act of intervention, involving engagement with and reassessment of Casanova's theory of world literature, has resulted, I hope, in a persuasive demonstration that her model requires modification. 'World literary studies' certainly offers a critical approach that draws attention to the material infrastructure of the literary world, and the resultant inequalities in the status of writers from nations at different positions within it. But Casanova's model, in its rather rigid established form, is insufficiently flexible to assist in the challenging work of recovering a writer for a dominated British nation. Her theory of a 'universalising literary autonomy', based on the historical achievement of de-historicised, aesthetic, literary centres in Paris, London and elsewhere, proves inadequate to the task. After all, the literary infrastructure in these centres does not function in ways that recognise and sustain the autonomy of writers distant from and indeed foreign to these centres. Casanova's theory therefore needs to be modified so as to incorporate analysis of the position of the literary field within the political and economic contexts of the particular dominated nation concerned. Critics need to develop ways of effecting such crucial adjustments, while retaining the viability of the overarching comparative model, and not simply focusing on the particularities of the individual nation. By the same token, Casanova's concept of 'pure criticism' does not allow for the ways in which ostensibly 'detached' aesthetic criteria, operated from the centre, function in fact to sustain the marginalisation of the dominated nation. Finally, her 'Irish paradigm' is based on a model of history that is too deterministic; it offers a useful set of critical tools, but these need to be used within a looser framework which allows for the possibility that the particular historical circumstances of an individual nation might change the way that different stages of the paradigm unfold. There cannot be a single theory that accounts for the emergence of national literary traditions across all dominated nations. Nonetheless, modified in ways that take into account these limitations, Casanova's theory of world literature has provided me with the means of considering Thomas in a different light, and to recover him for an English-language Welsh tradition that is currently in the process of emerging from the shadows of its Anglicisation.

Notes

Introduction

[1] Edward Thomas, 'The Patriot', *Nationalist* 3/29 (1909), 38. Hereafter *P*.

[2] Cited in Hazel Davies, 'Edward Thomas: twelve unpublished letters to O. M. Edwards', *National Library of Wales Journal*, 28/3 (1994), 343. Hereafter *TUL*.

[3] Edward Thomas, diary, 1900–1901, National Library of Wales, Aberystwyth, MS NLW 22900B, n. p.

[4] Edward Thomas, *The South Country* (London: J. M. Dent & Co., 1909), p. 71. Hereafter *SC*.

[5] Walter de la Mare, foreword, in R. George Thomas (ed.), *Edward Thomas: Collected Poems* (London: Faber and Faber, 2004), p. 249.

[6] Edna Longley, *Poetry in the Wars* (Newcastle: Bloodaxe, 1986), p. 113. Hereafter *PW*.

[7] Tony Conran, *Frontiers in Anglo-Welsh Poetry* (Cardiff: University of Wales Press, 1997), p. 30. Hereafter *F*.

[8] Robert Crawford, *Devolving English Literature* (rev. edn, Edinburgh: Edinburgh University Press, 2000), p. 6. Hereafter *DEL*.

[9] Michael Gardiner, *The Cultural Roots of British Devolution* (Edinburgh: Edinburgh University Press, 2004), p. 158. Hereafter *CRBD*.

[10] Kenneth O. Morgan, 'Welsh devolution: the past and the future', in Bridget Taylor and Katarina Thomson (eds), *Scotland and Wales: Nations Again?* (Cardiff: University of Wales Press, 1999), p. 200.

[11] Morgan, 'Welsh devolution', p. 201.

[12] Gwyn A. Williams, *When Was Wales?: a History of the Welsh* (London: Black Raven Press, 1985), p. 178. Hereafter *WWWH*.

[13] Tom Nairn, 'Scotland and Wales', *Planet*, 34 (1976), 1.

[14] Cited in John Harris, 'The war of the tongues: early Anglo-Welsh responses to Welsh literary culture', in Geraint H. Jenkins and Mari A. Williams (eds), *'Let's Do Our Best for the Ancient Tongue': the Welsh Language in the Twentieth Century* (Cardiff: University of Wales Press, 2000), p. 451.

[15] Dai Smith, *Wales! Wales?* (London: Allen and Unwin, 1984), p. 104. Hereafter *WW*.

[16] Saunders Lewis, *Presenting Saunders Lewis*, ed. Alun R. Jones and Gwyn Thomas (Cardiff: University of Wales Press, 1973), p. 118.

[17] Lewis, *Presenting Saunders Lewis*, p. 127.

[18] R. Tudur Jones, *The Desire of Nations* (Llandybie: Christopher Davies Ltd., 1974), p. 15. Hereafter *DN*.

[19] R. Tudur Jones, 'The Welsh language and religion', in Meic Stephens (ed.), *The Welsh Language Today* (Llandysul: Gomer Press, 1973), p. 64.

[20] Tudur Jones, 'The Welsh language and religion', p. 79.

[21] J. R. Jones, 'Need the language divide us?', in Janet Davies (ed.), *Compass Points: Jan Morris Introduces a Selection from the First Hundred Issues of 'Planet'* (Cardiff: University of Wales Press, 1993), p. 143. Hereafter *NLD*.

[22] Glyn Jones, *The Dragon Has Two Tongues: Essays on Anglo-Welsh Writers and Writing* (London: Dent, 1968), pp. 5–6. Hereafter *DTT*.

[23] Dai Smith, *In the Frame: Memory and Society 1910 to 2010* (Cardigan: Parthian, 2010), p. ix.

[24] Barbara Prys-Williams, *Twentieth-Century Autobiography: Writing Wales in English* (Cardiff: University of Wales Press, 2004), p. 1.

[25] M. Wynn Thomas, *Internal Difference: Twentieth-Century Writing in Wales* (Cardiff: University of Wales Press, 1992), p. xiii. Hereafter *ID*.

[26] Alyce von Rothkirch and Daniel Williams, introduction, in Alyce von Rothkirch and Daniel Williams (eds), *Beyond the Difference: Welsh Literature in Comparative Contexts* (Cardiff: University of Wales Press, 2004), p. 1.

[27] Ned Thomas, *The Welsh Extremist: a Culture in Crisis* (London: Victor Gollancz Ltd, 1971), p. 35.

[28] Geraint Evans, 'Crossing the border: national and linguistic boundaries in twentieth-century Welsh writing', in *Welsh Writing in English: a Yearbook of Critical Essays*, 9 (2004), p. 126.

[29] M. Wynn Thomas, *Corresponding Cultures: the Two Literatures of Wales* (Cardiff: University of Wales Press, 1999), p. 45. Hereafter *CC*.

[30] M. Wynn Thomas, introduction, in Tony Brown and Russell Stephens (eds), *Nations and Relations: Writing across the British Isles* (Cardiff: New Welsh Review, 2000), p. i. Hereafter *I*.

[31] See Katie Gramich, *Kate Roberts* (Cardiff: University of Wales Press, 2011).

[32] See Kirsti Bohata, *Postcolonialism Revisited* (Cardiff: University of Wales Press, 2004).

[33] Daniel G. Williams, 'Pan-Celticism and the limits of post-colonialism: W. B. Yeats, Ernest Rhys and William Sharp in the 1890s', in Tony Brown and Russell Stephens (eds), *Nations and Relations: Writing across the British Isles* (Cardiff: New Welsh Review, 2000), p. 1.

[34] Williams, 'Pan-Celticism and the limits of post-colonialism', p. 1.

[35] See for example essays by Benita Parry, Neil Lazarus and Crystal Bartolovich in Bartolovich and Lazarus (eds), *Marxism, Modernity and Postcolonial Studies* (Cambridge: Cambridge University Press, 2002).

36   Michael Cronin, 'Global questions and local visions: a microcosmopolitan perspective', in Alyce von Rothkirch and Daniel G. Williams (eds), *Beyond the Difference*, p. 187. Hereafter *GQ*.

37   John Harris, 'Anglo-Welsh literature', in Philip Henry Jones and Eiluned Rees (eds), *A Nation and Its Books: a History of the Book in Wales* (Aberystwyth: National Library of Wales, 1998), p. 368.

38   Theo D'haen, *The Routledge Concise History of World Literature* (London and New York: Routledge, 2012), p. 1. Hereafter *HWL*.

39   See Emily Apter, *The Translation Zone: a New Comparative Literature* (Princeton: Princeton University Press, 2006), and David Damrosch, *What Is World Literature?* (Princeton: Princeton University Press, 2003).

40   Franco Moretti, 'Conjectures on world literature', *New Left Review*, 1 (Jan–Feb 2000), 54.

41   Moretti, 'Conjectures on world literature', 66.

42   Christopher Prendergast, introduction, in Christopher Prendergast (ed.), *Debating World Literature* (London: Verso, 2004), p. vii.

43   Frances Ferguson, 'Planetary literary history: the place of the text', *New Literary History*, 39/3 (Summer 2008), 670. Hereafter *PLH*.

44   Pascale Casanova, *The World Republic of Letters*, trans. M. B. DeBevoise (Cambridge, MA: Harvard University Press, 2004), p. 293. Hereafter *WRL*.

Chapter One

1   Terry Eagleton, review of *The World Republic of Letters*, *New Statesman*, 11 April 2005, *www.newstatesman.com/node/150398*; Louis Menand, 'Literature's global economy', *New Yorker*, 26 December 2005, *www.newyorker.com/archive/2005/*.

2   Perry Anderson, 'Union sucrée', *London Review of Books*, 26/18 (2004), *www.lrb.co.uk/v26/n18/*.

3   Christopher Prendergast, 'The world republic of letters', in Christopher Prendergast (ed.), *Debating World Literature* (London: Verso, 2004), p. 8.

4   Debjani Ganguly, 'Global literary refractions: reading Pascale Casanova's *The World Republic of Letters* in the post-cold war era', *English Academy Review*, 25/1 (2008), 10.

5   See Chapter 3 of Declan Kiberd, *Inventing Ireland: the Literature of the Modern Nation* (London: Vintage Books, 1996).

6   Belinda Humfrey, 'Prelude to the twentieth century', in M. Wynn Thomas (ed.), *A Guide to Welsh Literature: Welsh Writing in English* (Cardiff: University of Wales Press, 2003), p. 7. Hereafter *PTC*.

7   John Kerrigan, *Archipelagic English: Literature, History, and Politics 1603–1707* (Oxford: Oxford University Press, 2008), p. 9. Hereafter *AE*.

8   See Chapter One of M. Wynn Thomas, *Corresponding Cultures: the Two Literatures of Wales* (1999).

9   Kate Jackson, *George Newnes and the New Journalism in Britain, 1880–1910: Culture and Profit* (Ashgate: Aldershot, 2001), p. 15.

[10] Jackson, *George Newnes and the New Journalism*, p. 15.
[11] Cited in Mary Hammond, *Reading, Publishing and the Formation of Literary Taste in England 1880–1914* (Aldershot: Ashgate, 2006), p. 8.
[12] For discussion, see Stephen Knight, *A Hundred Years of Fiction: Writing Wales in English* (Cardiff: University of Wales Press, 2004), p. 7.
[13] Kirsti Bohata, *Postcolonialism Revisited* (Cardiff: University of Wales Press, 2004), p. 133. Hereafter *PR*.
[14] Prendergast, 'The world republic of letters', p. 25; Debjani Ganguly, 'Global Literary Refractions: Reading Pascale Casanova's *The World Republic of Letters* in the Post-cold War Era', *English Academy Review*, 25/1 (2008), 6.

Chapter Two

[1] Brian James, 'The ancestry of Edward Thomas the poet (1878–1917)', *National Library of Wales Journal*, 28/1 (1993), 81–91. James's research into Thomas's family tree has proved not only that one of Thomas's ancestors was involved in the Newport Chartist Uprising in 1839, but also that he and Gwili were in fact related through Thomas's great-grandmother, Anne Jenkins, who was Gwili's aunt.
[2] John Davies, *A History of Wales* (rev. edn; London: Penguin, 2007), p. 430. Hereafter *HW*.
[3] R. George Thomas, *Edward Thomas: A Portrait* (Oxford: Clarendon Press, 1985), p. 17. Hereafter *ETAP*.
[4] Cited in Thomas Seccombe, foreword, in Edward Thomas, *The Last Sheaf* (London: Jonathan Cape, 1928), p. 7.
[5] Huw Walters, *Canu'r Pwll a'r Pulpud: Portread o'r Diwylliant Barddol Cymraeg yn Nyffryn Aman* (Caernarfon: Cyhoeddiadau Barddas, 1987), p. 148.
[6] Edward Thomas, 'How I began', in *New York Times*, 18 January 1913.
[7] *Poems* (1917) is reviewed by Edward Thomas's father, Philip Henry Thomas in *The Welsh Outlook*, 6/1 (January 1919), 18–19, but aside from its identification of Thomas's 'essentially Welsh' spirit, it focuses on its subject's 'passion for England', a dual allegiance that will be explored more fully in the final chapter of this study. The same is true of a 1927 review by Anglophone Welsh novelist Geraint Goodwin (author of *The Heyday in the Blood*), whose description of Thomas as a 'great Welshman' subsequently fails to make any connection between his Welshness and his aesthetic – see *The Welsh Outlook*, 14/11 (November 1927), 297–8. Although 'Barddoniaeth Edward Thomas' (The Poetry of Edward Thomas) by D. Llewelyn Walters – see *Tir Newydd* 11 (February 1938), 13–17 – is written in Welsh, it nonetheless accepts an Anglocentric reading of Thomas's work, placing it in the context of an English pastoral and elegiac tradition.
[8] Saunders Lewis, *Is There an Anglo-Welsh Literature?* (Caerdydd: Cyhoeddwyd gan y Gangen, 1939), p. 4. Hereafter *AWL*.
[9] See Roland Mathias, *A Ride Through the Wood: Essays on Anglo-Welsh Literature* (Bridgend: Poetry Wales Press, 1985), p. 72.

10 See Jane Aaron, *Nineteenth-Century Women's Writing in Wales: Nation, Gender and Identity* (Cardiff: University of Wales Press, 2010), and M. Wynn Thomas, *In the Shadow of the Pulpit: Literature and Nonconformist Wales* (Cardiff: University of Wales Press, 2010).

11 Tony Conran, *Frontiers in Anglo-Welsh Poetry* (Cardiff: University of Wales Press, 1997), p. 2.

12 Tony Conran, *The Cost of Strangeness: Essays on the English Poets of Wales* (Llandysul: Gomer Press, 1982), pp. 54 and 57. Hereafter *TCS*.

13 Alun Lewis, review of *The Trumpet and Other Poems*, *Horizon*, 3/13 (January 1941), 80.

14 R. S. Thomas, introduction, in R. S. Thomas (ed.), *Selected Poems of Edward Thomas* (London: Faber and Faber, 1964), p. 11.

15 Elis Jenkins, 'Edward Thomas: some of his Welsh friends', *National Library of Wales Journal*, 15/2 (1967), 147–56.

16 Patrick McGuinness, 'Leslie Norris's Water Voices', in Meic Stephen (ed.), *Leslie Norris: the Complete Poems* (Bridgend: Seren, 2008), p. 19.

17 Leslie Norris, review of *Edward Thomas: a Critical Biography* by William Cooke, *Poetry Wales*, 6/1 (Summer 1970), 47–52.

18 Jeremy Hooker, 'The writings of Edward Thomas: I', *The Anglo-Welsh Review*, 18/41 (1969), 20.

19 R. George Thomas, *Edward Thomas: Writers of Wales* (Cardiff: University of Wales Press, 1972), p. 68. Hereafter *ERG*.

20 Norris, review of *Edward Thomas: a Critical Biography*, p. 49.

21 Norris, review of *Edward Thomas: a Critical Biography*, p. 47.

22 Leslie Norris, 'The poetry of Edward Thomas', in Sam Adams and Gwilym Rees Hughes (eds), *Triskel One: Essays on Welsh and Anglo-Welsh Literature* (Llandybie: Christopher Davies Ltd., 1971), p. 173. Hereafter *LN*.

23 F. R. Leavis, *New Bearings in English Poetry: a Study of the Contemporary Situation* (London: Chatto and Windus, 1932), p. 55. Hereafter *NB*.

24 Terry Eagleton, *Literary Theory: an Introduction* (Oxford: Blackwell, 1983), p. 31.

25 Eagleton, *Literary Theory*, p. 31.

26 Jeremy Hooker, 'The writings of Edward Thomas: II', *The Anglo-Welsh Review*, 19/43 (1970), 64. Hereafter *WET*.

27 R. George Thomas, *Edward Thomas: a Portrait* (Oxford: Clarendon Press, 1985), p. 223. Hereafter *ETAP*.

28 John Powell Ward, 'Edward Thomas', *Poetry Wales*, 13/4 (Spring 1978), 5.

29 Powell Ward, 'Edward Thomas', 5.

30 Joan Harding and Derwyn Jones, 'Edward Thomas and Wales', *Poetry Wales*, 13/4 (Spring 1978), 102–3. Hereafter *JHDJ*.

31 Sally Roberts Jones, 'Edward Thomas and Wales', in Jonathan Barker (ed.), *The Art of Edward Thomas* (Bridgend: Poetry Wales Press, 1987), p. 77. Hereafter *ETW*.

32 Jeremy Hooker, 'Poetic Lands and Borderlands: Henry Vaughan to Robert Frost', in Alyce von Rothkirch and Daniel G. Williams (eds), *Beyond the Difference:*

Welsh Literature in Comparative Contexts (Cardiff: University of Wales Press: 2004), p. 218.

33   John Powell Ward, 'Borderers and borderline cases', in M. Wynn Thomas (ed.), *A Guide to Welsh Literature: Welsh Writing in English* (Cardiff: University of Wales Press, 2003), p. 107.

34   Powell Ward, 'Borderers and borderline cases', p. 107.

35   John Cann Bailey, review of *An Annual of New Poetry*, *Times Literary Supplement*, 29 March 1917, 151.

36   Walter de la Mare, foreword, in R. George Thomas (ed.), *Edward Thomas: Collected Poems* (London: Faber and Faber, 2004), p. 247. Hereafter *WDLM*.

37   From Robert Frost, *Collected Poems, Prose, & Plays* (New York: The Library of America, 1995), p. 205.

38   Cited in Julian Thomas, preface, in Edward Thomas, *The Childhood of Edward Thomas: a Fragment of Autobiography* (London: Faber and Faber, 1938), p. 10.

39   Robert P. Eckert, *Edward Thomas: A Biography and a Bibliography* (London: J. M. Dent and Sons, 1937), p. 164.

40   Eckert, *Edward Thomas*, p. 51. Another late 1930s publication on Thomas is John Moore's *The Life and Letters of Edward Thomas* (1939), which contains a foreword by former wartime Prime Minister, David Lloyd George. He had been a friend of Thomas's father, Philip Henry, prior to the latter's death in 1920, and perhaps unsurprisingly, given his own involvement in World War I recruitment, claims that 'only war itself' released Thomas's 'poetic flair'. See David Lloyd George, foreword, in John Moore, *The Life and Letters of Edward Thomas* (London: Heinemann, 1939), pp. xv–xvii.

41   Eleanor Farjeon, *Edward Thomas: the Last Four Years* (Oxford: Oxford University Press, 1958), p. 154. Hereafter *LFY*.

42   Rupert Brooke, *The Poetical Works*, ed. Geoffrey Keynes (London: Faber and Faber, 1970), p. 23.

43   Ralph Lawrence, 'Edward Thomas in perspective', *English*, 12/71 (1959), 177. Hereafter *RLP*.

44   Edna Longley, *Poetry in the Wars* (Newcastle: Bloodaxe, 1986), p. 113. Hereafter *PW*.

45   Peter Howarth, *British Poetry in the Age of Modernism* (Cambridge: Cambridge University Press, 2005), p. 10. Hereafter *BPAM*.

46   Edna Longley, 'The Great War, History, and the English Lyric', in Vincent Sherry (ed.), *The Cambridge Companion to the Literature of the First World War* (Cambridge: Cambridge University Press, 2005), p. 73. Hereafter *GW*.

47   Edna Longley, 'Going Back to Edward Thomas', in Guy Cuthbertson and Lucy Newlyn (eds), *Branch-Lines: Edward Thomas and Contemporary Poetry* (London: Enitharmon Press, 2007), p. 37.

48   Edna Longley, 'Notes', in Edna Longley (ed.), *Edward Thomas: the Annotated Collected Poems* (Newcastle: Bloodaxe, 2008), p. 265. Hereafter *ELN*.

49   Peter McDonald, 'Into the unknown', *Times Literary Supplement*, 21 November 2008, 5.

50 McDonald, 'Into the unknown', 5.
51 Peter McDonald, 'Rhyme and determination in Hopkins and Edward Thomas', *Essays in Criticism*, 43/3 (1993), 228.
52 McDonald, 'Rhyme and determination', 233.
53 Peter McDonald, *Mistaken Identities: Poetry and Northern Ireland* (Oxford: Oxford University Press, 1997), p. 216.
54 McDonald, *Mistaken Identities*, p. 194.
55 Michael Longley, *The Weather in Japan* (London: Jonathan Cape, 2000), p. 24.
56 Michael Longley, *Poems 1986–1983* (Harmondsworth: Penguin, 1976), p. 86.
57 Michael Longley, *Man Lying on a Wall* (London: Gollancz, 1976), p. 39.
58 Peter McDonald, *The House of Clay* (Manchester: Carcanet, 2007), p. 22.
59 Lucy Newlyn, '"The shape of the sentences": Edward Thomas's Tracks in Contemporary Poetry', in Guy Cuthbertson and Lucy Newlyn (eds), *Branch-Lines: Edward Thomas and Contemporary Poetry* (London: Enitharmon Press, 2007), p. 81.
60 Andrew Motion, *Philip Larkin* (London: Faber and Faber, 1993), p. 210.
61 Motion, *Philip Larkin*, p. 210.
62 McDonald, *Mistaken Identities*, p. 18.
63 Cited in McDonald, *Mistaken Identities*, p.125.
64 Seamus Heaney, *District and Circle* (London: Faber and Faber, 2006), p. 35.
65 Andrew Motion, *The Poetry of Edward Thomas* (London: Routledge and Kegan Paul, 1980), p. 5. Hereafter *PET*.
66 John Lucas, *Modern English Poetry from Hardy to Hughes: a Critical Study* (London: B. T. Batsford, 1986), p. 86.
67 Lucas, *Modern English Poetry from Hardy to Hughes*, p. 89.
68 Anthony Thwaite, *Twentieth-Century English Poetry: an Introduction* (London: Heinemann, 1978), p. 38. Hereafter *TCP*.
69 J. M. Coetzee, *Youth* (London: Secker and Warburg, 2002), p. 58.
70 Anthony Easthope, *Englishness and National Culture* (London: Routledge, 1999), p. 179. Hereafter *E*.
71 Edward Thomas, *Edward Thomas: the Annotated Collected Poems*, ed. Edna Longley (Newcastle: Bloodaxe, 2008), p 51. Hereafter *ACP*.
72 Martin Dodsworth, 'Edward Thomas, Seamus Heaney and modernity: a reply to Anthony Easthope', *English*, 49/194 (2000), 148.
73 Dodsworth, 'Edward Thomas, Seamus Heaney and modernity', 148.
74 Stan Smith, *Edward Thomas* (London: Faber and Faber, 1986), p. 13. Hereafter *ET*.
75 See Stan Smith, '"Literally for this": metonymies of national identity in Edward Thomas, Yeats and Auden', in Alex Davis and Lee M. Jenkins (eds), *Locations of Literary Modernism: Region and Nation in British and American Poetry* (Cambridge: Cambridge University Press, 2000), pp.113–34.
76 David Gervais, *Literary Englands: Versions of 'Englishness' in Modern Writing* (Cambridge: Cambridge University Press, 1993), p. 41. Hereafter *LE*.
77 Peter Howarth, *British Poetry in the Age of Modernism* (Cambridge: Cambridge University Press, 2005), p. 10. Hereafter *BPAM*.

[78]   Matthew Hollis, *Now All Roads Lead to France: the Last Years of Edward Thomas* (London: Faber and Faber, 2011), p. 161.

Chapter Three

[1]   Ian Norrie, *Mumby's Publishing and Bookselling in the Twentieth Century* (6th edn; London: Bell & Hyman Ltd, 1984), p. 14. Hereafter *MPB*.
[2]   John Gross, *The Rise and Fall of the Man of Letters: Aspects of English Literary Life Since 1800* (London: Weidenfeld and Nicolson, 1969), p. 199. Hereafter *RFML*.
[3]   John Davies, Nigel Jenkins, Menna Baines and Peredur I. Lynch (eds), *The Welsh Academy Encyclopaedia of Wales* (Cardiff: University of Wales Press, 2008), p. 712.
[4]   Philip Henry Jones, 'Two Welsh publishers of the Golden Age: *Gee a'i Fab* and *Hughes a'i Fab*', in Philip Henry Jones and Eiluned Rees (eds), *A Nation and Its Books: a History of the Book in Wales* (Aberystwyth: National Library of Wales, 1998), p. 173. Hereafter *TWP*.
[5]   Richard E. Huws, 'Spurrell of Carmarthen', in Philip Henry Jones and Eiluned Rees (eds), *A Nation and Its Books*, p. 191.
[6]   Huws, 'Spurrell of Carmarthen', p. 191.
[7]   Charles Parry, 'From manuscript to print: printed books', in R. Geraint Gruffydd (ed.), *A Guide to Welsh Literature c.1530–1700* (Cardiff: University of Wales Press, 1997), p. 263.
[8]   Glyn Tegai Hughes, 'Life and thought', in Branwen Jarvis (ed.), *A Guide to Welsh Literature c.1700–1800* (Cardiff: University of Wales Press, 2000), p. 2; p. 1.
[9]   Mary Ann Gillies, *The Professional Literary Agent in Britain, 1880–1920* (Toronto: University of Toronto Press, 2007), p. 23.
[10] Mary Hammond, *Reading, Publishing and the Formation of Literary Taste in England 1880–1914* (Aldershot: Ashgate, 2006), p. 4.
[11] Paul Delany, *Literature, Money, and the Market: from Trollope to Amis* (New York: Palgrave, 2002), p. 102.
[12] Stephen Knight, *A Hundred Years of Fiction: Writing Wales in English* (Cardiff: University of Wales Press, 2004), p. xi.
[13] Knight, *A Hundred Years of Fiction*, p. xi.
[14] Hywel Teifi Edwards, 'Victorian stocktaking', in Hywel Teifi Edwards (ed.), *A Guide to Welsh Literature c.1800–1900* (Cardiff: University of Wales Press, 2000), p. 210. Hereafter *VS*.
[15] Ieuan Gwynedd Jones, 'The nineteenth century', in Philip Henry Jones and Eiluned Rees (eds), *A Nation and Its Books*, p. 162.
[16] Kate Jackson, *George Newnes and the New Journalism in Britain, 1880–1910: Culture and Profit* (Aldershot: Ashgate), 2001, p. 1.
[17] Aled Jones, 'The Welsh newspaper press', in Hywel Teifi Edwards (ed.), *A Guide to Welsh Literature c.1800–1900*, p. 5.
[18] Aled Jones, *Press, Politics and Society: a History of Journalism in Wales* (Cardiff: University of Wales Press, 1993), p. 95. Hereafter *PPS*.

[19] Hazel Davies, 'Boundaries: the early travel books and periodicals of O. M. Edwards', in Hywel Teifi Edwards (ed.), *A Guide to Welsh Literature c.1800–1900*, p. 204. Hereafter *B*.

[20] Jones, 'The Welsh newspaper press', p. 8.

[21] Huw Walters, 'The periodical press to 1914', in Philip Henry Jones and Eiluned Rees (eds), *A Nation and Its Books*, p. 204.

[22] Walters, 'The periodical press to 1914', p. 206.

[23] J. O. Jones, 'The national awakening of Wales in its relation to the Welsh press', *Young Wales*, 1/11 (1895), 280. Hereafter *NAW*.

[24] Glyn Jones, *The Dragon Has Two Tongues: Essays on Anglo-Welsh Writers and Writing* (London: Dent, 1968), p. 52.

[25] Kenneth O. Morgan, *Wales in British Politics 1868–1922* (Cardiff: University of Wales Press, 1963), p. 68. Hereafter *WBP*.

[26] M. Wynn Thomas, *Transatlantic Connections: Whitman U.S., Whitman U.K.* (Iowa City: University of Iowa Press, 2005), p. 236.

[27] J. Hugh Edwards, 'Salutatory', *Young Wales*, 1/1 (1895), 1.

[28] Edwards, 'Salutatory', 1–2.

[29] Tom Ellis, 'Letter', *Young Wales*, 1/6 (1895), 142.

[30] Anon., 'Thoughts from Mazzini', *Young Wales*, 1/6 (1895), 175.

[31] W. Llewelyn Williams, 'O fon i fynwy', *Young Wales*, 1/9 (1895), 195. Hereafter *OFF*.

[32] Dai Smith, *Wales! Wales?* (London: Allen and Unwin, 1984), p. 19.

[33] David Lloyd George, 'National self-government for Wales', *Young Wales*, 1/9 (1895), 234.

[34] Dafydd Johnston, 'The literary revival', in Dafydd Johnston (ed.) *A Guide to Welsh Literature c.1900–1996* (Cardiff: University of Wales Press, 1998), p. 3 (hereafter *LR*), and Knight, *A Hundred Years of Fiction*, p. 54.

[35] Cited in *HW*, p. 453.

[36] Allan James, *John Morris-Jones: Writers of Wales* (Cardiff: University of Wales Press, 1987), p. 17. Hereafter *JMJ*.

[37] Allan James, *John Morris-Jones* (Caerdydd: Gwasg Prifysgol Cymru, 2011), p. 181.

[38] B. F. Roberts, 'Scholarly publishing 1820-1922', in Philip Henry Jones and Eiluned Rees (eds), *A Nation and Its Books,* p. 229.

[39] Cited in Davies, *B*, p. 200.

[40] Huw Walters, *Canu'r Pwll a'r Pulpud: Portread o'r Diwylliant Barddol Cymraeg yn Nyffryn Aman* (Caernarfon: Cyhoeddiadau Barddas, 1987), p. 179.

[41] Jeremy Hooker, *Imagining Wales: a View of Modern Welsh Writing in English* (Cardiff: University of Wales Press, 2001), p. 6.

[42] Cited in M. Wynn Thomas, *Transatlantic Connections*, p. 235.

[43] Cited in *VS*, p. 222.

[44] T. Robin Chapman, 'Poetry between the wars', in Dafydd Johnston (ed.), *A Guide to Welsh Literature c.1900–1996*, pp. 51–2.

[45] Meic Stephens (ed.), *The New Companion to the Literature of Wales* (Cardiff: University of Wales Press, 1998), p. 806. Hereafter *NCLW*.

[46] See Chapter 9 of Allan James, *John Morris-Jones* (2011), pp. 179–93.
[47] Thomas Marchant Williams, 'To the reader', *Nationalist*, 1/1 (1907), 1–2.
[48] Thomas Marchant Williams, 'Our point of view', *Nationalist*, 1/1 (1907), 4.
[49] Anon., 'Reviews', *Nationalist*, 1/10 (1907), 26.
[50] Anon., 'Reviews: *Y Traethodydd*', *Nationalist*, 2/15 (1908), 30.
[51] Thomas Marchant Williams, 'Our point of view', *Nationalist*, 2/14 (1908), 2.
[52] Anon., 'Reviews: *Y Geninen*', *Nationalist*, 1/4 (1907), 26.
[53] Edward Thomas, *The Childhood of Edward Thomas: a Fragment of Autobiography* (London: Faber and Faber, 1938), p. 105. Hereafter *CET*.
[54] Cited in Kay Seymour House, introduction, in James Fenimore Cooper, *The Pathfinder, or the Inland Sea* (New York: Penguin, 1989), p. xix.
[55] Cited in House, p. xix.
[56] Edward Thomas, *The Happy-Go-Lucky Morgans* (London: Duckworth & Co., 1913), p. 124. Hereafter *HGLM*.
[57] Edward Thomas, *Beautiful Wales* (London: A. & C. Black, 1905), p. 156. Hereafter *BW*.
[58] Edward Thomas, 'Reviews', 6 vols, Edward Thomas Collection (scrapbooks; Cardiff: Cardiff University Library, 1901–17), vol. 3, p. 6. Hereafter *R*, followed by volume and page number.
[59] Thomas's idiosyncrasies of place names and personal names in titles and text (here, for example, 'Llandebie' for Llandybie) are retained without comment throughout this and subsequent chapters.
[60] E. Cefni Jones, *Gwili: Cofiant a Phregethau* (Llandysul: Gwasg Gomer, 1937), p. 86.
[61] Jones, *Gwili*, p. 180.
[62] Edward Thomas, *Horae Solitariae* (London: Duckworth & Co., 1902), p. 45. Hereafter *HS*.
[63] Gwili, *Poems* (Cardiff: n. p., 1920), p. 94. Hereafter *GP*.
[64] Cited in *ETAP*, p. 80.
[65] Edward Thomas, *Letters from Edward Thomas to Gordon Bottomley*, ed. R. George Thomas (London: Oxford University Press, 1968), p. 155. Hereafter *LGB*.
[66] The poem was written in 1918 and withheld from publication until the war was over, eventually appearing as the third poem in Yeats's 1919 collection, *The Wild Swans at Coole*.
[67] Edward Thomas, 'At a Cottage Door', *Nationalist*, 3/30 (1910), 14.

Chapter Four

[1] Edward Thomas, *The Heart of England* (London: J. M. Dent & Co., 1909), p. 241.
[2] Edward Thomas, diary, 1909, National Library of Wales, Aberystwyth, MS NLW 22908B, n. p.
[3] Edward Thomas, letter to C. F. Cazenove, 8 December 1907, Cardiff University Library, Cardiff, ETC 209.
[4] Cathryn A. Charnell-White, *Bardic Circles: National, Regional and Personal Identity in the Bardic Vision of Iolo Morganwg* (Cardiff: University of Wales Press, 2007), p. 2.

5   Charnell-White, *Bardic Circles*, p. 78.
6   Edward Thomas, *Horae Solitariae* (London: Duckworth & Co., 1902), pp. 48 and 87. Hereafter *HS*.
7   Edward Thomas, *Rest and Unrest* (London: Duckworth & Co., 1910), p. 88.
8   Thomas, *Rest and Unrest*, p. 141.
9   Edward Thomas, *Light and Twilight* (London: Duckworth & Co., 1911), p. 151. Hereafter *LT*.
10 Cited in *ETAP*, p. 80.
11 Edward Thomas, *George Borrow: the Man and His Books* (London: Chapman & Hall, 1912), p. 267. Hereafter *GB*.
12 Eiluned Rees and Philip Henry Jones, preface, in Philip Henry Jones and Eiluned Rees (eds), *A Nation and Its Books: a History of the Book in Wales* (Aberystwyth: National Library of Wales, 1998), p. xii.
13 Edward Thomas, *The South Country* (London: J. M. Dent & Co., 1909), p. 131. Hereafter *SC*.
14 Edward Thomas, *Richard Jefferies: his Life and Work* (London: Hutchinson & Co., 1909), p. 224. Blodeuwedd, one of the main characters in the fourth branch of *The Mabinogion* is created from flowers by the magicians Gwydion and Math as a wife for Lleu Llaw Gyffes who is unable to have a human wife.
15 Edward Thomas, *Lafcadio Hearn* (London: Constable & Co., 1912), pp. 12 and 20.
16 Edward Thomas, *The Country* (London: B. T. Batsford, 1913), p. 1.
17 Thomas, *The Country*, p. 7.
18 Edward Thomas, *In Pursuit of Spring* (London: Thomas Nelson & Sons, 1914), p. 300.
19 Thomas, *In Pursuit of Spring*, p. 300.
20 Edward Thomas, *Icknield Way* (London: Constable & Co., 1916), p. 22. Hereafter *IW*.
21 Macsen is loosely identified with Magnus Maximus, a Roman commander in the fourth century AD. The text suggests that Elen, the Welsh woman he sees in a dream and later marries, is responsible for building roads between Roman forts in north and south Wales.
22 Edward Thomas, *Celtic Stories* (Oxford: Clarendon Press, 1911), p. 6. Hereafter *CS*.
23 Matthew Hollis, *Now All Roads Lead to France: the Last Years of Edward Thomas* (London: Faber and Faber, 2011), p. 189.
24 *NCLW*, p. 458
25 John Jones, 'The Ash Grove – Llwyn Onn', in *Folksongs of Various Countries*, *http://ingeb.org/songs/allhail.html*.
26 All the poems named in the following discussion may be found in the *Annotated Collected Poems*.
27 Edna Longley, 'Notes', in Edna Longley (ed.), *Edward Thomas: the Annotated Collected Poems*, p. 284.
28 R. S. Thomas, introduction, in R. S. Thomas (ed.), *Selected Poems of Edward Thomas* (London: Faber and Faber, 1964), p. 11.
29 Cited in *ETAP*, p. 70.

[30]	Sioned Davies (trans.), *The Mabinogion* (Oxford: Oxford University Press, 2007), p. 252.

Chapter Five

[1]	Declan Kiberd, *Inventing Ireland: the Literature of the Modern Nation* (London: Vintage Books, 1995), p. 51.
[2]	Edna Longley, 'The Great War, history, and the English lyric', in Vincent Sherry (ed.), *The Cambridge Companion to the Literature of the First World War* (Cambridge: Cambridge University Press, 2005), p. 74.
[3]	Daniel G. Williams, *Ethnicity and Cultural Authority: from Arnold to Du Bois* (Edinburgh: Edinburgh University Press, 2006), p. 128. Hereafter *ECA*.
[4]	Thomas, *R*, vol. 5, p. 32.
[5]	He reviewed Colum's *Wild Earth* on 13 April 1908 and *Thomas Muskerry: a Play* on 15 August 1910, both in the *Morning Post*; Colum's *Studies* in the *Daily Chronicle* on 22 February 1908, and his *Broad Sheet Ballads* in the *Saturday Westminster Gazette* on 21 March 1914.
[6]	Judy Kendall, *Edward Thomas: the Origins of His Poetry* (Cardiff: University of Wales Press, 2012), p. 73.
[7]	Cited in Stan Smith, *Edward Thomas* (London: Faber and Faber, 1986), p. 12.
[8]	Matthew Hollis, *Now All Roads Lead to France: the Last Years of Edward Thomas* (London: Faber and Faber, 2011), p. 74.
[9]	M. Wynn Thomas, *Transatlantic Connections: Whitman U.S., Whitman U.K.* (Iowa City: University of Iowa Press, 2005), p. 259. Hereafter *TC*.
[10]	Ernest Rhys's *Lays of the Round Table* was reviewed in the *Daily Chronicle* on 25 January 1906, *The Masque of the Grail* on 13 August 1908 and his travel book, *The South Wales Coast*, in the *Daily Chronicle* on 25 September 1911.
[11]	O. M. Edwards, 'Introduction', *Wales*, 1/1 (1894), 1.
[12]	Edward Thomas and Robert Frost, *Elected Friends: Robert Frost and Edward Thomas to One Another*, ed. Matthew Spencer, (New York: Handsel Books, 2003), p. 106. Hereafter *EF*.
[13]	Edward Thomas, etter to C. F. Cazenove, 4 April 1912, Durham University Library, Ms. Abbott 499.
[14]	Edward Thomas, 'Poems by Edward Eastaway', in *Poetry: a Magazine of Verse*, 9/5 (1917), 247–51.
[15]	Cited in Edna Longley (ed.), *A Language Not to Be Betrayed: Selected Prose of Edward Thomas* (Manchester: Carcanet, 1981), p. 118.
[16]	Ibid.
[17]	Clive Wilmer, 'Edward Thomas: Englishness and modernity', *PN Review*, 27/4 (March/April 2001), 59.
[18]	Edgar Jepson, *Memories of an Edwardian and Neo-Georgian* (London: Richards, 1937), p. 140.
[19]	Edward Thomas, *Edward Thomas: Selected Letters*, ed. R. George Thomas, (Oxford: Oxford University Press, 1995), p. 76.

20   Lawrence Rainey, *Institutions of Modernism: Literary Elites and Public Culture*
      (New Haven and London: Yale University Press, 1999), p. 28.
21   Jay Parini, *Robert Frost: a Life* (London: Pimlico, 2001), p. 150.
22   Peter Nicholls, *Modernisms: a Literary Guide* (Basingstoke: Macmillan, 1995),
      p. 69. Hereafter *M*.
23   Edward Thomas, diary, 1909, National Library of Wales, Aberystwyth, MS NLW
      22908B, n. p.
24   Edward Thomas, diary, 1904–1905, National Library of Wales, Aberystwyth, MS
      NLW 22903B, n. p., and diary, 1912, National Library of Wales, Aberystwyth, MS
      NLW 22911B, n. p.
25   Edward Thomas, *Maurice Maeterlinck* (London: Methuen, 1911), p. 309.
26   Cited in *M*, p. 74.
27   Thomas reviewed Maeterlinck's *Sister Beatrice* and *Ardiane and Barbe Bleue* in
      the *Daily Chronicle* on 30 December 1901; *The Buried Temple* in the same paper
      on 28 April 1902; *Old-Fashioned Flowers* in the *Morning Post* on 13 December
      1906 and again in the *Daily Chronicle* on 7 May 1907; *Life and Flowers* in the
      Morning Post on 25 April 1907 and in the *Bookman* in July 1907; *Joyzelle* in the
      Daily Chronicle on 7 May 1907; *Aglavaine and Selysette*, *Ardiane and Barbe
      Bleue*, *The Life of the Bee*, *The Treasure of the Humble* and *Wisdom and Destiny*,
      all in the *Daily Chronicle* of 19 February 1909; and *Death* in the same paper on
      23 October 1911.
28   Patrick McGuinness, *Maurice Maeterlinck and the Making of Modern Theatre*
      (Oxford: Oxford University Press, 2000), pp. 1 and 2.
29   Emile Verhaeren's verse featured in *The Welsh Outlook* in the May 1914, October
      1914, December 1914 and July 1915 issues, while many articles on Belgium
      appeared during these years. A favourable review of Edward Thomas's novel, *The
      Happy-Go-Lucky-Morgans*, which appeared in the November 1914 issue, narrowly
      missed appearing alongside Verhaeren's work.
30   Anon., 'Emile Verhaeren', *The Welsh Outlook* 1/10 (October 1914), 423.
31   This article is reprinted in the 'British Isles' section, edited by M. Wynn Thomas,
      of Gay Wilson Aleen and Ed Folsom (eds), *Walt Whitman and the World* (Iowa
      City: University of Iowa Press, 1995), pp. 55–6.
32   Ann L. Ardis, *Modernism and Cultural Conflict, 1880–1922* (Cambridge: Cambridge
      University Press, 2002), p. 46. Hereafter *MCC*.
33   Cited in Edna Longley, introduction, in Edna Longley (ed.), *A Language Not to
      Be Betrayed*, p. xii.
34   All four of Thomas's reviews of Wilde were published in the *Daily Chronicle*: *De
      Profundis* on 13 February 1904, *The Duchess of Padua* on 13 February 1908, *The
      Works* on 13 April 1908, and *Miscellanies and Reviews* on 1 February 1909.
35   Mark Lilly, *Gay Men's Literature in the Twentieth Century* (Basingstoke: Macmillan,
      1993), p. 29.
36   Edward Thomas, letter to C.F. Cazenove, 16 January 1912, Cardiff University
      Library, Cardiff, ETC 209.
37   Thomas reviewed Swinburne's *Channel Passage and Other Poems* in *World* on
      6 September 1904; *The Queen Mother and Rosamund* in the *Morning Post* on

5 March 1908; *The Duke of Gandia* in the May 1908 *Bookman*; *Age of Shakespeare* in the *Daily Chronicle* on 24 September 1908 and in the *Daily News* in the same month; and *Selections from the Poetical Works* in the *Daily Chronicle* in July 1913. He reviewed Symons's *Spiritual Adventures* in the *Daily Chronicle* on 11 January 1906; *The Fool of the World* in the same paper on 20 November 1906; *Studies in Seven Arts* in the *Morning Post* on 17 December 1906; a *Pageant of Elizabethan Poetry* on 7 January 1907 in the *Daily Chronicle*; *William Blake* in *Saturday Review* on 19 October 1907; *The Symbolist Movement in Literature* in the *Morning Post* on 14 May 1908; *The Romantic Movement in English Poetry* in the *Daily Chronicle* on 7 October 1909 and again in the *Morning Post* on 20 January 1910; and finally, *Knave of Hearts* in the February 1914 *Bookman* and in the *Daily Chronicle* on 23 April 1914.

[38] Thomas reviewed *Iolaus* in the *Daily Chronicle* on 22 April 1902; *Days with Walt Whitman* in the same paper on 7 June 1906; and *Sketches from Life in Town and Country* in *Saturday Review* on 27 June 1908.

[39] Martin Taylor (ed.), *Lads: Love Poetry of the Trenches* (London: Constable, 1989), p. 31. Hereafter *LLP*.

[40] Edward Thomas, *Richard Jefferies: His Life and Work* (London: Hutchinson & Co., 1909), p. 182.

[41] Thomas reviewed *Poems* in the *Daily Chronicle* on 15 September 1906; *The Chronicle of a Pilgrimage* in the *Morning Post* on 3 February 1910; *Before Dawn* in the *Daily Chronicle* on 4 September 1911 and in the October 1911 issue of *Bookman*.

[42] Thomas mentions Whitman in *Beautiful Wales* (p. 192), *Richard Jefferies* (p. 313), *The South Country* (p. 113 and p. 135) and *A Literary Pilgrim in England* (p. 87).

[43] Thomas reviewed Michael Field's *Borgia: a Period Play* in the *Daily Chronicle* on 19 July 1905; *Wild Honey from Various Thyme* in the *Morning Post* on 5 March 1908; *Queen Mariamne* in the *Daily Chronicle* on 24 April 1909; *The Tragedy of Pardon* in the same paper on 30 March 1911; and *Mystic Trees*, again in the *Daily Chronicle* in May 1913 and in *Bookman* in August 1913.

[44] Edna Longley, 'Notes', in Edna Longley (ed.), *Edward Thomas: the Annotated Collected Poems* (Newcastle: Bloodaxe, 2008), p. 232.

[45] *LGB*, p. 92. Thomas uses similar language to describe another extra-marital infatuation, this time with an eighteen-year-old woman, Hope Webb, of whom he later wrote, 'I liked her for her perfect wild youthfulness' (cited in Hollis, *Now All Roads Lead to France*, p. 263).

[46] Cited in Hugh Brogan, *The Life of Arthur Ransome* (London: Pimlico, 1992), p. 32.

[47] Declan Kiberd, *Inventing Ireland: the Literature of the Modern Nation* (London: Vintage Books, 1996), p. 41.

[48] Hollis, *Now All Roads Lead to France*, p. 196.

[49] Kiberd, *Inventing Ireland*, p. 41.

[50] Michael Hofmann, foreword, in Matthew Spencer (ed.), *Elected Friends: Robert Frost and Edward Thomas to One Another* (New York: Handsel Books, 2003), p. xxxvi.

[51] Hofmann, foreword, p. xxxvi.

Chapter Six

1   Edward Thomas, letter to Walter de la Mare, 30 August 1914, Bodleian Library, Oxford, MS Eng. Lett. c.376.

2   Edward Thomas, *The Letters of Edward Thomas to Jesse Berridge*, ed. Anthony Berridge (London: Enitharmon Press, 1983), p. 74.

3   Cited in *TUL*, p. 343.

4   'Wales' or 'Welsh', incidentally, explicitly occurs in 'Man and Dog', 'The Child on the Cliffs', 'Health', 'Words', and 'Roads'.

5   Ian Norrie, *Mumby's Publishing and Bookselling in the Twentieth Century* (6th edn; London: Bell & Hyman Ltd, 1984), p. 20.

6   C. F. Cazenove, letter to Edward Thomas, 17 August 1914, Durham University Library, Durham, MS Abbott 122.

7   Cited in Matthew Hollis, *Now All Roads Lead to France: the Last Years of Edward Thomas* (London: Faber and Faber, 2011), p. 159.

8   Cited in Judy Kendall (ed.), *Edward Thomas's Poets* (Manchester: Carcanet, 2007), p. 65.

9   Cited in Kendall (ed.), *Edward Thomas's Poets*, p. 65.

10 Edward Thomas, letter to parents, 9 July 1915, Cardiff University Library, Cardiff, ETC 161.

11 Letter from C. F. Cazenove to Edward Thomas, 26 August 1914, Durham University Library, Durham, MS Abbott 125.

12 Ian Baucom, *Out of Place: Englishness, Empire and the Locations of Identity* (Princeton: Princeton University Press, 1999), p. 4. Hereafter *OOP*.

13 Edward Thomas, diary, 1900–1901, National Library of Wales, Aberystwyth, MS NLW 22900B, n. p.

14 Edward Thomas, *The Isle of Wight* (London: Blackie & Son, 1911), p. 27.

15 Thomas, *The Isle of Wight*, p. 29.

16 Smith, Stan, *Edward Thomas* (London: Faber and Faber, 1986), p. 118. Hereafter *ET*.

17 Thomas and Conrad were acquaintances from 1906 until Thomas's death in 1917. They met regularly at literary lunches organised by the publisher Edward Garnett. On one occasion, when Conrad was ill, Thomas even ghost-wrote for him. According to Thomas's diary entry for 20 July 1910, he penned '1200 [words] for *Daily Mail* (as Conrad)', an article that appeared in the paper under the title 'Can Poetry Flourish in a Scientific Age?' on 30 July of the same year.

18 Michael Kirkham, *The Imagination of Edward Thomas* (Cambridge: Cambridge University Press, 1986), p. 130.

19 Cited in *WRL*, p. 240.

20 Raymond Williams, *The Country and the City* (London: Chatto and Windus, 1973), p. 255. Hereafter *TCC*.

21 Edna Longley, 'Notes', in Edna Longley (ed.), *Edward Thomas: the Annotated Collected Poems* (Newcastle: Bloodaxe, 2008), p. 283.

22 Hollis, *Now All Roads Lead to France*, p. 279.

Works Cited

Primary Sources: works by Edward Thomas

Poetry

Collected Poems (London: Selwyn and Blount, 1920).

Collected Poems of Edward Thomas, ed. R. George Thomas (London: Faber and Faber, 2004).

Edward Thomas: the Annotated Collected Poems, ed. Edna Longley (Newcastle: Bloodaxe, 2008).

Last Poems (London: Selwyn and Blount, 1918).

Poems (London: Selwyn and Blount, 1917).

'Poems by Edward Eastaway', *Poetry: a Magazine of Verse*, 9/5 (1917), 247–51.

Prose and Anthologies

'At a Cottage Door', *Nationalist*, 3/30 (1910), 10–16.

Beautiful Wales (London: A. & C. Black, 1905).

Celtic Stories (Oxford: Clarendon Press, 1911).

The Childhood of Edward Thomas: a Fragment of Autobiography (London: Faber and Faber, 1938).

Cloud Castle and Other Papers (London: Duckworth & Co., 1922).

The Country (London: B. T. Batsford, 1913).

Feminine Influence on the Poets (London: Martin Secker, 1911).

Four-and-Twenty Blackbirds (London: Duckworth & Co., 1915).

George Borrow: the Man and his Books (London: Chapman & Hall, 1912).

The Happy-Go-Lucky Morgans (London: Duckworth & Co., 1913).

The Heart of England (London: J.M. Dent & Co., 1909).

Horae Solitariae (London: Duckworth & Co., 1902).

'How I began', *New York Times*, 18 January 1913.

In Pursuit of Spring (London: Thomas Nelson & Sons, 1914).

Icknield Way (London: Constable & Co., 1916).

The Isle of Wight (London: Blackie & Son, 1911).

Keats (London: T. C. & E. C. Jack, 1913).

Lafcadio Hearn (London: Constable & Co., 1912).

A Language Not to be Betrayed: Selected Prose of Edward Thomas, ed. Edna Longley (Manchester: Caracnet, 1981).

The Last Sheaf (London: Jonathan Cape, 1928).

Light and Twilight (London: Duckworth & Co., 1911).

A Literary Pilgrim in England (London: Methuen, 1917).

Maurice Maeterlinck (London: Methuen, 1911).

Oxford (London: A. & C. Black, 1903).

'The Patriot', *Nationalist* 3/29 (1909), 38–43.

(Ed.), *Pocket Book of Poems and Songs for the Open Air* (London: E. Grant Richards, 1907).

Rest and Unrest (London: Duckworth & Co., 1910).

'Reviews', scrapbooks 1901–17, 6 vols, Edward Thomas Collection, Cardiff University Library, Cardiff.

Richard Jefferies: his Life and Work (London: Hutchinson & Co., 1909).

The South Country (London: J. M. Dent & Co., 1909).

Algernon Charles Swinburne: a Critical Study (London: Martin Secker, 1912).

(Ed.), *This England: an Anthology for her Writers* (London: Oxford University Press, 1915).

Published correspondence

Edward Thomas: Selected Letters, ed. R. George Thomas (Oxford: Oxford University Press, 1995).

Elected Friends: Robert Frost and Edward Thomas to One Another, ed. Matthew Spencer (New York: Handsel Books, 2003).

Letters from Edward Thomas to Gordon Bottomley, ed. R. George Thomas (London: Oxford University Press, 1968).

The Letters of Edward Thomas to Jesse Berridge, ed. Anthony Berridge (London: Enitharmon Press, 1983).

Unpublished diaries and correspondence

Diary, 1900–1901, National Library of Wales, Aberystwyth, MS NLW 22900B.

Diary, 1904–1905, National Library of Wales, Aberystwyth, MS NLW 22903B.

Diary, 1909, National Library of Wales, Aberystwyth, MS NLW 22908B.

Diary, 1912, National Library of Wales, Aberystwyth, MS NLW 22911B.

Letter to C. F. Cazenove, 8 December 1907, Cardiff University Library, Cardiff, ETC 209.

Letter to C. F. Cazenove, 16 January 1912, Cardiff University Library, Cardiff, ETC 209.

Letter to C. F. Cazenove, 4 April 1912, Durham University Library, Durham, MS Abbott 499.

Letter to C. F. Cazenove, 17 August 1914, Durham University Library, Durham, MS Abbott 122.

Letter to C. F. Cazenove, 26 August 1914, Durham University Library, Durham, MS Abbott 125.

Letter to parents, 9 July 1915, Cardiff University Library, Cardiff, ETC 161.

Letter to Walter de la Mare, 30 August 1914, Bodleian Library, Oxford, MS Eng. Lett. c.376.

Secondary Sources

Aaron, Jane, *Nineteenth-century Women's Writing in Wales: Nation, Gender and Identity* (Cardiff: University of Wales Press, 2010).

Anderson, Perry, 'Union sucrée', *London Review of Books*, 26/18 (2004), *www.lrb.co.uk/v26/n18/*.

Anon., 'Emile Verhaeren', *The Welsh Outlook* 1/10 (October 1914), 423–6.

Anon., 'Reviews', *Nationalist*, 1/10 (1907), 23–7.

Anon., 'Reviews: *Y Geninen*', *Nationalist*, 1/4 (1907), 26.

Anon., 'Reviews: *Y Traethodydd*', *Nationalist*, 2/15 (1908), 30.

Anon., 'Summer talk of literary London', *New York Times*, 3 August 1907.

Anon., 'Thoughts from Mazzini', *Young Wales*, 1/6 (1895), 175.

Anon., 'Topics of the week', *New York Times*, 1 September 1906.

Ardis, Ann L., *Modernism and Cultural Conflict, 1880–1922* (Cambridge: Cambridge University Press, 2002).

Bailey, John Cann, review of Gordon Bottomley (ed.), *An Annual of New Poetry* (London: Constable, 1917), *Times Literary Supplement*, 29 March 1917, 151.

Bartolovich, Crystal, and Neil Lazarus (eds), *Marxism, Modernity and Postcolonial Studies* (Cambridge: Cambridge University Press, 2002).

Baucom, Ian, *Out of Place: Englishness, Empire and the Locations of Identity* (Princeton: Princeton University Press, 1999).

Bohata, Kirsti, *Postcolonialism Revisited* (Cardiff: University of Wales Press, 2004).

Brogan, Hugh, *The Life of Arthur Ransome* (London: Pimlico, 1992).

Brooke, Rupert, *The Poetical Works*, ed. Geoffrey Keynes (London: Faber and Faber, 1970).

Casanova, Pascale, 'Literature as a world', *New Left Review*, 31 (Jan–Feb 2005), 71–90.

—— *The World Republic of Letters*, trans. M. B. DeBevoise (Cambridge, MA: Harvard University Press, 2004).

Cazenove, C. F., unpublished letters to Edward Thomas, Durham University Library, Durham, Abbott Collection, MS 122 and 125.

Chapman, T. Robin. 'Poetry between the Wars', in Dafydd Johnston (ed.), *A Guide to Welsh Literature c.1900–1996* (Cardiff: University of Wales Press, 1998), pp. 50–88.

Charnell-White, Cathryn A., *Bardic Circles: National, Regional and Personal Identity in the Bardic Vision of Iolo Morganwg* (Cardiff: University of Wales Press, 2007).

Coetzee, J. M., *Youth* (London: Secker and Warburg, 2002).

Conran, Tony, *The Cost of Strangeness: Essays on the English Poets of Wales* (Llandysul: Gomer Press, 1982).

—— *Frontiers in Anglo-Welsh Poetry* (Cardiff: University of Wales Press, 1997).

Cooper, James Fenimore, *The Pathfinder, or the Inland Sea* (1840; New York: Penguin, 1989).

Crawford, Robert, *Devolving English Literature* (rev. edn; Edinburgh: Edinburgh University Press, 2000).

Cronin, Michael, 'Global questions and local visions: a microcosmopolitan perspective', in Alyce von Rothkirch and Daniel G. Williams (eds), *Beyond the Difference: Welsh Literature in Comparative Contexts* (Cardiff: University of Wales Press, 2004), pp. 186–203.

Davies, Hazel, 'Boundaries: the early travel books and periodicals of O. M. Edwards', in Hywel Teifi Edwards (ed.), *A Guide to Welsh Literature c.1800–1900* (Cardiff: University of Wales Press, 2000), pp. 186–209.

—— 'Edward Thomas: twelve unpublished letters to O. M. Edwards', *National Library of Wales Journal*, 28/3 (1994), 335–45.

Davies, John, *A History of Wales* (rev. edn; London: Penguin, 2007).

Davies, John, and Nigel Jenkins, Menna Baines and Peredur I. Lynch (eds), *The Welsh Academy Encyclopaedia of Wales* (Cardiff: University of Wales Press, 2008).

Davies, Sioned (trans.), *The Mabinogion* (Oxford: Oxford University Press, 2007).

De la Mare, Walter, foreword in R. George Thomas (ed.), *Edward Thomas: Collected Poems* (London: Faber and Faber, 2004), pp. 246–53.

Delany, Paul, *Literature, Money, and the Market: from Trollope to Amis* (New York: Palgrave, 2002).

Deresiewicz, William, 'The literary world system', *Nation*, 3 January 2005, *www. thenation.com/doc/20050103/deresiewicz*.

D'haen, Theo, *The Routledge Concise History of World Literature* (London and New York: Routledge, 2012).

Dodsworth, Martin, 'Edward Thomas, Seamus Heaney and modernity: a reply to Anthony Easthope', *English*, 49/194 (2000), 143–54.

Eagleton, Terry, *Literary Theory: an Introduction* (Oxford: Blackwell, 1983).

—— 'Review of *The World Republic of Letters*', *New Statesman*, 11 April 2005, *www.newstatesman.com/node/150398.*

Easthope, Anthony, *Englishness and National Culture* (London: Routledge, 1999).

Eckert, Robert P., *Edward Thomas: A Biography and a Bibliography* (London: J. M. Dent and Sons, 1937).

Edwards, Hywel Teifi, 'Victorian stocktaking', in Hywel Teifi Edwards (ed.), *A Guide to Welsh Literature c.1800–1900* (Cardiff: University of Wales Press, 2000), pp. 210–231.

Edwards, J. Hugh, 'Salutatory', *Young Wales*, 1/1 (1895), 1–2.

Edwards, O. M., 'Introduction', *Wales*, 1/1 (1894), 1–2.

Eliot, Simon, 'Some trends in British book production, 1800–1919', in John O. Jordan and Robert L. Patten (eds), *Literature in the Marketplace: Nineteenth-Century British Publishing and Reading Practices* (Cambridge: Cambridge University Press, 1995), pp. 19–43.

Ellis, Tom, 'Letter', *Young Wales*, 1/6 (1895), 142.

Evans, Geraint, 'Crossing the border: national and linguistic boundaries in twentieth-century Welsh writing', *Welsh Writing in English: a Yearbook of Critical Essays*, 9 (2004), 123–35.

Farjeon, Eleanor, *Edward Thomas: the Last Four Years* (Oxford: Oxford University Press, 1958).

Feltes, N. N., *Literary Capital and the Late Victorian Novel* (Madison: University of Wisconsin Press, 1993).

Ferguson, Frances, 'Planetary literary history: the place of the text', *New Literary History* 39/3 (Summer 2008), 657–84.

Frost, Robert, *Collected Poems, Prose, & Plays* (New York: The Library of America, 1995).

Ganguly, Debjani, 'Global literary refractions: reading Pascale Casanova's *The World Republic of Letters* in the post-cold war era', *English Academy Review*, 25/1 (2008), 4–19.

Garlick, Raymond, *An Introduction to Anglo-Welsh Literature* (Cardiff: University of Wales Press, 1970).

Gardiner, Michael, *The Cultural Roots of British Devolution* (Edinburgh: Edinburgh University Press, 2004).

Gervais, David, *Literary Englands: Versions of 'Englishness' in Modern Writing* (Cambridge: Cambridge University Press, 1993).

Gillies, Mary Ann, *The Professional Literary Agent in Britain, 1880–1920* (Toronto: University of Toronto Press, 2007).

Gramich, Katie, *Kate Roberts* (Cardiff: University of Wales Press, 2011).

Gross, John, *The Rise and Fall of the Man of Letters: Aspects of English Literary Life Since 1800* (London: Weidenfeld and Nicolson, 1969).

Guest, Charlotte (trans.), *The Mabinogion* (London: J. M. Dent and Son, 1913).

Gwili, *Poems* (Cardiff: n. p., 1920).

Hammond, Mary, *Reading, Publishing and the Formation of Literary Taste in England 1880–1914* (Aldershot: Ashgate, 2006).

Harding, Joan, and Derwyn Jones, 'Edward Thomas and Wales', *Poetry Wales*, 13/4 (Spring 1978), 102–106.

Harris, John, 'Anglo-Welsh literature', in Philip Henry Jones and Eiluned Rees (eds), *A Nation and Its Books: a History of the Book in Wales* (Aberystwyth: National Library of Wales, 1998), pp. 355–70.

—— 'The war of the tongues: Early Anglo-Welsh responses to Welsh literary culture', in Geraint H. Jenkins and Mari A. Williams (eds), *'Let's Do our Best for the Ancient Tongue': the Welsh Language in the Twentieth Century* (Cardiff: University of Wales Press, 2000), pp. 439–62.

Heaney, Seamus, *District and Circle* (London: Faber and Faber, 2006).

Hofmann, Michael, foreword in Matthew Spencer (ed.), *Elected Friends: Robert Frost and Edward Thomas to One Another* (New York: Handsel Books, 2003), pp. xxxi–xl.

Hollis, Matthew, *Now All Roads Lead to France: the Last Years of Edward Thomas* (London: Faber and Faber, 2011).

Hooker, Jeremy, *Imagining Wales: a View of Modern Welsh Writing in English* (Cardiff: University of Wales Press, 2001).

Hooker, Jeremy, 'Poetic lands and borderlands: Henry Vaughan to Robert Frost', in Alyce von Rothkirch and Daniel Williams (eds), *Beyond the Difference: Welsh Literature in Comparative Contexts* (Cardiff: University of Wales Press: 2004), pp. 206–22.

—— 'The writings of Edward Thomas: I', *The Anglo-Welsh Review*, 18/41 (1969), 20–8.

—— 'The writings of Edward Thomas: II', *The Anglo-Welsh Review*, 19/43 (1970), 63–78.

House, Kay Seymour, introduction in James Fenimore Cooper, *The Pathfinder, or the Inland Sea* (New York: Penguin, 1989), pp. ix–xxix.

Howarth, Peter, *British Poetry in the Age of Modernism* (Cambridge: Cambridge University Press, 2005).

Hughes, Glyn Tegai, 'Life and thought', in Branwen Jarvis (ed.), *A Guide to Welsh Literature c.1700–1800* (Cardiff: University of Wales Press, 2000), pp. 1–22.

Humfrey, Belinda, 'Prelude to the twentieth century', in M. Wynn Thomas (ed.), *A Guide to Welsh Literature: Welsh Writing in English* (Cardiff: University of Wales Press, 2003), pp. 7–46.

Huws, Richard E., 'Spurrell of Carmarthen', in Philip Henry Jones and Eiluned Rees (eds), *A Nation and Its Books: a History of the Book in Wales* (Aberystwyth: National Library of Wales, 1998), pp. 189–96.

Jackson, Kate, *George Newnes and the New Journalism in Britain, 1880–1910: Culture and Profit* (Aldershot: Ashgate, 2001).

James, Allan, *John Morris-Jones* (Caerdydd: Gwasg Prifysgol Cymru, 2011).

James, Allan, *John Morris-Jones: Writers of Wales* (Cardiff: University of Wales Press, 1987).

James, Brian, 'The ancestry of Edward Thomas the poet (1878–1917)', *National Library of Wales Journal*, 28/1 (1993), 81–91.

Jepson, Edgar, *Memories of an Edwardian and Neo-Georgian* (London: Richards, 1937).

Jenkins, Elis, 'Edward Thomas: some of his Welsh friends', *National Library of Wales Journal*, 15/2 (1967), 147–56.

Johnston, Dafydd, 'The literary revival', in Dafydd Johnston (ed.), *A Guide to Welsh Literature c.1900–1996* (Cardiff: University of Wales Press, 1998), pp. 1–21.

Jones, Aled, *Press, Politics and Society: a History of Journalism in Wales* (Cardiff: University of Wales Press, 1993).

Jones, Aled, 'The Welsh newspaper press', in Hywel Teifi Edwards (ed.), *A Guide to Welsh Literature c.1800–1900* (Cardiff: University of Wales Press, 2000), pp. 1–23.

Jones, E. Cefni, *Gwili: Cofiant a Phregethau* (Llandysul: Gwasg Gomer, 1937).

Jones, Glyn, *The Dragon Has Two Tongues: Essays on Anglo-Welsh Writers and Writing* (London: Dent, 1968).

Jones, Ieuan Gwynedd, 'The nineteenth century', in Philip Henry Jones and Eiluned Rees (eds), *A Nation and Its Books: a History of the Book in Wales* (Aberystwyth: National Library of Wales, 1998), pp. 157–71.

Jones, J. O., 'The national awakening of Wales in its relation to the Welsh press', *Young Wales*, 1/11 (1895), 280–4.

Jones, J. R., 'Need the language divide us?', in Janet Davies (ed.), *Compass Points: Jan Morris Introduces a Selection from the First Hundred Issues of 'Planet'* (Cardiff: University of Wales Press, 1993), pp. 143–58.

Jones, John, 'The Ash Grove – Llwyn Onn', in *Folksongs of Various Countries*, http://ingeb.org/songs/allhailt.html.

Jones, Philip Henry, 'Two Welsh publishers of the Golden Age: *Gee a'i Fab* and *Hughes a'i Fab*', in Philip Henry Jones and Eiluned Rees (eds), *A Nation and Its Books: a History of the Book in Wales* (Aberystwyth: National Library of Wales, 1998), pp. 173–83.

Kendall, Judy, *Edward Thomas: the Origins of His Poetry* (Cardiff: University of Wales Press, 2012).

—— (ed.), *Edward Thomas's Poets* (Manchester: Carcanet, 2007).

Kerrigan, John, *Archipelagic English: Literature, History, and Politics 1603–1707* (Oxford: Oxford University Press, 2008).

Kiberd, Declan, *Inventing Ireland: the Literature of the Modern Nation* (London: Vintage Books, 1996).

Kirkham, Michael, *The Imagination of Edward Thomas* (Cambridge: Cambridge University Press, 1986).

Knight, Stephen, *A Hundred Years of Fiction: Writing Wales in English* (Cardiff: University of Wales Press, 2004).

Larkin, Philip, *Required Writing: Miscellaneous Pieces 1955–1982* (London: Faber and Faber, 1983).

Lawrence, Ralph, 'Edward Thomas in perspective', *English*, 12/71 (1959), 177–83.

Leavis, F. R., *New Bearings in English Poetry: a Study of the Contemporary Situation* (London: Chatto and Windus, 1932).

Lewis, Alun, review of Edward Thomas, *The Trumpet and Other Poems* (London: Faber and Faber, 1940), *Horizon*, 3/13 (January 1941), 78–80.

Lewis, Saunders, *Is there an Anglo-Welsh Literature?* (Caerdydd: Cyhoeddwyd gan y Gangen, 1939).

—— *Presenting Saunders Lewis*, ed. Alun R. Jones and Gwyn Thomas (Cardiff: University of Wales Press, 1973).

Lilly, Mark, *Gay Men's Literature in the Twentieth Century* (Basingstoke: Macmillan, 1993).

Llewelyn Williams, W., 'O fon i fynwy', *Young Wales*, 1/9 (1895), 195–99.

Lloyd George, David, foreword in John Moore, *The Life and Letters of Edward Thomas* (London: Heinemann, 1939), pp. xv–xvii.

—— 'National self-government for Wales', *Young Wales*, 1/9 (1895), 231–5.

Longley, Edna, 'The Great War, history, and the English lyric', in Vincent Sherry (ed.), *The Cambridge Companion to the Literature of the First World War* (Cambridge: Cambridge University Press, 2005), pp. 57–84.

—— introduction in Edna Longley (ed.), *A Language Not to be Betrayed: Selected Prose of Edward Thomas* (Manchester: Carcanet, 1981), pp. i–xxi.

—— 'Notes', in Edna Longley (ed.), *Edward Thomas: the Annotated Collected Poems* (Newcastle: Bloodaxe, 2008), pp. 141–322.

—— *Poetry in the Wars* (Newcastle: Bloodaxe, 1986).

Longley, Michael, *Man Lying on a Wall* (London: Gollancz, 1976).

—— *Poems 1966–1983* (Harmondsworth: Penguin, 1986).

—— *The Weather in Japan* (London: Jonathan Cape, 2000).

Lucas, John, *Modern English Poetry from Hardy to Hughes: a Critical Study* (London: B. T. Batsford, 1986).

McDonald, Peter, *The House of Clay* (Manchester: Carcanet, 2007).

—— 'Into the unknown', *Times Literary Supplement* (21 November 2008), 5–7.

—— *Mistaken Identities: Poetry and Northern Ireland* (Oxford: Oxford University Press, 1997).

—— 'Rhyme and determination in Hopkins and Edward Thomas', *Essays in Criticism*, 43/3 (1993), 228–46.

McGuinness, Patrick, 'Leslie Norris's Water Voices', in *Leslie Norris: the Complete Poems*, ed. Meic Stephens (Bridgend: Seren, 2008), pp. 15–26.

—— *Maurice Maeterlinck and the Making of Modern Theatre* (Oxford: Oxford University Press, 2000).

Marchant Williams, Thomas, 'Our point of view', *Nationalist*, 1/1 (1907), 3–4.

—— 'Our point of view', *Nationalist*, 2/14 (1908), 1–2.

—— 'Our point of view', *Nationalist*, 4/36 (1911), 1–3.

—— 'To the reader', *Nationalist*, 1/1 (1907), 1–2.

Marx, Karl, *Selected Writings*, ed. David McLellan (Oxford: Oxford University Press, 1977).

Mathias, Roland, *A Ride Through the Wood: Essays on Anglo-Welsh Literature* (Bridgend: Poetry Wales Press, 1985).

Menand, Louis, 'Literature's global economy', *New Yorker*, 26 December 2005, *www.newyorker.com/archive/2005*.

Moore, John, *The Life and Letters of Edward Thomas* (London: Heinemann, 1939).

Moretti, Franco, 'Conjectures on world literature', *New Left Review*, 1 (Jan–Feb 2000), 54–68.

—— *Graphs, Maps, Trees: Abstract Models for Literary Study* (London: Verso, 2005).

—— 'History of the novel: theory of the novel', *Novel*, 43/1 (Spring 2010), 1–10.

—— 'More conjectures', *New Left Review*, 20 (Mar-Apr 2003), 73–81.

—— 'Style Inc. Reflections on seven thousand titles (British novels, 1740–1850)', *Critical Inquiry*, 36 (Autumn 2009), 134–58.

Morgan, Kenneth O., *Wales in British Politics 1868–1922* (Cardiff: University of Wales Press, 1963).

—— 'Welsh devolution: the past and the future', in Bridget Taylor and Katarina Thomson (eds), *Scotland and Wales: Nations Again?* (Cardiff: University of Wales Press, 1999), pp. 199–220.

Motion, Andrew, 'Back – due to popular demand', *Guardian Review* (3 May 2008), 6.

—— *Philip Larkin* (London: Faber and Faber, 1993).

—— *The Poetry of Edward Thomas* (London: Routledge and Kegan Paul, 1980).

Nairn, Tom, 'Scotland and Wales', *Planet*, 34 (Nov. 1976), 1–11.

Nicholls, Peter, *Modernisms: a Literary Guide* (Basingstoke: Macmillan, 1995).

Norrie, Ian, *Mumby's Publishing and Bookselling in the Twentieth Century* (6th edn; London: Bell & Hyman Ltd, 1984).

Norris, Leslie, 'The poetry of Edward Thomas', in Sam Adams and Gwilym Rees Hughes (eds), *Triskel One: Essays on Welsh and Anglo-Welsh Literature* (Llandybie: Christopher Davies Ltd., 1971), pp. 164–78.

—— review of William Cooke, *Edward Thomas: a Critical Biography* (London: Faber and Faber, 1970), *Poetry Wales*, 6/1 (Summer 1970), 47–52.

Parini, Jay, *Robert Frost: a Life* (London: Pimlico, 2001).

Parry, Charles, 'From manuscript to print: printed books', in R. Geraint Gruffydd (ed.), *A Guide to Welsh Literature c.1530–1700* (Cardiff: University of Wales Press, 1997), pp. 263–76.

Powell Ward, John, 'Borderers and borderline cases', in M. Wynn Thomas (ed.), *A Guide to Welsh Literature: Welsh Writing in English* (Cardiff: University of Wales Press, 2003), pp. 91–119.

—— 'Edward Thomas', *Poetry Wales*, 13/4 (Spring 1978), 5–6.

Prendergast, Christopher (ed.), *Debating World Literature* (London: Verso, 2004).

Prys-Williams, Barbara, *Twentieth-Century Autobiography: Writing Wales in English* (Cardiff: University of Wales Press, 2004).

Rainey, Lawrence, *Institutions of Modernism: Literary Elites and Public Culture* (New Haven and London: Yale University Press, 1999).

Rees, Eiluned, and Philip Henry Jones, preface in Philip Henry Jones and Eiluned Rees (eds), *A Nation and Its Books: a History of the Book in Wales* (Aberystwyth: National Library of Wales, 1998), pp. xi–xiv.

Roberts, B. F., 'Scholarly publishing 1820–1922', in Philip Henry Jones and Eiluned Rees (eds), *A Nation and Its Books: a History of the Book in Wales* (Aberystwyth: National Library of Wales, 1998), pp. 221–33.

Roberts Jones, Sally, 'Edward Thomas and Wales', in Jonathan Barker (ed.), *The Art of Edward Thomas* (Bridgend: Poetry Wales Press, 1987), pp. 75–84.

Said, Edward, *Culture and Imperialism* (London: Vintage, 1994).

Seccombe, Thomas, foreword in Edward Thomas, *The Last Sheaf* (London: Jonathan Cape, 1928), pp. 7–11.

Smith, Dai, *In the Frame: Memory and Society 1910 to 2010* (Cardigan: Parthian, 2010).

—— *Wales! Wales?* (London: Allen and Unwin, 1984).

Smith, Stan, *Edward Thomas* (London: Faber and Faber, 1986).

—— '"Literally for this": metonymies of national identity in Edward Thomas, Yeats and Auden', in Alex Davis and Lee M. Jenkins (eds), *Locations of Literary Modernism: Region and Nation in British and American Poetry* (Cambridge: Cambridge University Press, 2000), pp.113–34.

Stephens, Meic (ed.), *The New Companion to the Literature of Wales* (Cardiff: University of Wales Press, 1998).

Taylor, Martin (ed.), *Lads: Love Poetry of the Trenches* (London: Constable, 1989).

Thomas, Julian, preface in Edward Thomas, *The Childhood of Edward Thomas: A Fragment of Autobiography* (London: Faber and Faber, 1938), pp. 7–10.

Thomas, M. Wynn, *Corresponding Cultures: the Two Literatures of Wales* (Cardiff: University of Wales Press, 1999).

—— *Internal Difference: Twentieth-Century Writing in Wales* (Cardiff: University of Wales Press, 1992).

—— *In the Shadow of the Pulpit: Literature and Nonconformist Wales* (Cardiff: University of Wales Press, 2010).

—— introduction in Tony Brown and Russell Stephens (eds), *Nations and Relations: Writing across the British Isles* (Cardiff: New Welsh Review, 2000), pp. i–iv.

—— *Transatlantic Connections: Whitman U.S., Whitman U.K.* (Iowa City: University of Iowa Press, 2005).

Thomas, Ned, *The Welsh Extremist: a Culture in Crisis* (London: Victor Gollancz Ltd, 1971).

Thomas, R. George, *Edward Thomas: A Portrait* (Oxford: Clarendon Press, 1985).

—— *Edward Thomas: Writers of Wales* (Cardiff: University of Wales Press, 1972).

Thomas, R. S., introduction, in *Selected Poems of Edward Thomas*, ed. R. S. Thomas (London: Faber and Faber, 1964), pp. 11–14.

Thwaite, Anthony, *Twentieth-Century English Poetry: an Introduction* (London: Heinemann, 1978).

Tudur Jones, R., *The Desire of Nations* (Llandybie: Christopher Davies Ltd., 1974).

—— 'The Welsh language and religion', in Meic Stephens (ed.), *The Welsh Language Today* (Llandysul: Gomer Press, 1973), pp. 64–91.

von Rothkirch, Alyce, and Daniel Williams, introduction, in Alyce von Rothkirch and Daniel Williams (eds), *Beyond the Difference: Welsh Literature in Comparative Contexts* (Cardiff: University of Wales Press, 2004), pp. 1–3.

Walters, Huw, *Canu 'r Pwll a 'r Pulpud: Portread o 'r Diwylliant Barddol Cymraeg yn Nyffryn Aman* (Caernarfon: Cyhoeddiadau Barddas, 1987).

—— 'The periodical press to 1914', in Philip Henry Jones and Eiluned Rees (eds), *A Nation and Its Books: a History of the Book in Wales* (Aberystwyth: National Library of Wales, 1998), pp. 197–207.

Williams, Daniel G., *Ethnicity and Cultural Authority: from Arnold to Du Bois* (Edinburgh: Edinburgh University Press, 2006).

—— 'Pan-Celticism and the limits of post-colonialism: W. B. Yeats, Ernest Rhys and William Sharp in the 1890s', in Tony Brown and Russell Stephens (eds), *Nations and Relations: Writing across the British Isles* (Cardiff: New Welsh Review, 2000), pp. 1–29.

Williams, Gwyn A., *When Was Wales?: a History of the Welsh* (London: Black Raven Press, 1985).

Williams, Raymond, *The Country and the City* (London: Chatto and Windus, 1973).

Wilmer, Clive, 'Edward Thomas: Englishness and modernity', *PN Review*, 27/4 (March/April 2001), 59–64.

Wilson Aleen, Gay, and Ed Folsom (eds), *Walt Whitman and the World* (Iowa City: University of Iowa Press, 1995).

Index